50 Successful
IVY LEAGUE
Application
Essays

Includes advice from college admissions officers and the 25 essay mistakes that guarantee failure

GEN and KELLY TANABE

HARVARD GRADUATES AND AUTHORS OF
Get into Any College, The Ultimate Scholarship Book and
Accepted! 50 Successful College Admission Essays

50 Successful Ivy League Application Essays
By Gen and Kelly Tanabe

Published by SuperCollege, LLC
3286 Oak Court
Belmont, CA 94002
www.supercollege.com

Credits: Cover: TLC Graphics, www.TLCGraphics.com. Design: Monica Thomas Layout: The Roberts Group, www.editorialservice.com

Trademarks: All brand names, product names and services used in this book are trademarks, registered trademarks or tradenames of their respective holders. SuperCollege is not associated with any college, university, product or vendor.

Disclaimers: The authors and publisher have used their best efforts in preparing this book. It is sold with the understanding that the authors and publisher are not rendering legal or other professional advice. The authors and publisher cannot be held responsible for any loss incurred as a result of specific decisions made by the reader. The authors and publisher make no representations or warranties with respect to the accuracy or completeness of the contents of the book and specifically disclaim any implied warranties or merchantability or fitness for a particular purpose. The accuracy and completeness of the information provided herein and the opinions stated herein are not guaranteed or warranted to produce any particular results. The authors and publisher specifically disclaim any responsibility for any liability, loss or risk, personal or otherwise, which is incurred as a consequence, directly or indirectly, from the use and application of any of the contents of this book.

ISBN13: 9781932662405

Manufactured in the United States of America
10 9 8 7 6 5 4 3 2 1

Library of Congress Cataloging-in-Publication Data

Tanabe, Gen S.
  50 successful Ivy League application essays / Gen and Kelly Tanabe.
    p. cm.
  ISBN 978-1-932662-40-5 (alk. paper)
  1. College applications--United States. 2. Private universities and colleges--United States--Admission. I. Tanabe, Kelly Y. II. Title. III. Title: Fifty successful Ivy League application essays.
  LB2351.52.U6T36 2009
  378.1'616--dc22
                          2009026129

TABLE OF CONTENTS

Chapter 1: 25 Essay Mistakes that Guarantee Failure   1

Chapter 2: Ivy League Admissions Officer Q&A   13

Chapter 3: Academic Passion   21
"Bacon" by Mariam Nassiri   21
"Beyond Plug-and-Chug Math" by Anonymous   24
"A Different Kind of Love" by Oana Emilia Butnareanu   26
"From Flaubert to Frisbee" by Aditya Kumar   29
"Raising the Bar" by Anonymous   32

Chapter 4: Books/Literature   35
"Rosencrantz and Guildenstern" by Fareez Giga   35

Chapter 5: Career   39
"Puzzles" by Anonymous   39
"Addressing Injustices" by Mathew Griffin   42
"My Unpopular Decision" by Shiv M. Gaglani   44
"Healing Beyond Borders" by Mathew Griffin   46
"Scientific Sparks" by Ariela Koehler   48
"Researching Cancer" by Anonymous   50

Chapter 6: Entrepreneurship   53
"The Computer Doctor" by Mathew Griffin   53

Chapter 7: Challenges   57
"Unshakable Worth" by Sarah Langberg   57
"No Longer Invisible" by Angelica   60
"Power of People" by Suzanne Arrington   63
"Self Mind" by Timothy Nguyen Le   66
"A Summer of Stem Cells" by Ariela Koehler   69
"All Worth It" by Anonymous   72

Chapter 8: Community Service   75
"Music from the Heart" by Anonymous   75
"Precious Planet" by Pen-Yuan Hsing   77
"Cuddle Buddies" by Anastasia Fullerton   80
"Best Reader" by Manika   82

Chapter 9: Family   87
"Box of Chocolates" by Alex Volodarsky   87
"Dear Santa" by Anonymous   91
"Lessons from the Immigration Spectrum" by Anonymous   93

Chapter 10: Heritage and Identity   97
"Heritage" by Anonymous   97
"Abuelo" by Angelica   100
"Anything Goes" by Jean Gan   102
"Strength from Family Struggles" by Anonymous   104

Chapter 11: Humor 109
"Exit Door" by Fareez Giga 109
"Crime Scene Report" by Lauren Sanders 111

Chapter 12: An Influential Person 115
"John Nash" by Jonathan Cross 115
"Then and Now: How the Perseverance of a Working, Single Mother
Molded the Persona of her Chinese-American Daughter" by Lisa Kapp 118

Chapter 13: Issues 123
"Sustainable Development in South Africa" by Steve Schwartz 123
"A Young Voice for Seniors" by Ariela Koehler 126

Chapter 14: Leadership 129
"Birthing a Business" by Jason Y. Shah 129
"Beyond Dictionary Definitions of Leadership" by Victoria Tomaka 132

Chapter 15: Personal Growth 137
"Beauty" by Anonymous 137
"Keeping up with the Beat of the Drum" by Shreyans C. Parekh 140
"Hurricane Transformations" by Jason Y. Shah 142
"The House on Wellington Avenue" by Jackie Liao 145

Chapter 16: Talent 149
"A Dramatic Coup" by Fareez Giga 149
"Music as My Second Language" by Jean Gan 150
"My Bedroom" by Fareez Giga 153
"A Special Performance" by Anonymous 155

Chapter 17: Travel 157
"Extra Page" by Lauren Horton 157
"Looking Beyond the Castle" by Brian Aguado 160

Chapter 18: Vignette 163
"Polar Bears" by Lauren Horton 163
"Moving" by Laura V. Mesa 165

Chapter 19: Why Our College 169
"Exploring Life's Intricacies" by Mathew Griffin 169
"Leveraging Potential" by Cameron McConkey 171
"Inspiration from an Energy Conversion Machine" by Anonymous 174

Chapter 20: Wait List Letter 177
"Wait List Supplement" by Pen-Yuan Hsing 177

Chapter 21: Advice on Topics from Ivy League Students 181

Chapter 22: Advice on Writing from Ivy League Students 199

Chapter 23: What I Learned from Writing the Essay 215

About the Authors 230

DEDICATION

To our readers—
we hope you achieve your dream!

ACKNOWLEDGMENTS

THIS BOOK WOULD NOT HAVE BEEN possible without the generous contributions of the Ivy League students who agreed to share their admission essays and advice in order to help others who hope to follow in their footsteps.

We would also like to thank the admissions officers for spending the time to impart some of their knowledge to our readers: Dr. Michele Hernandez, former assistant director of admissions at Dartmouth College and Eva Ostrum, former assistant director of undergraduate admissions at Yale University.

We would like to express our appreciation to Chenxing Han for assisting with the analysis of the students' essays.

Special thanks to the counselors: Mary Pinedo, Whitney High School, Cerritos, CA; Renee Brown, Brooklyn Technical High School, Brooklyn, NY; Tricia Bryan, John Marshall High School, Los Angeles, CA; Yamila Dielacher, El Camino High School, South San Francisco, CA; Stephanie Gabbard, Champion High School, Warren, OH; Linda Kimmel, Irvington High School, Fremont, CA; Lynda McGee, Downtown Magnets High School, Los Angeles, CA; Ann Meyer, Highlands High School, Fort Thomas, KY; Mary O'Reilly, Josephinum Academy, Chicago, IL; Lois Rossi, Uniontown Area High School, Uniontown, PA; Chris Ward, Lake Park High School, Roselle, IL; Carla Zielinski, Perkiomen Valley High School, Collegeville, PA and Carnegie Vanguard High School.

1

25 ESSAY MISTAKES THAT GUARANTEE FAILURE

FOR EVERY OPEN SLOT AT AN Ivy League college, there are 10 to 12 eager applicants vying for it–and you're one of them. On paper, most applicants appear very similar. All are well qualified academically with high grades and test scores and solid involvement in extracurricular activities.

Imagine the admissions officer who must choose which of these well-deserving applications to accept. How will he or she make the decision? Often, it's the essay. The essay is the one chance for you to share a piece of yourself that is not encapsulated in the dry numbers and scores of the application. It is your opportunity to demonstrate why you'd be a perfect fit at the college, how you'd contribute to the student body, and why the college should accept you over those other 11 applicants.

The essay is also the one part of your application that you have complete control over. You can write it the night before it's due and turn in a piece that is half-baked, or you can spend a little time on the essay and turn in one that can set you apart from the competition.

The truth is that you don't have to be a good writer to create a successful admissions essay. Nor do you need to have survived a life changing event or won a Noble Prize. Writing a successful admissions essay for an Ivy League college is actually much simpler.

The secret is that any topic can be a winner but it all depends on your approach. If you spend the time to analyze your subject and can convey that quality of thought that is unique to you through words, you'll have a powerful essay. It doesn't have to be beautifully written or crafted as the next great American novel. At its core the essay is not a "writing test." It's a "thinking test." So you do need to spend the time to make sure that your thoughts are conveyed correctly on paper. It may not be pretty writing but it has to be clear.

So how do you do this? While we can give you tips and pointers (which is what you'll read in the analysis section following every essay) the best method is to learn by example. You need to see what a successful end product looks like. While there is no single way to produce a winning essay, as you will read, there are some traits that successful essays share. You'll learn what these are by reading the examples in this book as well as the interviews with admissions officers. Then you can write a successful essay that is based on your own unique experiences, world view, way of thinking, and personal style.

Why are admissions essays so important to getting into Ivy League colleges? At their most basic level, essays help admissions officers to understand who you are. While grades, test scores, and academic performance can give the admissions officers an estimate on how prepared you are to handle the academic rigors of college, the essay offers the only way they can judge how your background, talents, experience, and personal strengths come together to make you the best candidate for their school. For you, the applicant, the admissions essays offer the best opportunity to share who you are beyond the dry stats of your academic record. It's kind of amazing actually. You start with a blank sheet of paper and through careful selection, analysis, and writing, you create a picture of yourself that impresses the admissions officers and makes them want to have you attend their school.

Ultimately, this book is designed to help you create a successful essay that gets you accepted. It will guide you toward writing that essay by sharing with you the successes of others who have written to gain admission to Ivy League colleges as well as other highly selective schools such as MIT, Stanford, Caltech, Duke, and the University of Chicago.

If you're like most students, you would like to know the magic formula for writing an admissions essay. Although we would love to be able to tell you, unfortunately, no such formula exists. Writing is so individual and the options so limitless that it's impossible to develop a combination that will work for *every* essay. However, this doesn't mean that we're going to send you off with laptop in hand, without some guidance. Throughout this book you are going to see the "right way" to do things.

We thought it would be useful to start off with a few common mistakes that other students have made. You'll want to avoid these. In fact, some of these mistakes are so bad that they will almost guarantee that your essay will fail. Avoid these at all costs!

1. **Trying to be someone else.** This may sound very obvious, and well, it is. But you'd be surprised at how many students don't heed this simple piece of advice. A lot of students think that they need to be who the admissions officers want them to be; but, in reality, the admissions officers want you to be you. They aren't looking for the perfect student who is committed to every subject area, volunteers wholeheartedly for every cause, plays multiple sports with aptitude, and has no faults. Instead, they want to learn about the true you. Present yourself in an honest way, and you will find it much easier to write an essay about your genuine thoughts and feelings.

2. **Choosing a topic that sounds good but that you don't care about.** Many students think that colleges seek students who have performed a lot of community service, and it is true that colleges value contributions to your community. However, this doesn't mean that you must write about community service, especially when it's not something that has played a major role for you. The same holds true for any other topic. It's critical that you select a

topic that's meaningful to you because you will be able to write about the topic in a complete and personal way.

3. **Not thinking before writing.** You should spend as much time thinking about what you will write as actually putting words on paper. This will help you weed out the topics that just don't go anywhere, determine which topic has the greatest pull for you, and figure out exactly what you want to say. It can help to talk yourself through your essay aloud or discuss your thoughts with a parent, teacher, or friend. The other person may see an angle or a flaw that you do not.

4. **Not answering the question.** While this seems simple enough, many students simply do not heed this. The advice is especially pertinent for those who recycle essays. We highly recommend recycling because it saves you time to write one essay that you use for many colleges, but the caveat is that you need to edit the essay so that it answers the question being asked. It turns admissions officers off when students submit an essay, even a well-written one, that doesn't answer the question. They think that the students either aren't serious enough about the college to submit an essay that has been specifically written or at least edited for that college, or that they just don't follow directions. Either way, that's not the impression you want to leave.

5. **Not sharing something about yourself.** As you know, the main purpose of the admissions essay is to impart something about yourself that's not found in the application. Still, many students forget this, especially when writing about a topic such as a person they'd like to meet or a favorite book or piece of literature. In these cases, they may write so much about why they admire the person or the plot of the book that they forget to show the connection to themselves. Always ask yourself if you are letting the admissions officers know something about yourself through your essay.

6. **Forgetting who your readers are.** Naturally you speak differently to your friends than your teachers; when it comes to the essay, some applicants essentially address the admissions officers with a too-friendly high five instead of a handshake. In other

words, it's important to be yourself in the essay, but you should remember that the admissions officers are adults not peers. The essay should be comfortable but not too informal. Remember that adults generally have a more conservative view of what's funny and what's appropriate. The best way to make sure you're hitting the right tone is to ask an adult to read your essay and give you feedback.

7. **Tackling too much of your life.** Because the essay offers a few hundred words to write about an aspect of your life, some students think that they need to cram in as many aspects of their life as possible. This is not the approach we recommend. An essay of 500 to 800 words doesn't afford you the space to write about your 10 greatest accomplishments since birth or about everything that you did during your three-week summer program in Europe. Rather, the space can probably fit one or two accomplishments or one or two experiences from the summer program. Instead of trying to share your whole life, share what we call a slice of your life. By doing so, you will give your essay focus and you will have the space to cover the topic in greater depth.

8. **Having a boring introduction.** Students have started their essays by repeating the question asked and even stating their names. This does little to grab the attention of the admissions officers. Sure, they'll read the whole essay, but it always helps to have a good start. Think about how you can describe a situation that you were in, convey something that you strongly believe in or share an anecdote that might not be expected. An introduction won't make or break your essay, but it can start you off in the right direction.

9. **Latching on to an issue that you don't really care about.** One of the prompts for the Common Application is, "Discuss some issue of personal, local, national, or international concern and its importance to you." The key to answering this question is to carefully think about these words: "its importance to you." This is what students most often overlook. They select an issue and write about the issue itself, but they don't really explain why it is important to them or how they see themselves making an impact. If you write about an issue, be sure to pick one that is truly

meaningful to you and that you know something about. You'll probably score extra kudos if you can describe how you have done something related to the issue.

10. **Resorting to gimmicks.** Applicants have been known to enclose a shoe with their essays along with a note that reads, "Now I have one foot in the door." They have also printed their essays in different fonts and colors, sent gifts or food and even included mood music that's meant to set the mood while the admissions officer reads the essay. A few students have even sent cash! While gimmicks like this may grab some attention, they don't do much to further the applicants, especially those few who've sent money, a definite no-no. It's true that you want your essay to stand out but not in a way in which the admissions officer thinks that you are inappropriate or just plain silly. If you have an idea for something creative, run it by a teacher or counselor to see what he or she thinks first.

11. **Trying to make too many points.** It's better to have a single, well thought-out message in your essay than many incomplete ones. Focusing allows you to go into depth into a specific topic and make a strong case for your position. Write persuasively. You can use examples to illustrate your point.

12. **Not being specific.** If you think about some of the best stories you've been told, the ones that you remember the most are probably filled with details. The storyteller may have conveyed what he or she thought, felt, heard, or saw. From the information imparted, you may have felt like you were there or you may have developed a mental image of the situation. This is precisely the experience that you would like the admissions officers to have when reading your essay. The key to being memorable is providing as many details as possible. What thoughts were going through your mind? What did you see or hear? What were you feeling during the time? Details help bring the admissions officers into your mind to feel your story.

13. **Crossing the line.** Some students take to heart the advice to share something about themselves, but they end up sharing too much. They think that they must be so revealing that they use

their essay to admit to something that they would never have confessed otherwise. There have been students who have written about getting drunk, feeling suicidal, or pulling pranks on their teachers. It's possible that in the right context, these topics might work. For example, if the pranks were lighthearted and their teachers had a good sense of humor about them, that's acceptable. But for the most part, these kinds of topics are highly risky. The best way to determine if you've crossed the line is to share your idea with a couple of adults and get their reactions.

14. **Repeating what's in the application form.** The essay is not the application form, and it is not a resume. In other words, the essay is the best opportunity that you'll have to either delve into something you wrote in the application form or to expound on something new that doesn't really fit on the application form. It doesn't help you to regurgitate what's already on the application form.

15. **Not having a connection with the application form.** While you don't want to repeat information from the application form verbatim in your essay, it's usually a good idea to have some continuity between the form and your essay. If you write an essay about how your greatest passion in life is playing the piano and how you spend 10 hours a week practicing, this hobby should be mentioned in the application form along with any performances you've given or awards you've won. It doesn't make sense to write about how you love an activity in the essay and then to have no mention of it in the application form. Remember that the admissions officers are looking at your application in its entirety, and they should have a complete and cohesive image of you through all the pieces, which include the application form, essay, transcript, recommendations, and interview.

16. **Not going deep enough.** One of the best pieces of advice that we give students is to keep asking, "Why?" As an example, let's say that you are writing an essay on organizing a canned food drive. Ask yourself why you wanted to do this. Your answer is that you wanted to help the homeless. Ask yourself why this was important to you. Your answer is that you imagined your family in this situation. You would greatly appreciate if others showed

compassion and helped you. Why else? Because you wanted to gain hands-on experience as a leader. The point of this exercise is to realize that it's not enough to just state the facts or tell what happened, that you organized a canned food drive. What makes an essay truly compelling is explaining the "why." You want the readers of your essay to understand your motivation. Keep asking yourself why until you have analyzed the situation as fully as possible. The answers you come up with are what will make your essay stronger.

17. **Not getting any feedback.** Practically every article that you read in a magazine, book, or newspaper or on the Internet has been edited. The reason is that writing should not be an isolated experience. You may know exactly what you want to convey in your own mind, but when you put it on paper, it may not come out as clearly as it was in your mind. It helps to get feedback. Ask parents, teachers, or even friends to read and comment on your essay. They can help you identify what can be edited out, what needs to be explained better, or how you can improve your work.

18. **Getting too much feedback.** Asking one or two people for feedback on your essay is probably enough. If you ask more than that, you may lose the focus of your writing. Having too many editors dilutes your work because everyone has a different opinion. If you try to incorporate all of the opinions, your essay will no longer sound like you.

19. **Trying to be extraordinarily different.** There are some people who are extraordinarily different, but the truth is that most of us aren't. What's more important than conveying yourself as the most unique person at your school is that you demonstrate self-analysis, growth, or insight.

20. **Ruling out common topics.** There are topics that admissions officers see over and over again such as your identity, your relationship with your family, extracurricular activities, and the Big Game. While these topics are very common, it doesn't mean that you shouldn't write about them. Your topic is not as important as what you say about it. For example, many students choose to

write about their moms or dads. A parent can be one of the most influential persons in a student's life, and it makes sense that this would be the topic of many students' essays. So don't rule out mom or dad, but do rule out writing about mom or dad in the way that every other person will write. Explain how your dad made banana pancakes every morning and what that taught you about family, or how your mom almost got into a fight with another mom who made a racist comment. Make a common topic uncommon by personalizing it.

21. **Forcing humor.** You've probably seen at least one sitcom on TV or one monologue by Conan O'Brien or David Letterman with a joke that fell flat. Maybe you groaned at the TV or gave it an un-amused expression. Keep in mind that the jokes on TV are written by professional writers who earn large salaries to be funny. Now, remember that the great majority of us are not headed down this career path. What this means is that you shouldn't force humor into your essay. If you're a funny writer, then by all means, inject some humor. Just be sure to ask an adult or two to read the essay to see if they agree with you that it is funny. If you're not humorous, then it's okay. You don't need to force it.

22. **Writing the essay the night before it's due.** Almost every student has done it—waited until the last minute to write a paper or do a project. Sometimes it comes out all right, but sometimes not so much. It is not wise to procrastinate when it comes to writing a college admissions essay. It takes time. Even if you are able to write an essay the night before it's due, it's still better not to. The best essays marinate. Their authors write, take some time away from it and then return to it later with a fresh mind.

23. **Failing the thumb test.** As you are writing your essay, place your thumb over your name. Could you put another name at the top because it could be an essay written by many other students? Or is the essay personal to you so that basically yours is the only name that could be at the top? If you fail the thumb test, it's time to rethink the topic or your approach to it. You want your essay to be unique to you.

24. **Forgetting to proofread.** Some students put the wrong college name in their essays, a mistake that could easily be avoided by

proofreading. Many more students have spelling, grammatical, or punctuation errors. While these types of errors usually aren't completely detrimental, they can be distracting at best and be signs to the admissions officers that you're careless and not serious about their college at worst. Avoid this by not only using your computer's spell check but by asking someone else to help proofread your essay. Twice is better.

25. **Not writing to the specific college.** In addition to learning about you, admissions officers also hope to learn how you would fit in at their college. Be as specific as possible about a college, especially if you are writing an essay about why you'd like to attend that particular college. Explain one or two things about the school that make it the best one for you. Make sure that what you are writing is not so general that it could be said of any other college. In other words, it's good to describe how you visited the campus and had a conversation about Marx with a sociology student. It's not as good to state that you want to go to Harvard because it offers a high quality education.

26. **Not spending time on the rest of your application.** Remember that the essay is one piece of the application. It can certainly help your chances of being accepted, but you need to have everything else in place as well. Sure, it takes time to work on the application form, recommendation letters, and interviews, but you are taking actions now that will affect the next four years of your life and beyond. It's worth the effort.

How to Use This Book

Now that you have a clear of idea of the mistakes to avoid in your essay, it's time to get some advice on what you *should do*. Let's go directly to the source—Ivy League admissions officers. In the next chapter, three former Ivy League admissions officers share in their own words what they seek in applicants and give you tips on how to make the strongest impression on them.

Then, see what makes a solid essay through the essays themselves. Of course, the point is not to copy these essays. It's to gain inspiration. It's to see what's worked in the past and to get your creativity flowing so that you can formulate in your mind how you can best approach your topic.

We've analyzed each of the essays too. You'll see that even essays written by students accepted at the premier colleges in the country are not perfect and have room for improvement. You'll also see the strengths of the essays so that you can make sure to incorporate similar characteristics.

By learning through example, you can create the most compelling and persuasive essay possible. You'll know what not to do, you'll understand what the admissions officers want and, perhaps most importantly, you'll be inspired to write your own successful Ivy League admissions essay.

IVY LEAGUE ADMISSIONS OFFICER Q&A

DR. MICHELE HERNANDEZ
Former Assistant Director of Admissions, Dartmouth College
Author of *A is for Admission*

Q: **Can you give students an idea of what happens to their applications and essays after they are received by the college?**

A: First, admissions officers collect all the different parts of the application. Then, all the pieces are scanned and date stamped. It's all done electronically like an electronic file cabinet. Once everything is assembled, admissions officers start to read them one by one (now they often do them on the computer instead of in hard copy).

Unlike many colleges, Dartmouth doesn't sort the applications at first into regional categories or schools. They are placed into completely random groups that correspond with a particular admissions officer's group of states.

Once an admissions officer reads one application folder, it is passed on to someone else who will also review it. If after two reads it's a tie, the file goes to committee or to the director. After reading all the applications, the admissions officers start meeting and discussing the merits of each applicant one by one through committee meetings.

Admissions officers don't only look at the applicants at the top end of an academic or extracurricular scale. Every single application is reviewed through this process.

Q: **What are some of the most common mistakes that students make when writing their essays?**

A: Some students simply don't spend any time on their essays. A lot of bright students think, "I'm number one so I don't need to take any time on the application." The result is that it looks rushed. You want to show some reflection, that you thought about your application. You don't want to have the appearance that you spent only five minutes on it. Some of the more obvious errors have been not spell checking or putting the wrong school down, but more often, it's that the essays are not interesting.

Another mistake is the admissions officer doesn't learn anything. If I read an essay and think, "That's nice but I don't know anything more about this student," you've failed. You have to share something interesting about yourself. Remember that it's not just one essay, but there are 5 to 6 smaller essays. It's not as limited as you think.

Q: **How important is the introduction?**

A: Introductions are nice, but the whole essay has to work. It has to grab you from the beginning like a newspaper lead. It has to make you want to keep going.

Q: **Can you think of an example of when an applicant wrote about an ordinary topic in an extraordinary way?**

A: One student wrote about shooting a squirrel. I'm sure his guidance counselor told him to not write about that. However, the essay was about growing up to be a man, a meditation on what it means to grow up. While the topic may have seemed like the plot of a bad play, it was a slice of life essay that told a lot about his family and about him. The topic doesn't matter as much as what you do with it.

Q: **Are there any topics or approaches to topics that students shouldn't write about?**

A: Any approach works if it works. Writing is so fluid. There are no hard and fast rules except to be honest about yourself. The magic formula is that there's no magic formula. The truth is that you don't have to be a fabulous writer either. The admissions officers are reading the essays more for content. They're almost speed reading them for content. Remember that this is not your chance to be Faulkner. This is your chance to write about something you're interested in. It'll be a lot more vivid if it's something you're interested in. This may sound obvious, but so many kids obsess about the writing style instead of worrying about the actual content and that's a mistake.

Q: **Do you recommend that students ask someone else to read their essay and give feedback?**

A: You need some feedback because what you think is funny may not be to other people. You don't want it to be over-edited where everything's perfect, and you don't need a professional editor. The essay could be a little unpolished, but I would have a friend or parent read it for diction and flow. You don't want an essay in which you can tell that an English teacher went through it 45 times.

Q: **How important is the essay? In your experience, has it ever made the difference between a student being accepted or not?**

A: It all depends on where you are. If you are very strong academically, the admissions officers are verifying whether you're the genius everyone says you are. For you, the essay doesn't matter as much. Also, if you're in the low end, it doesn't matter as much. It matters more for the students in the middle of the pool for that college. If we use the scale of 1 to 9, the essay matters a lot for the students who are rated 5, 6, or 7. The essays have made a difference for students, but there haven't been many students who have moved from the rejection to the accepted pile based solely on the essays.

Q: Is there anything else you'd like to add?

A: It's not just one essay that counts. It's the whole application. It doesn't matter how good your essays are if your teachers say you're not interesting. It has to do with how all the information (teacher recs, essays, school support, transcript) fits together. Your essays have to be in line with the rest of your application. The admissions officers are going to be suspicious if you have a brilliant essay but it doesn't match the rest of your application. Everything has to be in the same vein.

Also, if you've had extraordinary circumstances, you should write about them in a note. If you weren't involved in activities, explain that you were taking care of your autistic sister. You want admissions officers to know about anything unusual

> Dr. Michele Hernandez is the former assistant director of admissions at Dartmouth College and the author of *A is for Admission*, *The Middle School Years*, *Don't Worry You'll Get In* and *Acing the College Application*. She is with the president and founder of Hernandez College Consulting (www. hernandezcollegeconsulting.com).

EVA OSTRUM
Former Assistant Director of Undergraduate Admissions, Yale University
Author of *The Thinking Parent's Guide to College Admissions*
Founder of High School Futures

Q: What are some of the most common mistakes that students make when writing their essays?

A: Some schools ask students to write about a role model such as asking what single person they would have lunch with. The biggest mistake that students make is that they spend more time writing about the other person than themselves. I'd suggest starting from your own vantage point. How have you been affected? From my own life, if I were writing an essay, one person I've always admired is Nelson Mandela. Every day on the first day of school I read an inspiring quote from Nelson Mandela. One day a boy looked at me and said, reacting to the quote, "Miss, who *are* you?" Focus on how your own actions and outlook have changed as a result of that person whether you've met them face to face or only know their writing.

Another really common mistake is that students feel they have to write something that makes them look different. When you're applying to a highly selective college, there's nothing you can do that looks different based on the actions themselves. Every admissions officer has seen someone who does what you do. Instead, focus on what makes you you. That's really what admissions officers want to know. Don't tie yourself in knots to look exotic. It doesn't matter what your essay's about. It's how you write about it.

Q: How can you tell if a student's essay is authentic?

A: You look at their critical reading score. If they have a low critical reading and writing score and an essay that looks like it's written by a college professor or if the essay sounds like a very sophisticated person wrote it and the recommendations don't present the same image, these can be a red flag. For many years, there's been an understanding that students in a certain income bracket get coached. If you do nothing, you're putting yourself at risk. Remember though it's fine to have someone read your essay and give feedback on how it flows. It's not fine to have someone read your essay and do line by line edits. That would present you in a way that doesn't line up.

Q: What is one or two of the best introductions you remember? What made them so memorable?

A: There was one essay that a student wrote about when his father first took him for karate lessons. The first sentence was about how he had been a complete failure at every other sport. There was another one by a girl who wrote about how she was a comic book artist. She was applying to art school, and some schools don't consider it to be a serious art form. She grabbed me from the very beginning because her passion was so clear. The essays that grab me give me some kind of hook in the beginning to reel me in.

Q: Can you think of an example of when an applicant wrote about an ordinary topic in an extraordinary way?

A: One Yale applicant wrote about how every day on her way to school she passed a building where the pigeons rested. You would think that's a ridiculous topic, but it was so well written and engaging. It was about something mundane, but it really grabbed my attention.

It's important to tell a good story. Think about the stories you listen to in your life that your relatives tell or your friends tell. If they're well told, that's what catches your attention.

Q: Are there any topics or approaches to topics that students shouldn't write about?

A: Topics that deal with personal tragedy are difficult. Frequently the students are not far enough away from the event to write about it with any distance. They're not really telling a story. The essay is either a factual narration or therapeutic. I would be very wary of writing about a really serious, heavy topic. It can be done, but I think that the rule of thumb should be if the topic is still sensitive enough that you might wince a little bit, tear up, or cringe, maybe it's not a good topic. If you can talk about the event and maybe even have a sense of humor about it, that's a sign you're far enough away from it. Of course that doesn't mean you have to write about it with humor.

Q: How important is the essay?

A: There was at least one student where the essay was very significant. I fell in love with this student because of his essay, and I wanted him to go to Yale. I thought he would add so much to the school, but one of his SAT scores was weak. It's so competitive that if there's one chink in the armor, that can end it. I could've passed over him and no one would've objected, but I made such a case for this student. I fought for him, and he got in. However, it can't just be on the basis of the essay alone. His teachers also really loved him and thought he walked on water. There has to be some resonance between the essay, the teachers and the classes.

Q: Is there anything that a student might find surprising about what you are looking for in the essays?

A: I think students would be surprised to know that admissions officers aren't looking for anything exotic. The more specific examples you can use, the more you can make it a story with very specific details, the better. You want to be able to picture what the person looks like, what it would be like to sit in a room and have a conversation with the person. The essay should make the admissions officers feel like they've had a conversation with you and want to learn more. It's not more esoteric than that.

Eva Ostrum worked as an assistant director of undergraduate admissions at Yale University and wrote *The Thinking Parent's Guide to College Admissions*. She also founded and runs High School Futures, an organization that works on educational reform in urban high schools (www.hsfutures.org).

3

ACADEMIC PASSION

"Bacon"

Mariam Nassiri
Duke University

THE ALARM CLOCK IS, TO MANY high school students, a wailing monstrosity whose purpose is to torture all who are sleep-deprived. Those who believe this are misguided, and are simply viewing the situation from a twisted perspective. For when these imprudent early-risers blearily rub their eyes each morning, and search in vain for whatever is making that earsplitting noise, they are, without a doubt, annoyed. Why?

It isn't because the only thing they desire is to sleep a few extra hours, as many would presume. No, these kids are groggy and irritable because they are waking up to what they think will be another horribly boring day of school. If one of these foolish Sallys or Joes were, say, sleeping comfortably on a *Saturday* morning, I could certainly see something different happening. A beautiful breakfast of tantalizing vittles—eggs, hash browns, and the like—would be ready and waiting for them on their kitchen tables. But the scrumptious delight to outshine them all would be a slab of bacon, piled proudly for the taking. It would be that wafting, wondrous bacon smell that would draw dear, sweet Sally abruptly from her slumber—long before an alarm clock has the chance to pierce the air.

Oh, bacon: what a marvelous, glorious thing! I live for those heart-stoppingly good strips of succulence, so crispy and crunchy, so packed with perfection. The thought of having a plate of bacon every day, perhaps every school day, sends me into sheer waves of ecstasy!

To be sure, many others would also wax poetic about this lovely breakfast food. But precious few would share this same zeal for learning. I, however, can smugly decree that I do regard both very highly. I brightly waken every morning to the mellifluous joy that sounds from my alarm clock, a huge smile plastered on my face, and the yearning to learn in my heart.

When I board my school bus Monday through Friday, it is still pitch black outside. Busmates will groan about how even the day has not yet dragged itself out of bed; I only chuckle through their thirty-minute rant fest as we chug down the freeway. Opting to be part of a far-away Magnet school, after all, has its benefits. My peers may still not look forward to waking up earlier, but when we are all together in a classroom, we take on the "bacon mentality." I have the opportunity to choose from a wealth of diverse classes, and love arriving to school each day with the prospect of having a new Spanish History lesson—taught to me in Spanish, for a change. Teachers, driven by the enthusiasm of their Magnet students, are inspired to create new classes for advanced students, including those who have completed AP Spanish Literature and are still eager to learn more, or those who want to learn about a specific aspect of a subject—we now have a Middle Eastern History class. Not to be outdone, the post-AP exam period of my English Language class included an intensive literature study, where we laughed at good ol' Yossarian in *Catch-22*, and developed a strong attachment to Jay Gatsby. I'd like to think that *The Great Gatsby*'s pursuit of Daisy is not unlike my own pursuit of bacon. I've gobbled up new knowledge rapidly, hankering after it like any elusive bacon strip, and happily digesting any new bits of information.

But six classes a year are simply not enough to satisfy my hunger for knowledge. Just as I eat bacon all three meals of the day (when possible), I attempt to learn all days of the week. Rather than make another trip to some lackluster movie theatre on the weekend, I dedicate my time to reading another good book, or reviewing Economics with my friends. But high school is starting to smell like leftovers to me now; I want fresh, new, crisp learning. I want not to read a textbook written by a renowned professor: I want to hear him speak directly. I'm ready for the university, and hunger for all the new opportunities waiting for me! I've finished my breakfast, and now it's time to get going to school.

ANALYSIS

Mariam's essay "Bacon" uses lively language and plenty of humor to tell a story that highlights her eagerness to go to school. Her writing is casual and funny, and it conveys in a personal and genuine way her enthusiastic attitude. "Bacon" reminds us that topics do not have to be serious to be sincere.

The metaphor of bacon is a very memorable one in image, smell, texture, and taste. Mariam capitalizes on these features in her beautiful—and mouthwatering!—descriptors of a Saturday morning breakfast of eggs. With a touch of humor and a hint of parody, she writes, "Oh, bacon: what a marvelous, glorious thing! I live for those heartstoppingly good strips of succulence, so crispy and crunchy, so packed with perfection. The thought of having a plate of bacon every day, perhaps every school day, sends me into sheer waves of ecstasy!"

Just when this celebration of bacon begins to appear over-the-top, and readers are beginning to worry that Mariam swapped a food magazine piece with her college admissions essay, she links the succulent bacon metaphor with school: "To be sure, many others would also wax poetic about this lovely breakfast food. But precious few would share this same zeal for learning." Though Mariam takes a risk in waxing poetic over bacon, she does so with carefully calculated dramatic effect that ultimately pays off. We are convinced that the "yearning to learn" is deeply engrained in our bacon-lover and early-riser author.

Mariam's narrative also shows us the sacrifices she makes for attending a Magnet school far from home. Her use of the phrase "bacon mentality" is original and creative. Mariam's descriptions of her classes are specific enough to prevent them from reading like a list. Rather, she demonstrates the depth of her commitment in her classes by citing specific details like Yossarian in Catch-22. Mariam's essay demonstrates how she is able to fit impressive details of her life into a narrative framework, a strategy that can avoid the pitfall of sounding like bragging. Mariam follows the "show, don't tell" mantra when she mentions the Magnet school in the context of her long early-morning bus ride, and in celebrating her Spanish history class, which is impressively taught in Spanish.

At the end of the essay, the bacon metaphor may seem overdone to some readers, as Mariam has "gobbled up new knowledge rapidly, hankering after it like any elusive bacon strip" and has expressed a desire for "fresh, new crisp" learning to satisfy her "hunger for knowledge." She might have reduced the number of mentions of bacon and hunger. However, Mariam's essay ultimately stands out for its originality and unpredictable connections, like linking *The Great Gatsby* to—what else?—bacon.

"Beyond Plug-and-Chug Math"

Anonymous
MIT

I HAVE ALWAYS BEEN A MATH-SCIENCE girl. I sighed and sulked through classes on US History and French in eager anticipation of the formulas and applications I would be learning later in the day. I believe there are many factors which attribute to my success, two being my fascination and persistence.

When I was seven I once asked what math was good for and why I should learn it. The answer I received simply does not do math justice, "One day when you're in line at the grocery store the cashier will give you too little change and you'll be glad you learned this." Now in calculus I see the application of all these once foreign symbols, formulas, and letters. I am often amazed by the calculations I am able to do using the cumulative information acquired from nearly 12 years of education, such as how to maximize the volume of a box given a certain surface area. Math is not just plug and chug as many view it but it requires creativity and thinking out of the box to solve the problems encountered in the real world. Beauty lies in its simplicity and in the fact that proofs and observations are what brought the golden rectangle from ancient Greece, Pascal's triangle, and the Pythagorean Theorem as well as a host of other theorems, equations, and postulates. Math has made the impossible possible and the once long and tedious, simple and quick. The genius of it is amazing as well as the fact that any person is capable of applying and discovering it. I draw graphs and try to make shapes from functions for fun, count to 10 to calm down, and save money at the store, too. For all of these reasons and many more, I am fascinated by math.

I wasn't always good at math, contrary to what students in my classes might say. When I first showed interest in math in the 5th grade my parents laughed; middle school was even worse. Incoming 6th graders were given a test on the second day of school and depending on their scores were placed into a high or low speed math class. I was put in the slow speed math and missed a lot of class my first year, as a result my grade drifted from a B to a C to a C-, then I got help. I knew I liked math and I didn't want to do bad in it so I bought books and hired my older brother to help me. I eventually made it to a B+. Later, in the summer after my junior year, I took a course that covered nearly a year of Calculus. I was told that if I decided to take Calculus AB, I would be bored, so I went for a challenge. My strongest subject began to take up most of my time. I had to read review books, go online for help, and stay in during nutrition and lunch for extra instruction. It was hard, but my dedication paid off and I earned an A. This persistence and drive also help me excel in math.

ANALYSIS

In this essay, the author begins by stating that she has "always been a math-science girl." The honest confession that follows, "I sighed and sulked through classes on US History and French," underscores this point. She goes on to provide specific examples of her "fascination and persistence" regarding math, even causing a chuckle when she asks why math is useful to learn and receives an answer that doesn't "do math justice"—being able to count change at the grocery store. This is comical, providing an excellent contrast to algebra with its "foreign symbols, formulas and letters." The rendering of math as a "foreign" language shows us the fascination the author has with math and its applications. Her praise of math and vision for the potential of what to others might merely be a boring academic subject is memorable in its admiring tone: she notes the "creativity and thinking out of the box" math requires, and believes its "beauty lies in its simplicity." The references to specific math theorems, equations, and postulates further strengthen the author's assertion that she is intrigued by all the applications that math has for the real world, whether they are ordinary or academic. The strength of this author's examples lies in their accessibility to a general audience. She summarizes this nicely when she writes, "I draw graphs and try to make shapes from functions for fun, count to 10 to calm down, and save money at the store, too." The reference to saving money at the store nicely ties back to the original anecdote about math being undervalued in society.

The second half of the essay addresses the author's "persistence" in math, following a most persuasive first section that clearly convinces us regarding her "fascination" for this area of study. "I wasn't always good at math, contrary to what students in my classes might say," she writes. This first sentence of the second paragraph comes as a surprise, since we are accustomed to associating passion for a subject with skill in the field. This section shows that writing about a weakness and not meeting expectations can still make an effective essay topic. Though most people would not admit to getting a C- in class, this author does so in an honest way in order to show the amount of progress she has been able to make. While the improvement in her grades is impressive, this anecdotal information might have been even more interesting had she spent more time explaining the ups and downs of achieving higher grades and taking a summer calculus course. Still, details the essay mentions—such as staying in for lunch to get extra instruction—certainly attest to her dedication. Overall, this essay provides a full and balanced explanation of the author's passion for math as well as her arduous journey toward excellence.

"A Different Kind of Love"

Oana Emilia Butnareanu
Stanford University

WHEN I WAS FOUR YEARS OLD, I fell in love. It was not a transient love-one that stayed by my side during the good times and vanished during the bad-but rather a love so deep that few would understand. It was not the love for a person, but the love for a language. It was the love for Spanish.

Having been born and raised behind the Iron Curtain, in a country where Western influence was limited and the official and only language was Romanian, I was on my own. Everyone around me, especially my family, had trouble understanding what could possibly draw me to such a foreign and, in their opinion, unattractive language. But as they say, love is blind, and the truth of the matter is that *I* wasn't even sure what it was exactly that made Spanish so fascinating to me. The only thing I knew was that I absolutely adored hearing its perfectly articulated phrases, and trying to make sense of its sweet and tender words: serenades to my innocent ear.

Spanish entered through my door on June 16th, 1994, when a man from the local cable company came to connect our living room to the rest of the world. That day, I was introduced to "Acasa," a Romanian cable network dedicated to broadcasting Spanish language *telenovelas* (soap operas) to Romanian audiences. As I learned to read, I started associating the Romanian subtitles with the Spanish dialogue, and little by little, I began understanding the language. For a little girl who had yet to discover new aspects of her own language, this was quite an accomplishment, but no one around me felt the same way. My father, enraged at my apparent "obsession" with the language, scolded me incessantly, declaring that:

"We are immigrating to the United States, not to Mexico! You should spend your time learning English instead of watching that nonsense!"

Sadly, my family's objection was only the first of many hardships I was bound to encounter. When I was nine, my immigration to the US forced me to say goodbye to what had become a huge and indispensible part of me. I needed to hear Spanish, to listen to it daily, and although Los Angeles could be considered a Spanish speaker's paradise, my largely Romanian neighborhood allowed for little interaction with the language. For six years, destiny kept us apart and the feelings that Spanish had evoked in me soon faded away.

But high school brought about a new era in my life, an era in which my love for Spanish was revived and greatly amplified. For an hour a day, life was put on hold and I was able to speak and read Spanish more actively than ever. After two years of Advanced Placement Spanish, I not only understood the language to perfection, but spoke it flawlessly as well.

There are no words that can describe how proud and greatly accomplished I feel today at my ability to speak Spanish. During a recent trip to Mexico, I was mistaken more than once for one of the natives. One man, after seeing my Romanian last name, asked me if it was my husband's, for undoubtedly, he believed, I was Mexican. Given to a Romanian girl, whose family members were oblivious to the language, and who had learned it on her own despite their objections, this was the greatest compliment of all. In the United States, Spanish is the second most spoken language and a great asset for anyone who speaks it. It is not "nonsense," as my father had dubbed it, and being able to prove this to him has made me even prouder for loving Spanish.

My love of Spanish has influenced much of who I am today. The fight that I led against family objections and immigration to a new land has allowed me to develop an ambitious and aggressive spirit in the face of adversity. It has made me stronger, and taught me that I must always fight with unstoppable perseverance for all that is important to me. I am determined to use my love and passion for Spanish to make an impact on the world. Currently, Spanish is the primary language of 21 nations around the globe, and one of the six official languages of the UN. I want to be the link that connects these nations to the United States, and to the 40 million Americans whose native language is Spanish. I want to use my ability to speak Spanish to learn more about the people of these nations, both on a professional and personal level. No matter where the path of life takes me, I wish for Spanish to always be a part of me.

Through the years, Spanish has evolved into one of my most remarkable accomplishments. Today, I am prouder than ever of loving Spanish-of having something that distinguishes me from the rest, something that makes me unique. It is not often the case for a Romanian-American girl living in Los Angeles to exhibit such passion and devotion towards a language that is foreign to both her native and adoptive countries. Nevertheless, Spanish is a big part of whom I am today, and an even bigger part of who I will be in the future.

ANALYSIS

Oana's essay opens with a fresh perspective on a theme that is often overused and can easily become hackneyed—love. The first sentence surprises us: "When I was four years old, I fell in love." Her young age piques our curiosity, and she holds our suspense until the last sentence. Like many of the excellent essays in this book, the strength of this essay lies in its originality. Oana describes a love for the language of Spanish. Learning Spanish in itself may not seem particularly exceptional, but Oana's background as a Romanian provides an unusual and memorable juxtaposition to her Spanish-speaking abilities.

In her descriptions, Oana playfully and effectively uses terms relating to love. For example, she notes that "love is blind" and personifies Spanish as it "entered through [her] door on June 16th, 1994." The sentence, "for six years, destiny kept us apart" continues to perpetuate a personified sense of Spanish, the language, being a "lover" to Oana. These examples show the power of artfully expanding on a metaphor to provide richness and coherence to one's essays.

Oana's love for Spanish's sweet serenades contrasts with her family's feelings towards this foreign and "unattractive" language. She uses her father's comment to capture these negative sentiments with powerful dramatic effect: "We are immigrating to the United States, not to Mexico! You should spend your time learning English instead of watching that nonsense!" His criticisms only make Oana's accomplishments all the more admirable and memorable—how many other Romanian girls teach themselves Spanish through watching *telenovelas* while their family looks on disapprovingly?

Oana writes frankly of the "hardships" she encountered, first in the form of family resistance to learning Spanish and later in the form of lacking an environment for communicating in Spanish in her predominantly Romanian Los Angeles neighborhood. However, she demonstrates her dedication to Spanish during the "new era" of high school, when she studied actively for two years and astonishingly became fluent in the language.

Oana relates several amusing anecdotes from her trip to Mexico to corroborate her fluency in Spanish. We learn that she "was mistaken more than once for one of the natives." She might have chosen to tell us more from this trip in order to show ways in which she was able to "prove" to her father that Spanish was "not 'nonsense'."

In her penultimate paragraph, Oana relates her long process of learning Spanish to her "ambitious and aggressive spirit in the face of adversity" as well as to her further plans "to use [her] love and passion for Spanish to make an impact on the world." Oana could have ended her essay with this paragraph, since her final paragraph mostly reiterates what she has already said. While it can be tempting to use concluding paragraphs to recap what you have already written, it is best to end in a way that seems fresh, rather than regurgitating what has already been said.

"From Flaubert to Frisbee"

Aditya Kumar
Brown University

THIS SUMMER, I WENT TO THE Governor's Honors Program, also known as GHP, a six-week intensive college-like experience where the best and brightest students in Georgia gather to learn and grow as individuals. It was the best thing that has ever happened to me. That is something of a hackneyed phrase; people cheapen the extremes of language by constantly using superlatives for everyday occurrences, making it harder and harder to actually describe the few subtle and transcendent moments of life. In *Madame Bovary*, Flaubert claims that language is but a cracked kettle on which we play music for the bears to dance, while we dream of making the stars weep. The experiences we have never fit within the too-close confines of language; but I will try anyway. The classes that I attended were nothing like the classes that I would take normally. Nowhere else would the teachers encourage sixteen and seventeen year-olds to look for sexual imagery in Shakespeare, and then find even more than they did, without the exercise being sordid instead of literary. I attended classes named anything from Dirty Words: Clean Thoughts (a class on Profanity; the only course in which the use of profane or vulgar language was prohibited) to Teenage Female Angst: Beyond Holden Caulfield to *Buffy the Vampire Slayer*. All of them opened my mind to a brand-new way of looking at the world, and processing information. Thanks to the varying education that I received, I know that valuable information about life is not only in the "classics," but even appears in seemingly mindless and trashy zombie films.

While I learned a lot in the classrooms of GHP, I feel that most of my growth occurred outside of the classroom. I met the sort of people who will change the world, who will go forth into the world and, without making a big name, will do the things that make the world a better place. My best friends there were people that I would never have met; people I would never have known existed; people that I can now not imagine life without. One was a math major, an excellent athlete in every sport, and an accomplished singer; the running joke was that the only thing that he was bad at was failing. The other was a phenomenal writer, always ready to play an endearing trick on somebody, and the former's girl-friend. Both of them were fairly conservative Christians, and yet totally accepting of me for whom I was, despite any of my clashes with their beliefs. I did not limit myself though, and made it almost a mission to find and talk to as many of the people there, because I was sure that each and every one of them would have an interesting perspective on things. Once I was walking back from playing Frisbee, and was stopped to discuss what the ethical framework for life ought to be; just for fun. The experience that I had there has undeniably changed me forever.

ANALYSIS

Aditya's description of his six weeks at GHP make use of plenty of diverse and lively examples to demonstrate how this "was the best thing that ever happened" to him. The one-paragraph format that Aditya chooses can be difficult on the readers, since long paragraphs can be quite daunting. Aditya might have chosen to create a new paragraph with the sentence, "The experiences we have never fit within the too-close confines of language; but I will try anyway." Another logical place to begin a new paragraph would be with the sentence, "While I learned a lot in the classrooms of GHP, I feel that most of my growth occurred outside of the classroom." In general, multiple paragraphs help organize an essay to focus the content and provide flow to overall paper structure.

While the sentence, "It was the best thing that has ever happened to me," seems simplistic, Aditya quickly redeems himself from the cliché with a sentence that shows his mastery of the English language. He writes, "That is something of a hackneyed phrase; people cheapen the extremes of language by constantly using superlatives for everyday occurrences, making it harder and harder to actually describe the few subtle and transcendent moments of life." His reference to *Madame Bovary* demonstrates Aditya's ability to draw connections between ideas and thereby support his own assertions. The examples Aditya references are particularly strong because he relates them to one another, instead of simply rattling off a long list. It can be challenging to present a diversity of interests while also holding a core focus. Aditya's center appears in the form of literary and cultural analysis of many sources, from classics to "trashy zombie films." The reference to *Madame Bovary* also shows us that Aditya truly learned to open his "mind to a brand-new way of looking at the world, and processing information."

Had Aditya ended his essay here, we would have learned about his cognitive development but missed out on the social and emotional aspects of his GHP experience. The descriptions of the close friendships Aditya formed with a diverse group of people further strengthen our understanding of how Aditya grew to be an open-minded person. Aditya devotes quite a large amount of space to talking about the math major who couldn't fail and his writer girlfriend; he might have summarized this information more concisely in order to explain his own relationships to them. By writing that they totally accepted him, Aditya removes his personal agency; he could have reworded the essay to explain how *he* became more accepting of *them*.

The last sentence of the essay, "The experience that I had there has undeniably changed me forever," is somewhat abrupt. With limited space, it is important to have both a strong introduction and a strong conclusion that are not so open-ended that they could be generalized to everyone. The most compelling part of Aditya's essay is not that "The experience that I had there has undeniably changed me forever" but rather in the sophisticated literary analyses he made, the friendships he formed, and the Frisbee he played. When space is limited, err on the side of more detailed descriptions and fewer generalizations.

"Raising the Bar"

Anonymous
MIT

THIS PAST SUMMER I HAD THE opportunity to participate in a highly rigorous academic program at MIT called MITES, Minority Introduction to Engineering and Science. For six and a half weeks I lived with 68 other rising seniors and college undergrads. Though we were all warned about how hard the program would be, we were all at the top of our classes and refused to believe it- after all, who did they think we were? The first day we sat together in a small auditorium, unaware of each other and of what lay ahead. We were told that our confidence would be shattered, our minds blown away, and our lives changed forever. Still somewhat unmoved, we were not afraid.

By the second week of MITES valedictorians, nerds, bookworms, and techies alike were leaning on each other's shoulders at two in the morning crying over problem sets they had imagined only in nightmares. It is a well known fact that hard times bring friends closer together, but I would have never expected for these strangers to become my best friends, my support system, or even my family. The 16 hours days I was accustomed to at home did not last long. I was getting an average of four hours of sleep per night, finishing a book per week, zooming through subjects once foreign to me, and constructing a semi-autonomous robot from drill motors all at the same time.

We were each enrolled in 5 classes, my schedule consisted of Introductory Physics, Engineering Design, Chemistry, first year Calculus, and Humanities. In the month and a half we completed a semester of Physics and Chemistry each, a full year of Calculus, the material equivalent to a semester in AP literature, and introductory level engineering. The work was so intense that when I entered school in the fall I enrolled in second year Calculus, and maintained the only A in AP Physics, having no physics experience prior to MITES.

Since this program I have not been satisfied with the regular coursework given at my school. I am constantly on the lookout for new programs to enroll in and other teams, clubs, and groups to join. This academic school year marks the peak of my involvement in educational opportunities. I have somehow managed to find time for the Speech and Debate team, ACE mentoring team, swim team, Science Bowl team, California Honors Society and Scholarship Federation, Play Production, Jewish Student Union, GEAR-UP Mentoring Program, and folklorico dancing.

MITES was the most challenging experience of my life. The program is the single most pivotal point in my academic endeavors to date. The assistants we had had all gone through the program and agreed that even in college at Harvard, MIT, Caltech, and Princeton, nothing came close. The motivation and encouragement I gained from MITES has fueled my academic pursuits and pushed me to raise the bar.

ANALYSIS

Many students choose to write about a transforming summer education experience. In "Raising the Bar," the author describes the grueling, rigorous academic program at MIT in which she participated. Foreshadowing the difficulties that lay ahead, the author writes, "We were told that our confidence would be shattered, our minds blown away, and our lives changed forever. Still somewhat unmoved, we were not afraid." This fearless attitude gives way to "crying over problem sets." The essay aptly describes the intensity of the program by explaining how busy the days were. She found herself "finishing a book per week, zooming through subjects once foreign to [her], and constructing a semi-autonomous robot from drill motors all at the same time." While these tasks might seem like a list, they are necessary to account for the author sleeping only four hours a night. When describing an event with a scope that is quite broad—in this case, six weeks long—it is always helpful to hone in on a few highlights. Three is typically a good number of examples. This essay might be stronger had the author explained more about the robot construction, since this is an unusual activity that piques the reader's curiosity. As a major project, the robot may have merited more space in the essay. The author could have spent less time listing the classes she took, especially if she could list this elsewhere in the application. What is more compelling than any course title is her observation that "the work was so intense that when [she] entered school in the fall [she] enrolled in second year Calculus, and maintained the only A in AP Physics, having no physics experience prior to MITES." This demonstrates the extent to which her learning was accelerated because of the MITES experience.

At the end of the third paragraph, the author gives a long list of activities in which she is involved. It is unclear what some of the activities entail—for instance, the ACE mentoring team, or the GEAR-UP Mentoring program. These examples might be more appropriate in a resume or another section of the admissions essay. Choosing one main activity or event and elaborating on it is a strategy to help keep an essay focused. While it is tempting to list all of our accomplishments, it is more memorable to focus on just one, or a few. Ultimately, the author brings us back to her main point, that MITES was a pivotal point in her academic career. Having a main thesis helps tie together an essay. In this paper, the author summarizes by saying, "The motivation and encouragement I gained from MITES has fueled my academic pursuits and pushed me to raise the bar." When editing your own writing, ask yourself if your various examples, sentences, and paragraphs serve the main point. This helps create a coherent, tightly-woven essay.

BOOKS/LITERATURE

"Rosencrantz and Guildenstern"

Fareez Giga
Stanford University

"ROSENCRANTZ AND GUILDENSTERN ARE DEAD" IS an astounding, intellectually challenging, and humorous concoction. Stoppard cleverly captures the characters of Hamlet, written by Shakespeare, but creates somewhat of a comic tragedy. Clearly an oxymoron, but profoundly effective. The play focuses on the story of Hamlet, but from the viewpoint of Rosencrantz and Guildenstern, and it also takes the theories proposed in Hamlet and presents them in a comic, rather than sullen, manner. One of the most humorous scenes is when Rosencrantz, or Guildenstern, since the distinction is never truly made between the two, is laying on a table and thinking to himself what it is like to be "dead in a box." This scene proves to be hilarious, despite its deep meaning, and parallels the infamous "To be, or not to be" speech in Hamlet. Life's unanswerable questions are constantly being asked throughout the play, but by inserting these dubious inquiries within a comedy, Stoppard is able to captivate and preserve his audience's attention. In fact, the humor provides the wiring, which connects the messages of the play to our own chaotic existences. This brilliant literary work captures the essence of a tragedy within a comedy, something only few authors can accomplish. It is able to provide profound, theoretical ideas that have long been questioned into a comic perspective, and yet keep its integrity.

ANALYSIS

In just one short paragraph, Fareez engages with the literary work "Rosencrantz and Guildenstern are Dead" in a lively and creative manner. Early on, the essay pinpoints the "oxymoron" of the tragicomedy form, giving us a theme of contrasts that runs throughout the short essay response. Fareez demonstrates his familiarity with the work by highlighting a specific scene from the play. This is more effective than a summary; considering the limited space provided, a summary would take up too much space and could also seem too general. The subsequent analysis of this scene shows that Fareez is an active interpreter of the literary work, as well as an avid reader of other plays, as shown by the analogy he draws to Hamlet. Through the description and analysis of one specific scene, Fareez addresses a broader issue: the "intellectually exciting" aspects of literary work that the essay prompt asks him to explain.

The reference to "life's unanswerable questions" implies that these are the types of deep philosophical inquiries that Fareez himself participates in. He might have chosen to be more explicit about this, thereby linking his analysis of the play more directly to his own life. This would help address the "explain why" aspect of the essay question in greater detail. It is always important to address all parts of an essay question to show that you have read the prompt mindfully and given it careful consideration.

This essay relates to Fareez's other essay, "A Dramatic Coup" (Chapter 16), in that it describes his passion for drama and theater. Some students choose to write on completely different topics for their various essays, especially if they have a diversity of interests. However, it is also appropriate to focus on a particular passion or interest, especially if you plan on pursuing this in college or are applying to a special program in a school and wish to demonstrate your dedication to a specific field such as science, music, or service. Writing more than one essay on a specific passion/interest runs the risk of sounding redundant, so this approach may be more useful for shorter essays. In Fareez's case, he was able to demonstrate in "A Dramatic Coup" that he is a dedicated actor, and also show that he is able to approach theater from a more intellectual and philosophical angle in "Rosencrantz and Guildenstern." Read together, these two essays give us the sense that Fareez is a creative individual who is willing to tackle an interest from many different perspectives. Furthermore, one can predict that Fareez will be a valuable asset to Stanford's drama department, whatever area of study he ultimately chooses.

5

CAREER

"Puzzles"

Anonymous
Harvard University

WHEN MY GRANDMOTHER CAME TO VISIT five years ago, she brought me a 3,000 piece jigsaw puzzle. To most, this would not sound very exciting—it would be almost as bad as a shirt saying "My grandparents went to India, and all they bought me was this stupid shirt." My reaction to the puzzle was different. I cut open the cardboard box as soon as I could, and poured the pieces out onto my puzzleboard. I worked patiently on the puzzle for hours at a time, my excitement building as more and more of the picture was revealed. I cut down my sleep time until the image of a picturesque forest was complete. The puzzle overshadowed all else in my life, if only for that short period of time.

Working on puzzles has helped me gain focus, determination, and patience. I have learned to apply these qualities to every task I face, dealing with the outside world in the same fashion as I would a puzzle. My love for science stems largely from this; science requires the same logical and levelheaded approach that a puzzle does, and as evidenced by the many puzzles decorating my house, this is an approach which suits my skills and temperament. This intellectual stimulation, coupled with a desire to discover more about life's mysteries, compels me to pursue a career in scientific research.

This summer, I worked in a cardiology laboratory at UCLA, looking at proteins associated with HDL to understand how atherosclerosis can be averted. After some experiments provided questionable results, I was given the task of confirming that the viruses we were working with had been packaged and identified correctly. I spent weeks running DNA gels, looking for specific genes in each virus, but my results were inconsistent. I was frustrated, but instead of giving up on my assignment, I was even more determined to find an explanation. I considered every aspect of the experiment, working backwards until I reached the source—the primers I had used to amplify the DNA were nonspecific and ineffective, and thus useless in distinguishing the three genes of interest to us. Knowing this, I was able to alter my experiment accordingly, looking at protein content instead of DNA sequences. I finally showed that two of the three viruses were correct; the third, however, needed to be repackaged. My work was crucial to the undergraduate student I was working with, because he was able to redesign his experiment to account for this third virus.

Working in a lab was an exhilarating experience for me. Even though I gave up lying on the beach to instead play with viruses and chemicals, the compulsion to understand these proteins inspired and motivated me. I am tremendously proud of the piece I contributed to the atherosclerosis puzzle: a small piece, but integral nonetheless. The sense of accomplishment I felt because of my work in the UCLA lab was much the same as that which I felt upon completing the 3,000 piece puzzle my grandmother gave me. This feeling is one I hope to experience throughout my life, because the atherosclerosis puzzle is most assuredly not the last such puzzle I will work on.

ANALYSIS

The writer's essay takes a tangible theme—puzzles—and uses it in a variety of ways to demonstrate her interests, passions, and values. Her writing is engaging because it plays with many different senses of the word "puzzles," so the theme doesn't feel tired or redundant. She begins her essay with a reference to a 3,000-piece jigsaw puzzle that her grandmother gave her. Her subsequent use of humor ("To most, this would not sound very exciting—it would be almost as bad as a shirt saying 'My grandparents went to India, and all they bought me was this stupid shirt'") effectively draws readers in. This statement also sets up an expectation that most people would not be thrilled by this gift but that the writer is *not* "most people." We can see that she is devoted to completing the impressively large puzzle by her mention that she even sacrificed sleep in pursuit of her goal.

In her second paragraph, the writer links this pastime to her intellectual interests. She makes a clear and compelling comparison between puzzles and scientific research, noting that both require a "logical and levelheaded approach." She demonstrates self-knowledge when she notes that this "suits [her] skills and temperament." This analysis is very explicit and may seem to violate the "show, don't tell" rule; but in her case, it helps us make the connection between puzzles and science—a connection that might not be immediately clear—and does so with precisely the "logical and levelheaded approach" that she describes. It is important to remember that rules like "show, don't tell" are meant as guidelines but can be flexibly interpreted. It is best not to sacrifice one's personal voice for writing "rules," which are best thought of as *recommendations*.

The beginning of the third paragraph takes us away from puzzles but aptly illustrates her dedication to a career in scientific research. Using an appropriate level of vocabulary, she describes her research at a UCLA cardiology lab. This demonstrates that she can explain complex ideas in clear and concise terms, a great strength for any researcher. The laboratory provides a different context for us to see the writer's response to challenging problems as well as a tireless resolve to solving any mystery.

The final paragraph nicely wraps up the essay by referencing the 3,000-piece jigsaw and her lab work to illustrate the broader theme of solving puzzles. We can see that the writer is both proud of her work (it is "integral") and humble (it is "a small piece" of the atherosclerosis puzzle), and she is eager to apply her spirit of curiosity and enthusiasm to her future college endeavors.

"Addressing Injustices"

Mathew Griffin
Brown University

MY REASONS FOR WANTING TO BE a doctor are very similar to why most people choose their career path: I want to make things fairer. People such as social workers are out to help make the world a little less unjust. It's not necessarily injustice from other people that I want to fight as these people do, but injustice from other factors. Many people who are close to me have been struck down from their future in ways that it's impossible for them to recover. My aunt was a great artist and loving mother before she developed severe schizophrenia. She now locks herself in her house for weeks at a time and remains isolated from her family. My friend Eric, who was once in his school's varsity basketball league, cannot play his senior season because a car accident left him nearly paralyzed. Finally, my friend Vince's depression has stripped him of his will to live, and despite attempts of over a dozen psychiatrists and medications he still spends most of his days aimlessly lying in bed. While I try very hard to cheer him up by talking to and entertaining him I am deeply concerned about his future. This trend is something that I'm seeing almost everywhere. More and more people are becoming depressed and hopeless, and I want to be able to put life and happiness back into them.

Not only do I see these injustices in my life, when I'm volunteering at my local hospital my desire to help become even more emboldened by the people I meet. A new grandmother I met recently had her spine shattered when she fell from a ladder back onto a table. As I talked to her, I remembered how many times I've seen pictures of my grandmother lifting me and my cousins and caring for us, and became overcome with emotion. While I don't believe her ability to care for her grandchildren will be destroyed, I know that she won't have the same opportunities as other grandparents and the inequality of the situation makes me extremely upset. I want nothing more than to give back her ability to walk and lift her grandkids. I believe being a doctor can allow me to bring this closer.

ANALYSIS

This essay demonstrates Mathew's commitment to social justice. Rather than making justice an abstract or philosophical issue, the essay shows us how it is directly relevant to Mathew's life by giving this injustice many faces: those of his aunt, his friends Eric and Vince, as well as the people he has met through volunteerism. While a long list of these people probably would not be interesting to read, Mathew has fit them into his essay as characters in stories. He does this by keeping the personal profiles distinct (his aunt has schizophrenia, Eric was paralyzed in a car accident, Vince is depressed). Furthermore, the organization of this short essay helps separate the people about whom he writes into two categories: 1) those who are close to him and 2) those who are in the wider community. In this way, Mathew shows the influences that are closest to home before branching out to the bigger community. As Mathew's essay demonstrates, writing about one's personal experiences is an effective way to rein in a topic as all-encompassing as justice.

The beginning of Mathew's essay makes a generalization. He states, "My reasons for wanting to be a doctor are very similar to why most people choose their career path: I want to make things fairer." Mathew might have started with simply: "I want to make things fairer." Since the essay questions specifically ask why he is interested in medicine, referencing all professions and careers beyond medicine broadens the scope of the answer rather than narrowing it. Furthermore, it is best to avoid sweeping generalizations in order to respect the plurality of beliefs in the world. For instance, many people may not choose their career paths to make things fairer; some may be motivated by money or fame. "Things" is also a bit vague, as is the phrase "other factors"— Mathew's might have clarified these terms so we can have a stronger sense of what sources of injustice he is hoping to fight.

Mathew takes advantage of the essay prompt to write about his volunteer work at a recent hospital. His story about the grandmother he met is heart-touching because Mathew is willing to share his personal reaction: "As I talked to her, I remembered how many times I've seen pictures of my grandmother lifting me and my cousins and caring for us, and I became overcome with emotion." This gives us a sense of Mathew's deep sense of caring for others.

"My Unpopular Decision"

Shiv M. Gaglani
Harvard University

SINCE I HAVE ALWAYS BEEN INTERESTED in science and technology, I subscribed to many research magazines, including *Popular Science* and *Scientific American*. However, until 10th grade, I never had the opportunity to contribute to medical research—something that I had always wanted to do. Then, one day I read an article titled "Print Me a Pancreas, Please" in *Popular Science*, which described novel tissue engineering research involving modification of off-the-shelf inkjet printers to print out living cells in a "bioink" solution. Having read much about tissue engineering, I realized this "organ printing" approach could potentially address problems of traditional tissue engineering methods, such as the need to precisely place specific cell types in 3D scaffolds. I was so excited that I came up with a few ideas of my own about advancing the printer capabilities. I was impelled to contact the researchers at the Medical University of South Carolina (MUSC) and Clemson University (CU).

I corresponded with the professor at MUSC and visited his lab multiple times, but realized that the actual printers were kept at CU. Therefore, I contacted the researchers at CU, who did not reply to about 50 of my e-mails. Not the one to give up easily, I called the Principal Investigator (PI) and expressed my eagerness to contribute to the research. After seeing my resumé and computer-aided designs ("Roadmap to Organ Printing"), he invited me to meet him at his lab on October 18th, which conflicted with my school's Homecoming dance. To my friends' bewilderment I made the "unpopular" decision to miss the dance. They could not understand why I preferred driving 26 hours to meet a researcher and miss all the fun at the once-a-year dance. To me, this was clearly the right choice. I was trading a great school experience to literally get my hands into cutting-edge medical research.

The PI was so impressed with my original CAD designs ("Roadmap to Organ Printing") and my resume that he invited me to research at his lab. Over Christmas and other school breaks, I learned many laboratory techniques, conducted novel research, and independently succeeded in "printing" the first functional 3D branching tube of smooth muscle cells (a rudimentary blood vessel). This research helped me win many science competitions and honors, including 2nd Place in Medicine and Health at the Intel International Science and Engineering Fair and become the Top Florida Presenter at the National Junior Science and Humanities Symposium. My computer-aided designs were published in *Biomaterials Forum* and the *Journal of Thoracic and Cardiovascular Surgery*.

This remarkable experience inspired me to perform many additional research projects and I consider it a turning point in my life. It has increased my passion for research and my determination to be a physician and work on devices or pharmaceuticals that improve people's quality of life. I have also become more confident in my research efforts and am able to contact any researcher to pursue a position in their laboratory. I have realized that there are many opportunities for students like myself to contribute to labs and brainstorm solutions for current problems.

ANALYSIS

Shiv demonstrates motivation and drive in this essay about his passion for research in science and technology. Many essays about academic interests focus on schoolwork or extra-curricular activities such as Science Clubs or math competitions. Shiv's story deviates from the norm by showing how "academic" interest is also a passion in his free time—the references to *Popular Science* and *Scientific American* illustrate this hobby. The most unique element of Shiv's story is his bold initiative in contacting the researchers at MUSC and CU after reading the "Print Me a Pancreas, Please" article. Shiv writes about his response to this article in concise, clear terms. "Having read much about tissue engineering, I realized this "organ printing" approach could potentially address problems of traditional tissue engineering methods, such as the need to precisely place specific cell types in 3D scaffolds." While somewhat complex, the ease with which he uses terminology demonstrates Shiv's familiarity with the topic.

The second paragraph of the essay presents many small but delightfully informative details that show Shiv's determination in pursuing research. We learn that he sent 50 emails to researchers, then, undaunted by the lack of a response, called the PI and arranged a personal meeting. He drives an astonishing 26 hours to meet the researcher, and "made the 'unpopular' decision to miss the dance." Shiv's resolve is clear: "To me, this was clearly the right choice. I was trading a great school experience to literally get my hands into cutting-edge medical research." These details distinguish Shiv from his peers.

The third paragraph also provides details that show Shiv's distinctive accomplishments, including his original computer-aided designs and science competition awards. However, these details read like a list and could easily be included in a resume. It might be more compelling to write about the meaning of an award rather than simply listing its name, as Jason's essay "Birthing a Business" (Chapter 14) shows. Shiv briefly mentions the laboratory techniques he learned on his way to achieving his award. Strong essays not only summarize the end product (an award) but also describe the process, the means to achieving the end.

Shiv's essay does a nice job of combining specific references to his research and larger, overarching goals. By presenting the story of the "turning point" of the university research experiment, Shiv compellingly illustrates his entrepreneurial instinct and passion for applied research that is directed toward finding solutions to real-world problems.

"Healing Beyond Borders"

Mathew Griffin
Brown University

WHILE HEALING PEOPLE WILL BE MY main priority as a doctor, I don't want to only help individuals overcome disease after disease. For true change I must work on a much larger scale. I plan on being involved in research, and drawing ideas and information from my patients and sharing it with researchers to find answers about the ailments that plague the human mind. By being a voice from the front lines I hope that I can catalyze the development of treatments and cures. Additionally, I want to become an advocate for public health. If a government is doing something that is detrimental to the health of its citizens, someone needs to point it out, and fight for a better alternative. Unless I do this then the people I help will continue to get sick regardless of how much I help.

Still, my main task as a doctor is to help patients, and I want to help as many of them as I can. Seeing the reality of the health of the world is very important to me if I am going to properly improve it. I have been so fortunate to live in a place where medicine is so refined, and I am even more blessed to know that I have the chance to help spread this refinement. While issues such as world hunger are constantly being improved, doctors in other countries are scarce and locals are still being trained in ancient ways and often hurting their patents more than helping. I want to give back my blessings a hundred-fold and spread better medicine. First, I want to see the health of our world as I help it by joining Medecins Sans Frontieres as soon as I can. Only after I help things first hand can I make a mature decision on how I should try to help the world as a whole. I feel the experiences that I get from my education and the experiences helping people across the world will give me a very strong ability to know how to help to the best of my abilities. Today I am already planning for this journey by teaching myself foreign languages. I hope that by the time I am ready to help people, knowing many languages will help me bond with my patients and truly make me a doctor without borders. I plan on fighting for health for as long as I can, and I want to help every person I can regardless of background, money or stigma.

ANALYSIS

In "Healing Beyond Borders," Mathew makes good use of a small amount of space to answer the two questions in the essay ("What is your vision of a physician?" and "How do you view your role as a future physician?"). When there is more than one specific question in an essay, it can be tempting to answer them separately as in a survey/questionnaire; but for college essays, it is best to take advantage of the format allotted to write a coherent piece. Mathew's essay does an excellent job of providing a strong thesis sentence to address both questions in a single argument: he places healing people as his main priority, but he also wants to "work on a much larger scale."

Mathew goes on to explain what this "larger scale" work would look like, giving us a vision of his role as a future physician. He writes about his desire to research mental health issues and to become "an advocate for public health." He then extends the "larger scale" beyond the U.S. to global proportions. However, rather than writing abstractly about "the world," which can sound idealistic but lacking in substance, Mathew pinpoints a specific way in which he can engage in global healthcare: Medicins Sans Frontieres. This reference demonstrates Mathew's research of healthcare on a worldwide scale, and the sentence "Today I am already planning for this journey by teaching myself foreign languages" demonstrates his commitment to this goal. Aspirations in college essays are strengthened by concrete "evidence" that you are already making progress toward these goals. Mathew could have mentioned the specific foreign languages he is studying to further define those places to which he is most drawn.

Overall, this essay gives us a strong sense of Mathew's commitment to global medicine. The essay could be strengthened by using more specific examples rather than generalized statements, such as the statement that "doctors in other countries are scarce and locals are still being trained in ancient ways and often hurting their patients more than helping." When writing about other cultures, it is important to be sensitive and avoid passing negative value judgments. Universities tend to be diverse places with people from many different backgrounds, making culturally sensitivity important for communicating with peers.

"Scientific Sparks"

Ariela Koehler
MIT

GROWING UP WITH SEPARATED PARENTS HAS not been the easiest life, but it has been my life. When I was younger, I'd hate going out to eat with my dad and seeing a family of four happily enjoying a meal. If my mother and father ever went out together to a restaurant, it was with me, once a year for my birthday, and was usually interspersed with various disagreements.

It was when I was in first grade that I began to realize that, although my parents had their differences and no longer loved each other, I was the one thing that united them. I had no basis to be envious of what I thought of as "complete" families.

Both my mother and father, wanting the best for me, recognized early on my love and fascination with all things scientific. They worked to create opportunities for me to pursue my interest. My mother would read at bedtime, at my request, nature field guides instead of nursery rhymes. The two of us often made long journeys at 3:00 A.M. to witness meteor showers in the clear skies of the mountains. She encouraged me to set up experiments around the house, which I happily did—measuring the growth of palm tree saplings and dissecting owl pellets to extract the mouse bones inside. An environmental scientist, my father could not wait to transfer all of his scientific knowledge into my young head. Needless to say, many of his spontaneous lectures were far above my grasp—I still vaguely remember a quantum physics talk he gave me when I was eight—but they inspired me to learn more on my own.

My thirst for scientific knowledge grew over the years, without limits in any one specific area. Then, in January four years ago, my

Aunt Diane died after a five-year battle with breast cancer. It was during my aunt's illness that I realized I could use my natural love of science to benefit others facing similar challenges.

I have continually pushed myself closer to this goal by excelling in my AP science classes, studying biotechnology at UC Davis through the COSMOS program, and competing as a member of my school's Science Bowl Team. This past summer, I had the opportunity to intern at the Reijo Pera Lab at Stanford University through the Stanford Institutes of Medicine Summer Research Program. During this two-month internship, I worked with human embryonic stem cells to explore the function of PRDM1, a potentially-useful gene in the creation of regenerative medicines.

The scientific spark my parents recognized years ago has shaped my life, and with it, I wish to shape the lives of others. I aspire to become a biomedical researcher, a career that harnesses my long-time fascination of science and my commitment to improve the quality of life for those facing medical challenges. It would be a privilege to work alongside scientists, exploring new treatments and technologies to create exciting new options for patients and their families.

ANALYSIS

Ariela fits a great deal of information about herself and her family into her response to the essay prompt, which asks for a description of "the world you come from" and an explanation of how "that world shaped your dreams and aspirations." These challenging questions require writing about outside influences as well as one's personal goals. Ariela does a wonderful job of focusing the essay by presenting us her family life—mostly in the first three paragraphs—and explaining how this nurtured a "thirst for scientific knowledge"—described in the last three paragraphs. While she also mentions her school (AP science classes), clubs (Science Bowl Team), and summer opportunities (an internship at Stanford), these all fit within the context of Ariela's family life, particularly her parents who encouraged the "scientific spark" they saw in their daughter. This central thesis holds the short essay together.

The introduction to "Scientific Sparks" presents an intimate view of Ariela's life growing up with separated parents. Her realization that "I was the one thing that united" her parents provides a nice segue into the third paragraph, in which she describes her parents' many efforts to support her scientific interests. The specific details Ariela provides are fun and memorable: bedtime nature field guides instead of nursery rhymes, 3 a.m. meteor showers, owl pellet and palm tree experiments, a lecture on quantum physics at the age of 8.

Each of the paragraphs provides a glimpse of Ariela's life growing up. This chronological ordering is clear and effective, helping to move the essay from past experiences to future aspirations. Ariela's use of turning points helps drive the narrative along. For example, she describes the realization in first grade that her parents no longer love each other; then she tells about her Aunt Diane's death, which helped her see that she "could use [her] natural love of science to benefit others." The subsequent examples, which are somewhat list-like, nonetheless show us ways in which Ariela has applied science to health issues. Her experience at the Riejo Pera Lab best supports this point. Ariela might have chosen to write more about her summer internship at Stanford as an iconic project rather than listing so many others. For instance, it is unclear what the COSMOS program is, though she may have written about this elsewhere in her essay.

The end of Ariela's essay provides an excellent, succinct summary that directly addresses the essay questions. Through mentioning her parents, she describes her "world," and through stating her intention of becoming a biomedical researcher, she shows how the two major themes in her essay—a love for science and desire to help people—are related.

"Researching Cancer"

Anonymous
Harvard University

I TROD THE MUD IN THE misty spring rain. It was Qing Ming, the holiday in China when we honored our deceased ancestors. On the ground of the cemetery, drenched flowers lay in my grandfather's remembrance. That morning—a month before my sixth birthday—I clung tightly to my mother's sleeves and finally learned why he passed away.

My grandfather had been a victim of cancer. Because the diagnosis came too late, all treatment was futile. As my mother whispered this to me with grief in her eyes, I stomped angrily in the mud. I blamed the doctors who couldn't find the tumor in time to save him. That rainy morning launched my dream to help cure cancer—a common wish, but one that fueled a life-changing pursuit. Knowing that the best protection against cancer was to detect it as early as possible, I examined the widely used methods of detection. I read about mammography and was astounded to learn that it failed to detect a large percentage of cases. As I wondered how to make detection more accurate, I heard about a research internship program at ____ Cancer Center. I jumped at the opportunity.

There, my mentors encouraged me to investigate cancer's genetic causes. I became intrigued by a gene suspected to play a role in the onset of breast cancer. We examined a process of gene-silencing—known as methylation—that changed DNA structure while keeping the sequence itself intact. Through a series of assays, we pinpointed the methylated sites in the gene sequence that distinguished cancerous breast cells from healthy cells. These were markers of disease!

The thrill came from knowing the vast clinical applications of the discovery. Finding such markers is a step toward the individualization of cancer treatment. Genomics-based diagnostics would detect cancer earlier than traditional procedures. Also, since methylation does not change the DNA sequence, it is reversible. Therapeutics could target these sites and minimize harm to healthy tissue.

Personalized cancer diagnostics promise a new dawn, but they are not yet reality. Many more genes need to be studied before we can fully comprehend the roots of the disease. Awed by the complexity of cancer, I realized that my dream was much more intricate than I imagined. However, my youthful passion in medicine did not dwindle. Instead, it strengthened and matured into a strategy. As my vague goals shaped into specific inquiries, my curiosity became insatiable. The joy of uncovering the unknown affirmed my love for science. My generation will keep pushing the boundaries of knowledge, and nothing would give me more fulfillment than continuing to fight in the war on cancer.

I recall that rainy Qing Ming morning when I gazed at my grandfather's gravesite. I wish I could tell him about the adventure he inspired. This war will be arduous, but every little "eureka!" along the way is a portent of victory.

ANALYSIS

The author of this essay might have taken the boring approach of just describing where she worked and what she did while researching, but she found a way to tie her research to a personal experience. By explaining in detail why the research was intellectually challenging to her, the author gave readers clues to her character. From her childhood experience, we understand her motivation for wanting to help find a cure for cancer. Learning about her grandfather's death sheds light on why she sought out an internship at the cancer center and why she now has an interest in pursuing a career in the field. It always adds meaning to a student's career goals when we understand the roots of his or her interest. Many students make the mistake of sharing lofty dreams such as finding the cure to cancer but don't back them up with actual actions that show that they are working toward making a difference. This student not only presents the global problem but demonstrates how she has and will continue to play a role in addressing it.

As the author describes her internship, she clearly explains what she did to research cancer. Most importantly, she outlines it in a way that is understandable to a layperson. As readers, we can easily conceive the subject's intellectual hold on her. This student's writing provides enough detail that we understand the complexity of her research but not so much that we are bogged down with too much information. It's not enough to just state what you did; it's more compelling to explain why.

In the fifth paragraph, the student ties her past experiences to her future plans. She explains that she intends to pursue a career in the sciences and to continue cancer research. Admissions officers like to understand the direction that students are taking so that they can visualize how they will contribute to society while undergraduates and after graduation as well. They want to know why you are pursuing a career field and what you hope to achieve as a part of it.

In the last paragraph, the student refers back to her personal experience. She wraps up the essay in a highly relatable way by connecting her grandfather's death to the intellectual excitement of cancer research as it applies to her career plans. She packs a lot into a short amount of space but does so in a way that flows smoothly and keeps our interest.

6

ENTREPRENEURSHIP

"The Computer Doctor"

Mathew Griffin
Brown University

EVERY TIME I DRIVE INTO A client's driveway, there's always that moment. That moment where I must shed any doubt I have and become adamant. That moment where I realize that, people are depending on me, and I must do my best to help them. And that moment where, with tool bag to my side, I must prepare to face whatever problem is waiting for me in their house. This time is no different. As with the hundreds of other problems I've faced, I must remember that every problem has a solution, and I can find it.

When I am greeted by a middle-aged woman as I approach the house, my remaining doubts evaporate. Once I see the individual I am about to help I become saturated with resolve. However, all she will see from me is a smile as I ask her how she is. I then ask her what the problem is, and she leads me to her computer. She tells me that her computer is shutting down randomly, and then leaves as I begin to work.

With a simple push of the power button, the process begins. Unfortunately, for this case, just as quickly as it starts—the computer shuts off. Never discouraged, I dismantle it to look for obvious signs of damage. However, everything here appears normal: wires secure, circuits shining.

But there's another test that may work. Eyes focused on the inside of the computer, I turn it on again. I have only a moment before it succumbs to its ailment again. Additionally, each time it starts could be damaging, so I have to make this count. When the sound of electricity surging through the computer begins, I immediately notice a vital fan failing to twirl: the computer is simply overheating. With a quick pull of the power I anesthetize the computer and operate. Using a replacement and screwdriver from my bag, I give the computer a new fan. Then, I start the computer nervously, but it starts perfectly.

My confidence and determination sweat off as accomplishment. I quickly look for the woman. She can tell I solved her problem as I walk towards her with a grin, and she smiles too.

This case is one of the hundreds I've solved over the past few years, all without a single failure to find a practical solution. I started my business because after seeing how grossly overcharged the community was by corporate technicians, I believed it would be a practical and great way for me to help the community and have a job. After fixing computers for my school for a year, school officials quickly noticed and spread word of my work, allowing my business to spread like wildfire throughout the local communities. With determination (and some creativity) I've solved some very unordinary and strange problems. I'd like to use this same willpower to help people in even better ways. No matter how impossible the problems I encounter may seem I will always remember what I tell myself when I fix computers: every problem must have a solution, and I can find it.

ANALYSIS

Mathew's essay is powerful because he doesn't just tell us about his entrepreneurship venture but actually gives us a sense that he's taking us to his work by narrating the process. This essay is also strong because Mathew demonstrates attributes that are desirable for an aspiring doctor—determination, problem-solving skills, and an eagerness to help others—using an example unrelated to the sciences and medicine. Since Mathew also wrote about science and medicine in "Exploring Life's Intricacies" (Chapter 19) and "Addressing Injustices" (Chapter 5), this essay diversifies his portfolio of essays while still connecting well with the overall theme of applying specifically to a pre-medical program.

Mathew's narrative grips us from the very beginning. He begins with a suspenseful sentence: "Every time I drive into a client's drive-way, there's always that moment." The immediate question that comes to mind is this: "What moment?" The image of a high school student driving to a client's house also raises our curiosity about what job this mature and responsible high school student is doing. Essays that challenge our expectations are often the most memorable: in Mathew's case, most high school students are studying; those who run their own businesses are rare.

The essay underscores the importance of Mathew's business. We can see this as he explains, ". . . people are depending on me, and I must do my best to help them." Matthew demonstrates his commitment to this vow as he describes his process of determining the computer's problem. The use of "doctor" terminology helps connect this essay to Mathew's career goal and provides a coherent metaphor for the paper. For instance, he mentions his "tool bag," which is reminiscent of a doctor's instrument bag, and writes about the computer as if it were a patient: "I anesthetize the computer and operate." This essay not only builds suspense and has us cheering for Mathew as he works to solve the problem, but the writing also allows us to share in the satisfaction and sense of accomplishment he feels at accomplishing his goal.

The final paragraph does a wonderful job of providing a more expansive context for the story we have just read. In essays that focus on one specific incident, it is often helpful to include a more general conclusion so that readers can understand the broader objective of this anecdote. Mathew does that well when he writes, "This case is one of the hundreds I've solved over the past few years, all without a single failure to find a practical solution." Mathew's mention of the school officials who recommended his work adds extra credibility to his business and cleverly provides an informal recommendation to attest to his determination and creativity.

7

CHALLENGES

"Unshakable Worth"

Sarah Langberg
Princeton University

PART OF ME IS MISSING. IT'S an identifiable, yet indescribable absence. It is odd how I can find more information about the initial supposed creators, Adam and Eve, than I can about my own. I don't know my father, and I doubt that I ever will. He left two weeks after I was born because I lacked a certain male member. Fidelity to personal convictions was more important to him than a life that he had just shepherded into this world. Because of his definitive choice, I will only be able to associate with him as a support check number until I am eighteen years of age. After that, who knows?

When I was eleven, my mother decided to call this long-gone man in search of owed child support. After eleven years of nothingness, financial distress caused my mother call this absolute last resource. In my house, we had an early 90s telephone that had a speaker/mute function. I can still see that outdated piece of technology in the corner of my mind. That speaker/mute function granted me the only contact with my father that I have ever known.

I was a mischievous child; I knew that day that my mother was physically on the phone with my birthfather. I was naïve. I thought that hearing my father's voice would fill the void created by years of absence. I thought that hearing his voice would allow me to place my father on the same grand plateau as other fathers who had always been there for their children, loved their children. I snuck into the room with the technical phone and silently listened in on the conversation. I felt smart and sly as I pressed the button that put the stranger's voice on the speakerphone. "Hah," I thought, "he can't hear me, but I can hear him." Maybe if he would have known the simple fact that his daughter was listening, maybe then some shred of human decency would have shined through.

Those few moments provided me with the only ounce of a man that comprises half of my biology that I will ever know. Unfortunately, the stranger didn't know I was listening. Like my life before, he never knew that I was there. As he yelled at my mother, I could hear the fear in her voice as he responded to her pleas with such malice. My mother tried to convey to my father that I was not just his incarnation to be provided for, but rather, a spectacular human being. As I sat there, listening intently to the conversation, I felt validated as a daughter by my mother's words, but shattered as a human being by my "father's" insolence.

In the moments that followed, that little girl, initially so excited at the prospect of finally being able to physically hear her creator, was eternally crushed. "Just because she exists doesn't mean I have to love her; it doesn't mean I have to know her. I don't love her, and I never will." Crash. Is it possible for the strongest muscle in your body to simply break in half? One of my genetic halves had declared that he loathed my very existence. Those words succeeded to shatter my heart into a million pieces. I didn't know how to react. I turned off the phone and slithered back to my room. How could someone be so heartless? How could someone that heartless be a part of me? No words.

I have been sobered by pain in a way that no psychological study ever could attempt. I may never know my father because of his decision, and in turn, he will never know me. In the end, his loss will be the greater one. My "father's" shining example of misconduct ironically guides me as a moral, ethical person. Rather than searching for any fault within myself, I use my father's failure as a tool. I take an earnest and honest stance in life. I know my great worth. I have nothing to prove to anyone, including myself.

ANALYSIS

Sarah's essay is written with candor about a difficult and highly personal topic—growing up without her father. She presents her thoughts in a way that elicits admiration for her strength, rather than pity. In writing about tragedies and tribulations that affect us but are outside of our control, it is important to think carefully about what kind of tone to use, and what kind of reader response this tone invites. For example, if Sarah had chosen to write an essay entirely fixated on the extreme anger she felt toward her father, readers may have felt alienated; if she wrote an essay that conveyed only sadness, we might have felt pity for her. The strength of Sarah's essay is that she is honest in displaying a spectrum of emotions. She conveys both confidence and vulnerability, which humanizes her story and also suggests to readers that she has invested valuable time and energy in a process of maturation and healing from the pain that she has experienced growing up.

The opening paragraph of the essay gives us a sense of the emptiness that Sarah has experienced: she writes about "an identifiable, yet indescribable absence." The paragraph is slightly risky in that it devotes several sentences to describing her father's decisions to leave her family, though the space allotted for the entire essay is limited. In this case, though several sentences seem to be redundant in telling the basic fact that Sarah's dad left two weeks after she was born, they work to create a sense of loss, of something "missing." This is an excellent reminder that not all sentences need to convey new information; they can also help create a mood or portray emotion. Sarah's first sentence creates a sense of bitter irony and sadness around the situation with her father, setting the context for the dialog with "this long-gone man."

The story about the phone conversation builds suspense. We, like 11-year-old Sarah, wonder how her dad will react, and hold expectations that he might redeem his absence. Sarah mentions the "speaker/ mute function," a more memorable symbol than simply "the phone." The suspense continues with the foreshadowing sentence, "Maybe if he would have known the simple fact that his daughter was listening, maybe then some shred of human decency would have shined through."

The remainder of the essay focuses on Sarah's reactions to the phone conversation. The second to last paragraph is particularly powerful in the way she juxtaposes the conversation she overhears with her emotional reactions: "Crash," "No words," and questions like "How could someone be so heartless?" deliver an intense, almost raw honesty, revealing a glimpse of this pivotal scene in Sarah's life.

Had she ended her writing here, this essay may not have felt very relevant to admissions officers. However, in the final paragraph, Sarah shows how she has internalized important lessons from the hurt she has experienced. The sense of self-worth and validation she conveys—"I know my great worth, I have nothing to prove to anyone"—is particularly effective after the painful story she has shared, an important lesson in the power of contrasts.

"No Longer Invisible"

Angelica
University of Chicago

I WISH I WAS INVISIBLE. I wish I was invisible. I wish I was invisible. One of my biggest fears has always been going to an unfamiliar place, but each time I have had the satisfaction of knowing that at the end of the day I can go home. I am a shy person, and it has always been difficult for me to adjust to a new environment. Transitioning from eighth grade to high school was especially difficult for me because my high school was, in fact, a boarding school, which meant that that feeling of satisfaction was no longer present at the end of the day but postponed to the end of the week. Living at LFA was a completely new world for me and nothing I had experienced could have prepared me for it.

With confused eyes and nothing less than a nauseous sensation in my stomach I entered my first day of high school. Growing up, I had always gone to school with people who looked like me, sounded like me, and dressed liked me, but here I quickly learned that I was the minority. I was not alone in this. Two of my friends came to LFA with me and, with this in mind, my shyness and I did not think it necessary to make new friends. Besides being one of the only schools with its own ice rink and providing only the latest technology for its students, it suddenly hit me that my new home had countless possibilities, but, before those possibilities could be realized, I had to take initiative. I learned a very important lesson at LFA: you will only get out of life as much as you put into it. Stepping out of my comfort zone allowed me to discover an interest and skill for volleyball and hidden leadership as the captain of the JV team. I became a tutor and friend for young Hispanic students at the Nuestro Center, and they reminded me how important it is to give back to the community. After numerous all nighters, I developed a system where I could get all of my homework done and still be able to get involved with sports and extracurriculars without having to sacrifice any sleep time.

Towards the end of my sophomore year a family member's sickness unfortunately forced me to leave my school and return home. I left LFA and joined my new family, Mirta Ramirez Computer Science Charter High School. Containing a student body that was 99 percent Hispanic, I was no longer the minority. I had unconsciously become accustomed to the LFA way of life because, in my mind, this tiny mustard yellow building with no more than four windows could not possibly compare to my old home. I was right. No, my new home was not as big nor as fancy, but I discovered that was not a setback. Although the resources were not directly visible nor as easily accessible, I learned that obstacles did not exist for students there. Most, if not all, of the students had the same hunger for knowledge as I had.

This summer my school announced that the building which we had been using had fire code violations and we could not return to our building in the fall. Throughout the summer my school did not have a building and did not find one until a few weeks after school started. By that time I had already taken a decision to, once again, leave my home and join yet another family. What I realized on my first day at Josephinum Academy, was that my shyness had not tagged along and I was eager to go to school. The nauseous feeling had left my stomach and enthusiasm had entered. I had already gained and learned so much from the people I had met in my two previous schools that I could not wait to continue my journey and embark on yet another discovery.

The knowledge that I have gained from these three schools is something I will take with me far beyond college. My roommate, across-the-hall mates, and classmates have influenced my life as much as I hope to have impacted theirs. It is evident to me that they have helped me develop into the very much visible person I am today. I have learned to step outside of my comfort zone, and I have learned that diversity is so much more than the tint of our skin. My small mustard colored school taught me that opportunity and success only requires desire.

I would be an asset to your college because as I continue on my journey to success, I will take advantage of every opportunity that is available to me and make sure to contribute as much as I can too. Now I am visible. Now I am visible. Now I am visible, and I want to be seen.

ANALYSIS

Angelica's essay is reminiscent of Jason's "Hurricane Transformations" (Chapter 15) in that it relates a story of self-transformation as she changes schools. The first paragraph opens with a memorable repetition: "I wish I was invisible. I wish I was invisible. I wish I was invisible." This mantra demonstrates the fear Angelica has of going to an unfamiliar place. She honestly confesses a shortcoming she has: "I am a shy person, and it has always been difficult for me to adjust to a new environment." In these admissions essays, it is appropriate to share perceived weaknesses. However, it is best not to dwell on these weaknesses excessively. In Angelica's case, she describes her shyness in order to help us trace her progress as she slowly becomes less introverted.

At the beginning of the second paragraph, we get a palpable sense of the distress Angelica's shyness causes her through her description of her "confused eyes" and nauseous stomach. She humorously describes the insular attitude she takes at her new school, LFA: ". . . my shyness and I did not think it necessary to make new friends." The transition to the next sentence is somewhat abrupt; Angelica might have considered using a paragraph break or adding another sentence so readers can see *how* she came to realize she "had to take initiative." However, she does a wonderful job of illustrating several ways in which she stepped out of her comfort zone by describing her leadership on the volleyball team and her community service as a tutor. Angelica wisely uses two concrete examples rather than writing a long list. Her ability to juggle extracurriculars and schoolwork without sacrificing sleep suggests that she will continue to manage her time wisely and pursue a well-balanced lifestyle in college.

This second paragraph also hints at the importance of Angelica's Hispanic ethnicity. She writes, "I was the minority" at LFA, and describes her work at the Nuestro Center. This is a creative way to write about one's heritage without exaggerating its importance. Race/ethnicity play different roles in people's lives, so there can hardly be a rule for how much or how little to factor this into one's essays. Perhaps the best rule of thumb is to write about this to the extent that you feel necessary in order to genuinely convey your most important point.

In Angelica's case, the fact that she comes from a Hispanic family is a backdrop to the more important point: she has a "hunger for knowledge" that refuses to be set back even in her predominantly Hispanic school that is not nearly as well-resourced as LFA. The metaphor of a "new family" and "new home" effectively demonstrate Angelica's ability to adapt. In the third school she moves to, we find out that Angelica's "shyness had not tagged along . . . The nauseous feeling had left [Angelica's] stomach and enthusiasm had entered." This reference to the nervous sensations Angelica mentioned in the second paragraph is an excellent way to show us how her feelings and thoughts have changed. Angelica's ability to relate parts of her essay together helps tie the narrative into a coherent whole. By referencing back to earlier sections of the story, she prevents her essay from reading like a narrated timeline of her past. The most powerful example of this strategy is at the end of her essay, where Angelica writes, "Now I am visible," bringing the theme of the piece back full circle.

"Power of People"

Suzanne Arrington
Columbia University

I BELIEVE IN PEOPLE. THIS CONVICTION drives my action and ambitions, and defines me in a world of cynicism and doubt. I have seen the power of people and their ability to come together in times of need and joy and sorrow. I know that ultimately, humans strive for belonging and community; thus, while loneliness and anger may always be in existence, so will be togetherness and bliss. My strong faith in humanity stems from my witnessing of the best in human qualities while doing the MS150 and during Hurricane Ike, and pushes me to pursue a career in helping others. Both of these events have allowed me to see humanity at its best, performing selfless acts of benevolence.

For the past four years, I have participated in the BPMS150 bike tour from Houston to Austin. This 175 mile ride raises funds for the National MS Society, which sponsors medical research for multiple sclerosis and aids the families of its victims. I can say from experience, the ride is grueling; enormous hills, headwinds, fatigue, and body aches are prevalent throughout. Yet every year, over thirteen thousand riders decide to put their minds and bodies through two days of torture so that they can help those who live with it every day. I have raised, over four years, more than eight thousand dollars to benefit the MS Society, and have never regretted any of the painful training or the ride itself. The view at the starting line is one of the most empowering I have ever witnessed: thousands of people, all of them with their hands on their handle bars, one foot poised on a pedal. All are ready to experience exhaustion for the benefit of others, like my father. He was diagnosed with MS when I was four, and is a constant motivator for me. I witnessed him become blind in one eye, and struggle with a body that refuses to function normally. I participate in this ride every year for him, as do thirteen thousand others. The power of people will ultimately help my father to receive better medical treatment, and maybe even one day, be cured.

While writing this essay, I was also able to observe and be a part of amazing human efforts. Hurricane Ike devastated Southeastern Texas, particularly the Houston and Galveston areas. Much of my extended family lives in Galveston, and so was forced to evacuate. Without hesitation, my parents opened up our home to aunts, uncles, grandparents, cousins, and pets. This is the environment in which I have always lived; our home is anyone's shelter, our food is anyone's nourishment. Together, our entire family weathered the storm, and comforted one another. My aunt's home received electrical power prior to my home, and so she eagerly welcomed us to stay with her. Large scale displays of altruism could be seen in the hundreds of University of Houston students handing out food and water to those affected by the hurricane. During times of need, people band together for safety and solace. Community is instinctual; dismiss the notions of survival of the fittest. People truly desire closeness with one another.

In the future, I hope to pursue a career in public health. I love studying science and math, and I would like to use this passion to benefit large numbers of people. Many go without basic medical treatment, and this causes a huge discrepancy in quality of life and health in the population. Even if this problem can never completely be solved, I want to help remedy this as much as possible. With small deeds and cooperative effort, humans can accomplish immense good. I know this because I believe in people, and I have seen them at their finest.

ANALYSIS

Suzanne begins her essay with a four-word sentence that is powerful for its simplicity and frankness: "I believe in people." She goes on to explain why this assertion of her beliefs distinguishes herself from the people around her. Several of the statements Suzanne makes are quite grand; for example, she states that "humans strive for belonging and community; thus, while loneliness and anger may always be in existence, so will be togetherness and bliss." Still, she avoids the pitfalls of generalization by honing in on two specific examples: the MS150 and Hurricane Ike. One minor point to comment on here is that it is best to spell out all acronyms when first using them in an essay. Most people probably do not know what the MS150/BPMS150 is, so Suzanne could have made this clear by referencing a 150-mile benefit bike tour.

The second paragraph does an excellent job of demonstrating what Suzanne does for the MS150, her feelings toward the event, and her personal motivation for participating in this "grueling" bike tour's "two days of torture" for four years. This description is particularly strong because Suzanne not only relates her own experience, but also shows that there are 13,000 other people dedicated to the same cause. This adds evidence to the faith in humanity that she describes in the first paragraph. When making broad claims, it is necessary to provide a broad base of evidence and support. Suzanne certainly accomplishes this in describing her fundraising achievements for the MS Society. Her essay is made more compelling by sharing the story of her "constant motivator," her father.

The transition between the second and third paragraph is somewhat jarring. After the sentence, "The power of people will ultimately help my father to receive better medical treatment, and maybe even one day, be cured," Suzanne could have chosen to write about her future career goals in public health. This link makes more sense logically than the current sentence preceding her career plans, "People truly desire closeness with one another." Luckily, because Suzanne referenced both the bike tour and Hurricane Ike in her introduction, the paragraph about the Hurricane is not entirely incongruous. It would simply have fit the flow of the essay better, had she chosen a more specific and compelling transition sentence rather than "While writing this essay, I was also able to observe and be a part of amazing human efforts."

The power of the Hurricane Ike story is similar to the strength of the MS150 description in that Suzanne presents her individual perspective along with a sense of collective effort. Overall, Suzanne does an excellent job of conveying two profound experiences to illustrate her conviction that "With small deeds and cooperative effort, humans can accomplish immense good."

"Self Mind"

Timothy Nguyen Le
Yale University

JULY 22 LAST YEAR WAS MEANT to be a typical Sunday. Just like every Sunday, my mother and I were getting ready to visit my older brother at his Waikiki apartment, where we would talk for a little while. But July 22nd was different. That chilly morning, we got a phone call from his roommate telling us my brother was going to the emergency room. As we drove to Queen's Hospital, I didn't know what to think. Although I tried to assure myself that nothing serious could have happened to him, anxiety clouded my mind.

My brother, Tyson, emigrated from Vietnam with my mom and my other older brother to the United States in 1990, with dreams of a new life and fresh opportunities. He enrolled in high school with virtually no knowledge of the English language. Even though he had to simultaneously manage a part-time job at McDonald's, he excelled in academics and was the top of his class in calculus.

At 34 years old, he was the epitome of health: he ran marathons every year, had a healthy diet, and never smoked or drank alcohol. When I got to the ER and saw him lying in the hospital bed, he looked like the Tyson that I always knew. Nothing seemed wrong. He just seemed tired, and he didn't have the energy to speak.

However, coming back from an MRI scan, my brother seemed different. His eyes were unfocused and dazed, as if he didn't see the room in front of him. Uneasiness and fear rushed down my spine. I shouted for help, just as my brother's body started to spasm. I felt a profound emotion surging up in me, one that I had never experienced before--a wrenching sense of trepidation, laced with sickening adrenaline. The seizure took control of his body, and he began to foam at the mouth. His body seized up, but I was frozen still. I didn't know what to do. I felt useless and terrified.

Tyson told me, when I was just a kid, not to work while I was in high school. I was young, though, and still wanted to work because I wanted to make money, like him. During his high school years, he took on a part-time job after school, even though it meant he had to come home late every night. Often, he would stay up through the early hours of the morning, determined to complete his schoolwork. He held down the job, despite its exhausting physical toll, because he had to: he had to assist with the bills and support my mom, so that she could take English classes at the local community college. Tyson said that I didn't have to work, because he would always be there to support me.

While my brother was in the hospital, my mother and I went there every day from before dawn to late at night, when the streets were empty. Tyson had developed severe brain inflammation as a result of the seizure. He had dozens of tests done: X-Rays, MRIs, blood tests, spinal taps, a bronchoscopy, and even a brain biopsy. A labyrinth of IV tubes, wires, and cables were hooked up to his body, monitoring his life signs and feeding dozens of chemicals and solutions into his bloodstream. The doctors kept him constantly sedated. His brain inflammation was life-threatening, and he caught a case of severe pneumonia. His doctors had to place him on life support. In three weeks, my brother had gone from being in the best shape of his life, from being a veritable Superman, to laying on his deathbed.

When I was a kid, I was a crybaby. I cried when I didn't get the toy I wanted. I cried when I didn't get the food I wanted. However, at some point during my childhood, around the age of six, I stopped crying. No matter how much I was teased or pushed around, I never cried. No matter how much I was mocked about my clothes, or my ethnicity, I didn't cry.

August 11 last year was the first time since childhood that I cried. It was the day that my brother passed away. And it was the first time that I ever saw my mom cry. It was a traumatizing experience, and for a while I was depressed that such a tragedy could occur so arbitrarily to someone like my brother: someone who was strong, someone who was healthy, someone who lived by a strong moral code and never sacrificed his values for material rewards. But after a while, I realized that the circumstances of his death were not a refutation of his beliefs, but instead, a reminder of their importance. Even though we cannot control the twists and turns of life, we must deal with them as best we can. My brother, even though he didn't know English, enrolled in school and ultimately excelled. And at the same time, to help our mother go to school on the side, he took on a part-time job. Certainly he must have wished that he hadn't faced those disadvantages, but he didn't complain. Rather, he faced the realities of his situation head-on, and succeeded. Tyson's death was a tragic reflection of the cold, random chance of nature, but it was in no way any verdict on his philosophy: instead, I realized, it served as a clear reminder to me that the worst can happen to even the best, and that the strength of an individual lies in his ability to maintain his values when faced with such difficult situations. Today, I still hold onto the lessons that my brother taught me through his actions: to put the needs of your family first, to always persevere in the face of adversity, and to never compromise your ideals for petty desires. To lose heart in these values because of his death, then, would be a harsh disservice to Tyson's legacy.

ANALYSIS

In "Self Mind," Timothy takes on the role of author and brother, describing his brother's death with poignancy and honesty. Utilizing his gift for storytelling, Timothy shares the rawness of his emotions, creating an essay that contrasts despair and hope, admiration for his brother and devastation for his loss. Much of the essay is somber, a tone that is apropos for the essay topic, but Timothy prevents the heaviness from becoming excessively depressing by relating parts of his past and Tyson's past, along with the broader philosophical lessons he learned from the painful experience of losing his brother. Timothy, like Sarah in her essay "Unshakable Worth," (Chapter 7) creates a powerful essay from family tragedy in a way that invokes admiration rather than pity.

The introduction of Timothy's essay sets an ominous mood without being overly melodramatic. We wonder why "July 22nd was different," feel the "chilly morning," and share Timothy's uneasiness as anxiety clouds his mind. Timothy goes on to give us a sense of who Tyson is. Without explicitly stating that he admires his brother, we can sense Timothy's respect for his brother's ability to overcome language and financial barriers as a newly arrived immigrant from Vietnam.

This narrative is particularly compelling because it combines different styles of narration and different paces of storytelling. For example, the first paragraph sets the scene for a specific day while creating a mood of slight discomfort. The second paragraph describes one of the crucial people in this story and takes a time scale of several years. The third paragraph continues explaining Tyson's story and brings us back to the ER, to the immediacy and urgency of the situation on July 22 last year. In the fourth paragraph, the pace of the narrative changes dramatically, especially when we arrive at this sentence: "Uneasiness and fear rushed down my spine. I shouted for help, just as my brother's body started to spasm." Timothy's short sentences help create a sense of paralysis as he describes how he felt at the time: "I didn't know what to do. I felt useless and terrified." While it is true that long sentences can provide the structure for complex descriptions, short and simple sentences are effective in conveying powerful emotions.

Timothy's essay uniquely bounces between the terrifying and distressing scene in the emergency room and paragraphs about Tyson's hard work and life philosophies. Timothy writes about both with vivid detail and heartfelt sincerity. The interludes where we learn about Tyson's struggles help alleviate the emotional intensity of the situation.

Though death is often avoided as an essay topic in the U.S., Timothy writes about it with dignity and grace. In revealing that after age six, he never cried, "no matter how much I was mocked about my clothes, or my ethnicity," Timothy shows us that he, like his brother, also faced challenges as an immigrant. This intimate fact also crystallizes Timothy's grief when his brother dies. Amazingly, Timothy is able to end the essay on a strong and optimistic note (just as Sarah does), one that highlights his love for his family and his perseverance in the face of adversity.

"A Summer of Stem Cells"

Ariela Koehler
MIT

"IT APPEARS ALL YOUR CELLS ARE DEAD."

Only shock prevented the tears from streaming down my face. My cells were dead. After being accepted into the competitive Stanford Institutes of Medicine Summer Research Program (SIMR), and spending approximately 170 hours of the past month manipulating human embryonic stem cells (hESCs), I was back to square one—with only one month of my internship remaining. How in the world was I going to make up for lost time?

As I asked myself the question, I thought back to exactly how I had spent those 170 hours, working to develop the stem cells which now, under the microscope, were hollow with the absence of life.

I started my internship a little overwhelmed by the fancy hoods, automatic pipettes, and high-speed centrifuges. But by the first of the 170 hours, I had familiarized myself with the equipment and begun my quest to find the function of PRDM1—a gene thought to control replication in hESCs. First though, I needed to make a growth medium for the hESCs. I painstakingly measured to the ten millionth of a liter, testing the accuracy of each measurement multiple times before finally dispensing it into the medium solution. After I had plated the hESCs on my new medium, I waited with bated breath for the results.

To my joy, two days later, my cells were thriving and even outgrowing their new home. Known for their ability to quickly replicate, it was logical they would need to be frequently transferred. The difficult part was that, as part of my experiment to find the purpose of PRDM1, I had different strains of hESCs (some serving as "control" strains) which could not be mixed. Transferring hESCs is a process requiring great concentration and coordination. It took me about three hours the first time. By the end of the month, though, transferring was second nature and my cells were doing well—I had inserted a fluorescent protein into their DNA to verify the hESCs containing the resistant vector were living, as hypothesized. I had successfully created hundreds of stable hESC colonies of different strains. Everything seemed to be going so well . . .

But now was not the time to reminiscence. I snapped out of my daydream and refocused on the situation at hand.

"Ariela? I know taking the news the first time can be hard, but keep in mind, you probably didn't do anything wrong. You know how sensitive they are . . . this sort of thing is common when working with stem cells."

"I know," I said, smiling genuinely this time, "I'm ready to try again."

My project was not completed by the end of the summer, but through hard work, I was able to replicate parts of the experiment to produce valuable data. Although the experiment did not go as planned, I am proud of myself for persevering. As Thomas Edison said, "Our greatest weakness lies in giving up. The most certain way to succeed is always to try just one more time."

ANALYSIS

"A Summer of Stem Cells" uses lively dialogue and careful detail to show us how Ariela responded to a major setback during her summer research at SIMR. The introduction, "It appears all your cells are dead," is gripping and mysterious. We subsequently learn of the astonishing 170 hours Ariela has devoted to her research project with human embryonic stem cells. Ariela's colloquial tone serves to draw readers in so that we sympathize with her plight. We also wonder how in the world Ariela will make up for the lost time now that she is "back to square one."

Where "Scientific Sparks" (Chapter 5) used a straightforward chronological narrative effectively, "A Summer of Stem Cells" provides a refreshing twist by going back in time. This tactic also invigorates our understanding of "170 hours." Generally, numbers are more meaningful when they are contextualized. Had Ariela not described how she spent the 170 hours, this detail may have seemed like bragging, or alternatively might have been dismissed. However, by describing "fancy hoods, automatic pipettes, and high-speed centrifuges" and the painstaking ways in which she used this professional equipment on her "quest," Ariela gives us a stronger understanding of her dedication and focus. She sets up suspense by writing, "I waited with bated breath for the results," a statement that invites the reader to share in her nervous and eager anticipation.

By writing about the learning process in the lab with such careful detail, Ariela shows us that she possesses the "great concentration and coordination" necessary for conducting scientific research. We are swept into her optimism: "Everything seemed to be going so well . . ." Here, the ellipses provide a transition back to the moment when Ariela discovers the devastating fact that her stem cells are dead. It would be helpful to know who speaks to Ariela—Is it her lab manager? A voice in her head?—to reassure her that she "probably didn't do anything wrong" and that "this sort of thing is common when working with stem cells."

This essay demonstrates that it is possible to write a compelling essay based on experiences related to a circumstance that might be deemed a failure or a project where performance didn't reach one's expectations. Ariela writes with admirable honesty when she admits that her project was not completed by the end of the summer. However, we understand that her perseverance paid off, as she was able to "produce valuable data." Since the original essay asked about "something that you have created," Ariela might have explained in greater detail what this "valuable data" was. However, her choice to show an experiment that she created that did not go as planned is a unique response. It is memorable because many people are afraid to admit their mistakes. By ending on a Thomas Edison quote, Ariela shows that she is following the persistent spirit of the famous scientist-inventor in her passionate pursuit of scientific knowledge.

"All Worth It"

Anonymous
Cornell University

HE'S IN MY ARMS, THE NEWEST addition to the family. I'm too over-whelmed. "That's why I wanted you to go to Bishop Loughlin," she says, preparing baby bottles. "But ma, I chose Tech because I wanted to be challenged." "Well, you're going to have to deal with it," she replies, adding, "Your aunt watched you when she was in high school." "But ma, there are three of them. It's hard!"

Returning home from a summer program that cemented intellectual and social independence to find a new baby was not exactly thrilling. Add him to the toddler and seven year old sister I have and there's no wonder why I sing songs from Blue's Clues and The Backyardigans instead of sane seventeen year old activities. It's never been simple; as a female and the oldest, I'm to significantly rear the children and clean up the shabby apartment before an ounce of pseudo freedom reaches my hands. If I can manage to get my toddler brother onto the city bus and take him home from day care without snot on my shoulder, and if I can manage to take off his coat and sneakers without demonic scream-ing for no apparent reason, then it's a good day. Only, waking up at three in the morning to work, the only free time I have, is not my cup of Starbucks.

We were already different at age fourteen. She gave birth to me and went to an alternative high school; I established closeness with new friends in a competitive high school. She and my then present father were taking care of me; I was studying the environmental effects on the onset of schizophrenia. She took her daughter to preschool, and I vowed to never let anything get in the way of my academics. Even though I'm taking courses that prepare me for a career in the medical field, a path I would not pursue even at risk of spontaneous combus-tion of Earth, there is no excuse for me to fail. After all, my family has a reputation for failure, and if I don't push myself, no one else will. When I think of me not choosing the effortless Bishop Loughlin High School and traditional fun with friends and preferring the intense courses, dedication to achievement, and overall feeling of self-worth, I cannot believe my mother still can't accept my choice.

One thing I've learned growing up in Brooklyn is that disappointment happens often. The bike I rode to school in the morning wasn't there when I went to get it in the afternoon. That's Brooklyn. Instead of seeing movies with friends on weekends, I work hard and attempt to keep the little kids out of my mom's hair. That's Brooklyn. Instead of going outside to my backyard, I remember I don't have one, and settle for the 12' by 6' concrete space in front of my house. That's Brooklyn. My Brooklyn doesn't feature flowers of the freshest air or people who smile and say hi. Instead, there's what might have been Orbit gum on the floor among the other thousand wads, a pool of strangely colored vomit, and the monotonous working class boarding the subway to the job it will complain about when it returns home.

If there's anything that Brooklyn has taught me, it's "just do it." I owe it to myself to keep trying, not because I have to, but because I want to prove to myself that I can. I'll have to endure the requirements of helping to raise my siblings and other responsibilities. After the chaos and traffic and noise have settled, I know I've made the right choice, even if my mother hasn't. And it's all worth it.

ANALYSIS

This essay opens with a conversation that abounds in conflict. Though this unconventional opening poses a risk of being confusing or unclear, it contains enough hints to pique the reader's curiosity. We wonder why the narrator feels overwhelmed. We sense the author's frustration at being encouraged to go to Bishop Loughlin instead of Tech and wonder why her mother doesn't agree with her. Finally, we feel curious about the emotions and situations behind the outburst, "It's hard!"

Like Lisa's essay, "Then and Now" (Chapter 12) and Jackie's "The House on Wellington Avenue," (Chapter 15), the author does not complain about the challenging circumstances surrounding her upbringing. This essay is particularly striking because it doesn't speak explicitly about poverty or teen pregnancy in an abstract way, but the author tells us the story of the direct lived experience: taming the "demonic screaming" of a younger sibling, cleaning up a "shabby apartment," waking up at 3 a.m. to do schoolwork.

The paragraph that begins "We were already different at age fourteen" could be more explicit about who comprises "we." Eventually it does become clear that the author is comparing herself to her mother. The author uses striking visual language to render the stark contrasts between her teenage years and her mother's. While her mother spent teenage years rearing children, the author chose "intense courses" and dedicated herself to academic achievements. This essay resembles "Lessons from the Immigration Spectrum" (Chapter 9) in that the author does not complacently accept the label of "underprivileged" but rather rises above the limitations, refusing to fail. The author of this essay highlights her determination when she writes, ". . . if I don't push myself, no one else will." In the first half of the essay, we see why her single mom does not push herself to succeed. In the fourth paragraph, the author powerfully illustrates why the entire neighborhood she grew up in did not foster success.

In describing how "disappointment happens often" in Brooklyn, the author chooses small examples to illustrate larger problems in the neighborhood. The disappearance of her bike hints at crime; her sacrifice of weekend outings indicates the intergenerational strains of teen pregnancy; the wads of gum and "strangely colored vomit" show the general state of disrepair. And "the monotonous working class/subway" illustration further demonstrates the author's general despair with her surroundings. The repetition of the phrase "That's Brooklyn" is a unique and memorable way to separate the different observations that the author makes about the dismal conditions of her neighborhood. This phrase shows the author's attitude of "just do it" even in circumstances where many would give up. The phrase also helps prevent the paragraph from reading like a long litany of complaints. The varied sentence lengths of this essay make it stylistically captivating. For instance, the last sentence, "And it's all worth it," is surprising and direct, capturing the author's keen resolve to overcome challenges. This essay is exceptional in its ability to use small, personal details to illustrate broader social issues that face a neighborhood full of disappointments. The intimate personal stories that the author shares make this essay a moving and compelling account of her strength and determination.

8

COMMUNITY SERVICE

"Music from the Heart"

Anonymous
Caltech

THE GREATEST JOY OF MUSIC IS to share it with others. Unfortunately, the pleasure of performing is often forgotten when players become more concerned with the technicalities and notes. I also once thought that I knew all the important keys to successful piano playing: practice, technique, dedication, and a love for what I do. Focused on the details, I lost sight of my audience.

During my sophomore year, my friend invited me to join "Music from the Heart," a group that showcased its musical talents to senior citizens. Although I accepted the invitation to support her, I began to regret my choice as the first performance approached. Not knowing how the seniors would respond to my performance, especially when I made a mistake, performing before the seniors became a terrifying thought.

Although my first performance went smoothly, it was hard to know whether the seniors enjoyed the pieces or the performance. While the group performed, the seniors would talk to each other, pausing to clap at the end of each piece. Trying to impress the audience, I eventually grew accustomed to preparing a showy piece as the monthly performance approached.

So used to this monthly routine, I doubted that this performance would be different from the previous ones when I was ready to perform my favorite piece one summer day. While waiting for my turn, I glanced around the room, noting with some uneasiness the growing number of seniors gathered around the piano. Amidst the crowd of chattering seniors, one woman's rapt attention to the performance caught my interest. She greeted each performer with a wide toothy smile and made a small comment about the composition. Uncertain of her expectations, I watched for her reaction when I rose to introduce my piece, "Clair de Lune" by Claude Debussy.

"Ooh, I love that song," was all she said in response.

A smile crossed my face when I discovered that she shared my enthusiasm for the composition. To demonstrate to her how much I enjoyed the song, I played my best to convey what made this moonlight song so special to me. My minor concerns on technicalities slowly dissipated as the song progressed. All that mattered then was playing the song I loved as well as I could. For the first time, I felt contented with my performance, undisturbed by mistakes.

The performance was far from perfect. However, none of the seniors commented that the rhythm was too slow or the notes were wrong like the audition judges would normally do. Although they still chattered softly during the performance, they all smiled and clapped. A few of them would say that the song was lovely. They appreciated my efforts to entertain them and eagerly asked the group to return soon. Just the delighted smile on the woman's face made the performance worthwhile.

It was the seniors' appreciation for what I did that brought them back to the piano each month, and my love for what I did that drew me to it. The monthly performance was not just a musical showcase; it was my chance to give back to the community and to help enrich the seniors' life. The true joy in my life is not just sharing music, but devoting myself to community services as a volunteer.

ANALYSIS

This student's introduction served its purpose. It probably made the admissions officers curious. What happened when she made the mistake of focusing on the technicalities of playing music rather than the enjoyment of it? It probably made them want to read more to find the answer.

As the author of this essay explains how she volunteered for Music from the Heart, she also reveals her honest feelings—how she has apprehension about performing and how she wasn't sure if the seniors were enjoying it because of their chatting during the performance. Many students think that you need to present yourself in a light that makes you appear almost perfect, but sharing these kinds of doubts actually makes the essay more interesting, personable and honest. Being perfect is not very compelling, but letting the reader know that you have minor insecurities adds some complexity. This also reveals a lot about the way that you think and how you view your own personality.

During the crux of the story, we can see the student change from focusing on how well she performs technically to sharing her enthusiasm for the music. She describes the internal dialogue that she has with herself, trying to perform with as much enthusiasm as possible when the seniors react to her playing. It's easy to understand why she enjoys playing for the seniors and how their smiles and thanks make it worth the time that she spends each month.

For essays on community service, it's critical to demonstrate that you are not just doing community service because it looks good on a resume or because a parent or your school is forcing you to, but that you actually enjoy the work and put your whole self into it. From this essay, the admissions officers could tell that this student gains as much from the experience as her audience does, and that she's likely to continue such service in college and beyond.

"Precious Planet"

Pen-Yuan Hsing
Duke University

"HELLO! WHAT'S YOUR NAME?" "PEN-YUAN HSING." I see The Expression, then hear The Response: "What?" Starting the first grade in the US without knowing a single word of English, going back to Taiwan three years later incapable of recognizing a single Chinese character is not exactly an ideal circumstance for blending in. For many years, I was always the quiet one sitting in the corner, the one who few people talked to, the one out of the loop. I was the "local alien."

I opt to join the Earth Science Club during my first year in Lishan High School, as I always had an interest in astronomy, which happened to be the focus of that year's club activities. I didn't know the weekly gathering time of our club was also an elective Earth Science course that students from other high schools could attend. I certainly did not realize what a big impact this arrangement would have on me.

Near the end of the first semester, I was approached by a girl from a neighboring school who attended this earth science course. She asked if I wanted to join her on an environmental survey of Taiwan's Keelung coast conducted by an organization called Taipei WetNet. For a moment I hesitated, I literally had no experience in responding to invitations. What suddenly came out of my mouth surprised me, "Sure, what time?"

For the next three years I spent in Taipei WetNet, I gained not only a close friend, knowledge about the problems our environment faced, but perhaps most importantly found a group of people who shared the same convictions, who are passionate about the same thing, the plight of our precious planet. A year after being introduced to this organization, I was its coordinator and presented my first academic paper at an environmental education conference. I learned that I don't always have to be the quiet one in the corner, that I do and can have things to share with everyone else. I don't have to fear.

I often think about how I managed to say yes on that fateful day. Was it just because of a pretty face? Or maybe there has always been a special part of me that wanted to get out, and she was instrumental in "flipping the switch." This eye-opening experience and what I learned from it is what I desperately want to share with the world.

Perhaps, somewhere out there is another quiet person in the corner just waiting to be found. A switch waiting to be flipped. You just have to find it, flip it, and make the world a brighter, warmer place.

ANALYSIS

Pen-Yuan begins his essay with an apparent shortcoming—not being about to blend in as the "local alien," "the quiet one sitting in the corner," "the one out of the loop." This introduction is reminiscent of Angelica's essay, "No Longer Invisible," (Chapter 7), in which she describes her intense shyness. Like Angelica, Pen-Yuan chooses to describe a weakness in order to demonstrate a gradual transformation in personality from introvert to extrovert and leader.

There is a bit of an abrupt break between Pen-Yuan's comment about feeling like a "local alien" to joining the Earth Science Club. It is often challenging to seamlessly transition between the introductory paragraph in an essay to the first body paragraph. While it is not essential to explicitly link these two paragraphs, being mindful of this transition can make the essay read more smoothly and logically.

Pen-Yuan does a nice job of using short snippets of conversation to add a lively tone to his essay as well as a means to highlight pivotal points. For instance, he opens the essay with, "Hello! What's your name?" and describes the confused "What?" that comes in response to "Pen-Yuan Hsing," a short exchange that underscores his feeling of being a "local alien." Later on, when he blurts out "Sure, what time?" in response to the invitation to join Taipei WetNet, we see another crucial turning point in Pen-Yuan's life.

As we move from the third to the fourth paragraph, the story line jumps from Pen-Yuan joining Taipei WetNet to his concluding three years with the organization. This section could be more effective if Pen-Yuan describes some of the events in which he participated during the three years. This might give the reader a sense of his engagement and involvement before he concludes, "I gained not only a close friend, knowledge about the problems our environment faced, but perhaps most importantly found a group of people who shared the same convictions, who are passionate about the same thing, the plight of our precious planet." Examples might have helped more compellingly demonstrate this passion for protecting the planet and his experiences working with a group.

Pen-Yuan illustrates his transformation from a loner to an integral member of the Taipei WetNet group when he writes, "I learned that I don't always have to be the quiet one in the corner, that I do and can have things to share with everyone else. I don't have to fear." He concludes his essay by urging us to reach out to "another quiet person in the corner just waiting to be found" in order to "make the world a brighter, warmer place." Because we know the personal story behind this request, it appears more meaningful and sincere. Overall, Pen-Yuan's essay convincingly portrays the story of personal transformation from shy student to fearless leader using the specific, memorable example of his dedicated environmental work with Taipei WetNet.

"Cuddle Buddies"

Anastasia Fullerton
Stanford University

THE COLD MID-AUGUST SAN FRANCISCO BAY fog was just begin-ning to roll in over Piedmont as I snapped the cover shut on Jennings Burch's book "They Cage the Animals at Night," the most recent addi-tion to my "get ready for 7th grade summer reading extravaganza." It is a story about a young boy who lives in various orphanages and foster homes with only his stuffed animal, Doggie, for companionship. My cousin from Connecticut had told me that it was a fabulous book, but little did I know how it would touch my life and the lives of others.

As I gazed across my room at the pile of stuffed animals I had been collecting since I was young, an idea came to me. I would collect stuffed animals for children like Jennings. First, I contacted local agencies that support children suffering from abuse and neglect and told them about my idea. They said that the stuffed animals would be very helpful in therapy and would certainly lift children's spirits.

I decided to call my project "Cuddle Buddies." Now I actually had to come up with the "buddies"! I wrote articles for the local and school newspapers, telling Jennings' story and asking for donations of stuffed animals. My phone rang off the hook; schools, families, local business-es and toy manufacturers all wanted to help. Much to my delight this project took the Bay Area by storm. By the second week my living room looked like a zoo with animals tucked in every corner and on top of each chair. Every time my mom and I made deliveries to the agencies, the kids would be waiting for their Cuddle Buddies with their eyes down, too shy to look but shaking with excitement.

Six years after its launch, Cuddle Buddies continues to expand. Each year I solicit from more toy companies and communities. Now over 25,000 stuffed animals have been donated to agencies in the Bay Area and Connecticut, emergency units, two orphanages in Africa and one in Germany. At the Saidia Children's Home in Kenya, Simon, a seven year old, whose parents died from AIDS, couldn't sleep at night. When the Cuddle Buddies were laid out for him to choose from, Simon selected a grey koala bear and soon after was sleeping through the night. My heart ached when I learned that a young girl in Oakland had stopped cutting herself so she could get the big black dog that she wanted so badly. I never dreamed that Cuddle Buddies would be used in these ways.

Knowing that I would be going on to college and that others my age could do what I have done, I decided to expand Cuddle Buddies. To spread the word beyond the Bay Area I designed a website, www.cuddlebuddies.net, and contacted newspapers and TV stations across the nation. The response was overwhelming. I heard from kids, parents, agencies and even The Girls Scouts. I am now helping to establish two dozen Cuddle Buddies chapters from Utah to North Carolina.

This has been a great experience. I have learned how to follow through on an idea, how to champion a cause and how to deal with setbacks. But most importantly, I have learned how easy it is to positively impact a life and the joy that comes from it. I will go to college with these lessons in mind and hope to continue my work with Cuddle Buddies, even as I engage in a whole new set of exciting academic and nonacademic pursuits.

ANALYSIS

"Cuddle Buddies" chronicles Anastasia's leading role in the development of a social enterprise. This story is probably compelling for admissions officers at Stanford, where there is a growing interest in social entrepreneurship. Anastasia's impressive story demonstrates her creativity and commitment to growing a vision, a valuable asset as a leader in whatever "exciting academic and nonacademic pursuits" lie ahead for her.

The introduction draws us in with its careful attention to detail: we can see the San Francisco fog, sense its chilliness, and witness Anastasia's passion for reading. The last sentence, "little did I know how it would touch my life and the lives of others," foreshadows the creation of Cuddle Buddies. What is particularly remarkable about this story is Anastasia's young age—she is only in 7th grade. It is quite a dramatic jump from the small scene in the book, *They Cage the Animals at Night,* and the decision to provide animals for therapy. Anastasia could have added a few more sentences to explain how she started the ball rolling on her project. In particular, it is surprising that she contacted local agencies—here it may help to specify which ones—as one imagines that most teenagers might simply tell their friends an idea and never actually act to make the vision a reality.

The third paragraph uses vivid imagery and active language to make the reader feel a part of the creation and expansion of "Cuddle Buddies." Anastasia does an excellent job of using lively phrases so that we feel we are also participants in the process as the phone "rang off the hook," the living room became "like a zoo" and the project "took the Bay Area by storm." It is impressive that this storm has hardly abated six years later. Admissions officers often admire stories about long-term commitment, especially when the author can demonstrate continual growth throughout this process. As Anastasia's third paragraph shows, this growth has certainly occurred: personally, Anastasia has learned management skills as her organization has expanded internationally, having donated 25,000 stuffed animals. Anastasia gives a face to this statistic by relating the story of Simon with his gray koala and the girl in Oakland who chooses the big black dog. This is concrete proof that this idea does "lift children's spirits."

The link to Anastasia's website is an excellent way to distinguish her from other prospective students. The website demonstrates her professionalism, much as the business card in Jason's story, "Birthing a Business" (Chapter 14) shows his willingness to go above and beyond expectations. Anastasia wraps up her essay nicely by noting, "I have learned how to follow through on an idea, how to champion a cause and how to deal with setbacks," skills she can apply as she pursues her education after high school.

"Best Reader"

Manika
University of Pennsylvania

THE GIANT BROWN BEAR WAS CREEPING quietly behind the blissfully pink duck ready to wring his bare paws around her neck and throw her into a pot of boiling stew.

We turned the page.

While I chuckled at the impracticality of a bear boiling water to eat a duck, especially a pink duck, I lifted my head to find Matthew tiptoeing about the room exhibiting the meanest, most ferocious look his cute face could conjure. All the while, little Monica sat huddled next to my arm honestly afraid to turn the page and find her favorite pink creature in a bear's "tummy."

It was one of those moments of my hours spent reading with children at the library when it dawned just how much, as a "grown up," I was missing.

I remembered the Thursday when Victoria bounded into the Reading Room showcasing in her small hands a golden certificate from school.

"Best Reader," it glistened. A smile came across my face as I looked into the eyes of the petite 7-year old who just last year had been held back in first grade because her reading was not up to par.

It was the same smile that had filled my face six months prior, when Victoria joined the reading program and I saw the other volunteers instantly point at me. Our supervisor had agreed with them, knowing I would use my patient disposition and friendly way with children to motivate our new student. I had nodded vigorously, smiling, not only because I was proud of the confidence they had in me, but because nothing would make me happier than taking on the challenge of helping Victoria improve her reading.

After spending the first session responding to an unrelenting stream of questions, I recognized that Victoria's talkative nature and impatience for answers overshadowed her desire to sit down and read. I treasured her energy and insatiable curiosity and fueled it with my own enthusiasm. Yet, for every interest she presented, I took her to scan the library shelves in search of a related book. I watched her eyes grow with excitement as I tirelessly helped her press through the stories, a journey in search of her answers. Some of the books I chose were difficult for her, but we read through them together, challenging limits and quenching the thirst for knowledge. In books, I told her time and again, she would find all she wanted to know.

Taking her certificate in my hands, I couldn't help but be proud that part of this glittering piece of paper was likely my doing.

My thoughts were interrupted by Victoria's chant. "I got best reader!" she exclaimed over and over jumping between feet as her arms waved from side to side. Without hesitation, I followed. Holding her certificate up for all to see, I matched my footing with hers as we hopped the length of the room giggling.

Whether it is victory celebrations or talking in different voices, whenever I am with these kids, I find myself being pulled into their childhood world—a world of simplicity, of undying curiosity, and of pure innocence. It is a world in which if everything is not perfect, it definitely can be. And with a simple "prayer to God" or "kiss on the boo-boo" it will be.

Though I go in each week to be these kids' teacher, I come out, having been their student. They have introduced me to a side of me I never realized existed.

As I enter college, it is not only my intelligence or my accumulated knowledge, but also the kid in me who will bring success. This child will jump to try every new activity with an enthusiasm that cannot fade. She will ask questions of everything she sees, of everything she hears and of everything she reads. She will dream big and for every step she stumbles upon towards that dream, she will get right back up and step again, this time, a little more carefully. And she will do all this, approach every life hurdle or triumph with a smile- a big contagious smile.

ANALYSIS

The unconventional first sentence of this essay grabs the reader's attention and creates a double-take effect with its absurd and comical juxtaposition of giant bear, pink duck, and boiling stew.

"We turned the page," the even shorter paragraph that follows, reveals the context of the first sentence—a children's book. Such child-like and active language makes us feel that we are in the room, reading over Manika and Monica's shoulders. These sentences create a sense of whimsy and wonder that help us see the reading room from the perspective of a child.

Manika next contrasts childhood curiosity with a young adult's perspective on life. Observing Matthew and Monica, she reflects, "It was one of those moments of my hours spent reading with children at the library when it dawned just how much, as a 'grown up,' I was missing." This single sentence feels a little choppy, even after the first two short paragraphs. While using short sentences to indicate a change in mood or pace is often an effective writing tool, it is best to use it sparingly. Manika draws upon this style several times, including the single-sentence paragraph that begins "taking her certificate in my hands" that is set off by yet another new paragraph with the note, "my thoughts were interrupted by Victoria's chant." In some ways, the short sentence structure has limited Manika's avenue for sharing details. For example, Manika writes about all she is missing out on as a "grown up." She might have used more complex sentences at this point to elaborate on her feelings and to give us a better sense of what the significance of that moment meant to her.

Manika does an excellent job of explaining her volunteer work in this essay. She manages to include other people's perceptions of her through her supervisor's knowledge that she had a "patient disposition and friendly way with children." She also includes her person reaction: "I had nodded vigorously, smiling, not only because I was proud of the confidence they had in me, but because nothing would make me happier than taking on the challenge of helping Victoria improve her reading." These sentences demonstrate Manika's enthusiasm and dedication to helping Victoria learn. The charming scene of dancing with Victoria and her "best reader" certificate not only sweetly celebrates her only accomplishments as a tutor, but also provides the reader with a glimpse of Manika's unselfishness in acknowledging her student's hard work. Manika's essay demonstrates an ability to empathize with younger children and even learn from their "words of simplicity" and "undying curiosity." This essay is successful because Manika describes a volunteer activity in a way that suffuses it with spirit and energy, so that we not only learn about her volunteer job but also about her ebullient personality.

9

FAMILY

"Box of Chocolates"

Alex Volodarsky
The Wharton School, University of Pennsylvania

EVERY SUNDAY MORNING, THE LOCAL STARBUCKS plays host to what my mom likes to call "mother-son bonding time." This Sunday is no different. My mom and I sit down with our regular Chai Latte and Caramel Frappuchino, and absorb the aroma of the coffee beans and the gentle rays of the winter sun.

"So Alex, what are we going to do for dad's 50th birthday?" When my mom asks a question about upcoming plans, she doesn't expect an answer; she already has something in mind. Many years ago, my mom started a family tradition of making gifts personal: poems, songs, skits. At first I didn't understand why we were wasting so much time when we could just buy a gift card from the local mall. But my outlook changed when I turned twelve. For my birthday, my parents gave me a poster, a product of their many hours on Photoshop. With long hair, sideburns, and a slim suit, I had become the fifth member of the Beatles crossing Abbey Road. Every morning when I wake up, this poster opposite my bed is the first thing I see, and I start off the day with a smile. Since then, I have needed little persuasion to start working on the next gift project. Actually, I even look forward to these times, when my parents find their inner children, and the trivial worries of life simply whisk away. My dad, both figuratively and literally, ditches his office suit and proper manners, and dons a red woman's wig and high heels to practice a scene. My mom stops scolding my sister and me, and joins us in our ruckus, doing the jitterbug and blowing on a harmonica. These are the moments in my family when there are no children or adults, just four people who give in to their creative urges.

"How about throwing Dad a party, and making him a movie?" my mom asks as I use my straw to fish for any remaining coffee at the bottom of the cup. "Just think of a movie you like and we'll parody it." A big fan of "the-life-is-like-a-box-of-chocolates" theory, I suggest my favorite movie, Forrest Gump. She smiles. "OK, but only if you play Forrest."

When we come home, my mom takes down a box, heavy with the dust of age, scribbled with messy Russian lettering. I peer over her shoulder as she empties onto the living room floor the contents: my dad's life story in black and white. Within minutes, I am completely immersed in the photographs I have never seen before. As I gape at a picture of a bearded teenager laughing with his friends, I do a double take. Is this the same clean-shaven man who helped me to prove the theorem that all right angles are congruent and always tells me to tuck in my shirt? I shake my head in disbelief as I thumb through some pictures of my dad and his friends with guitars in the forest singing songs around a camp fire. My mom explains that the Soviet government didn't approve of these songs, so the woods became their only refuge. I am now starting to understand why my dad, limited in what he could sing or say as a youth, pushes my sister and me to ask probing questions, survey news from all sides of the political spectrum, and watch controversial movies. Looking down at one of the pictures of my dad in the forest, it just hits me: the movie should be called "Forest Guy."

With each picture comes its own story, and collectively, they create a collage of my dad's past that I had never known. But even more surprises await me as I watch documentaries about Russian leaders in the 20th century. To truly parody Forrest Gump, some "great" Communist leaders must be part of Forest Guy's life, just as Kennedy and Nixon were part of Forrest Gump's. Coming up with bizarre ideas of how my dad met the Communist leaders is the most entertaining part of our moviemaking. My stomach throbs with laughter as I conceive the impossible notion of my dad bullying Gorbachev into destroying the Berlin Wall.

Along with Russian history, I also discover part of my family's: while discussing the horrors of Stalin's reign with my mom, I am shocked to hear that my father was born in exile, and one of his uncles died in Stalin's concentration camp for joking about Communists. It's hard to believe that someone can be killed for cracking a joke, when cracking a safe will only get you a few years in jail. Luckily, when I am joking about Lenin and Stalin in my film, my only worry is crowd response.

It is the day of the party, and as I look around at the apprehensive crowd, my instincts yell, "Run, Alex! Run!" Soon, the lights dim, and my anxiety grows. I am watching the viewers as intensely as they are watching the screen. As each joke is met with uproarious laughter and table slapping, my breaths become calmer and my fingers stop shaking. Twenty-five minutes later, I hear the long awaited ovation. I gaze from table to table at the sea of smiles, but one face catches my attention. It is my dad's, showing complete disbelief that something so grandiose could be done about him and for him. All these weeks I had been so focused on the guests' reactions that I never thought about my dad's. Although he is trying hard to contain himself, I see a tear sneak from the side of his eye. It is the first time I have seen my dad cry.

Yes, life is a box of chocolates. Some are delicious, some too bitter for your taste. But the best are like the one I picked that day; they seem like any other chocolate, but when you bite into them, they surprise you with an unexpected flavor.

ANALYSIS

In this extraordinarily creative essay, Alex reveals a gift for storytelling that jumps nimbly from seriousness to humor, cavorts from one surprise to another, and weaves in vivid descriptions, evocative metaphors and historical references. Many people might find it hard to imagine an essay that begins in a Starbucks and takes us through Forest Gump and Stalinist atrocities to end with a metaphor about a box of chocolates. However, Alex's ability to tie all these memorable details together coherently makes this essay stand out.

Alex opens with an introduction that stimulates our senses: we can smell the fragrant "aroma of the coffee beans" and feel the "gentle rays of the winter sun." Effective descriptions detail not only the visual scene, but also appeal more completely to our other senses. In describing his weekly Sunday "bonding time" with his mother, Alex gives us a sense of the deep connection he has to his family. As the essay unfolds, more clues reveal glimpses of Alex's dedication and commitment to his family. Touching and charming examples make Alex's family come alive for his readers. Instead of the nondescript labels of "mother" and "father," Alex provides tangible and memorable images of these people—his father in a red wig and high heels, his mother playing harmonica. These details perfectly illustrate "four people who give in to their creative urges." Though these family gatherings and gift projects might not show up on a resume, Alex does a wonderful job of showing us how they are central to his character. It's important to remember that a compelling personal essay may draw upon aspects of your life that might not fall under standard ideas of academic accomplishments and extracurricular activities.

The paragraph in which Alex discovers elements of his dad's past in Soviet Russia is a creative way for Alex to show us an aspect of his heritage. This paragraph could easily focus on Alex's dad while leaving out information about Alex himself. However, Alex wisely chooses to discuss his dad's relationship to himself: for example, we suspect that Alex is someone who asks probing questions, surveys the news critically, and watches controversial movies. In this paragraph, Alex masterfully weaves together elements of his own past and his dad's past while illustrating his personal interests and strengths. These seemingly disparate pieces of information are brought together by the story of the gift project, which itself is focused on film.

With rich detail, Alex describes the process of watching documentary films and creating the "Forest Guy" film for his father. This section is particularly interesting because Alex not only describes what happened, but also analyzes his own learning and emotional responses. The range and authenticity of these emotional responses is impressive (from stomach-throbbing laughter to tears on Alex's dad's face), and makes for a varied and lively reading experience. The cultural reference to Forrest Gump is a clever one that helps Alex wrap up his essay with a metaphor from the story. However, it is important to be careful to use commonly known cultural references or explain their context and not to assume that your reader will understand the reference. Jonathan Cross (Chapter 12) demonstrates this nicely when he references John Nash.

"Dear Santa"

Anonymous
Princeton University

EVERY YEAR, MY CHRISTMAS WISH LIST would read, *"Dear Santa, all I want for Christmas is a baby brother."* At age nine, I knew Santa *had* to be real because, one day, my mom announced that she was pregnant. After ten years of being an only child, I could not have anticipated how much my life would change because of a little brother. I received the honor of naming him, and I chose Jason. In retrospect, I should have named my brother "Ivan the Terrible."

Jason followed me *everywhere* like an irritating shadow. My grievances to my mom were countless, especially after Jason drew all over my bedroom walls and murdered my pet fish, Goldie. My mom's typical response was, "Well, isn't this what you've always wished for?"

Jason's mischief reached a new height one morning when I became the victim of a five year old with scissors. I stared into the bathroom mirror and dunked my head under cold water to make sure I was not dreaming. What I saw enraged me! In the middle of the night, Michael had cut off five inches of my long, black hair from one side of my head. I stood in horror, and stormed to the kitchen where I found the rest of my family calmly eating breakfast. I flashed a menacing stare at my brother, who snickered across the table. "You're going to pay for this!" I screamed. Furious beyond words, I could not even begin to describe my rage. Instead, I ran back to the bathroom and huddled on the floor.

"What am I going to do?" I was irate and panicked at the same time. As a freshman in high school, I was very sensitive about my appearance. I had been hesitant to cut my hair past the "tips to take away the split-ends" trim, because my hair had been the same length for seven years. I agonized over the situation and concocted my swift counter-attack. Instead of chopping off his hair, I found inspiration to appease my anger in the pages of *Teen* magazine and considered trendy hairstyles. My brother was stunned because I did not retaliate. Victory was mine.

Because of experiences such as this, I have learned to adapt, to keep my focus, and to solve problems with little or no resources. I approach tough situations with objectivity and determination. Like many other experiences with my brother and at school, I have dealt with difficult situations and turned them into positive opportunities for change. I am flexible with the circumstances given to me, and I strive for the best outcome. Despite the craziness Santa's gift brings, Jason's continuous surprises provide laughter to my life. As for my hair, I did cut off the five inches from the other side, and I actually cherished the new look better. Thanks, Santa.

ANALYSIS

The author's wit shines through in this punchy, concise essay. In fact, her humor is immediately evident in the first paragraph when shining expectations for a long-wished-for baby brother are thwarted by the blunt sentence, "In retrospect, I should have named my brother 'Ivan the Terrible'." She uses italics and exclamation points effectively in her writing to punctuate key words and to express her mood. For instance, from the statement "Jason followed me *everywhere* like an irritating shadow," the exaggeration of "everywhere" heightens our understanding of the intensity of her irritation. The exclamation point at the end of "What I saw enraged me!" underscores the author's anger. Excessive use of word-stylization and punctuation can be distracting in an essay, but *thoughtful* use can enhance writing. In her case, these were particularly appropriate because her essay conveyed a more casual, informal tone.

Stylistically, the author also varies her sentence length to excellent dramatic effect. In particular, the contrast between longer descriptions of what was going on and short remarks such as "You're going to pay for this," the thought of "What am I going to do?," and the proud conclusion, "Victory was mine" draw us into the immediacy of the story. She chose to illustrate one very specific event from her many "grievances" (from bedroom wall vandalism to goldfish murder)—her brother cutting off her hair. This specific anecdote demonstrates how it is possible to write an essay that doesn't describe a transformation of years or even a weeklong summer camp. Though the event the author describes in this essay probably transpired in a matter of hours, she still made this a meaningful topic for her paper. This shows us that there's really no "best" timeframe or topic for writing a personal essay. The author's essay takes a specific topic of a very short timeframe, relates it to a longer timeframe (we know she has had long hair for seven years and is sensitive about her appearance as many high school freshmen are) and shows more generalized, almost "timeless" if you will, aspects of her overall character. We can contrast this to Jason Y. Shah's approach in "Hurricane Transformations" (Chapter 15), in which he tells a story of change that occurs over many months.

The writing styles are different; yet, both essays effectively show us positive traits in the authors' characters.

The strength of this author's essay is that she conveys a specific event with a lively narrative pace and snappy dialogue then ultimately creates a broader conclusion that helps us understand how this specific incident illustrates that she has "learned to adapt, to keep [her] focus, and to solve problems with little or no resources." Though the overall tone of her essay may seem to focus on annoyance and anger at her brother, ultimately she demonstrates her resilience and her capacity for forgiveness in noting, "despite the craziness Santa's gift brings, Jason's continuous surprises provide laughter to my life." Her comment that she preferred her new hairstyle further demonstrates how she turns difficult situations into advantageous opportunities. "Thanks, Santa" is a catchy way to end the essay. It can be tempting to end with a long "summary" sentence, but she shows how even two words can make for a memorable and satisfying ending.

"Lessons from the Immigration Spectrum"

Anonymous
MIT

MY FAMILY HAS TAKEN LIVING IN the big city as a reason for why we should never give up. Here in Los Angeles there are countless individuals and families along all points on the immigration spectrum from recent arrivals to recent citizenship. Residing in this great city has provided me with diversity, opportunity, acceptance, and an abundance of role models to follow through all troubles- big and small.

I always thought that I had it the worst out of all my family members because I was never allowed to get anything lower than what my brother or a cousin had gotten in a class. My parents figured if they could do it, so could I, and if not on my own then with a little of their help. It was not until recently that I realized the truth in this. In my short life I have seen my father go from speaking no English, to excelling in it. I have heard countless stories about migrant farmers such as Cesar Chavez and my grandfather who had nearly nothing, yet persisted and succeeded.

Growing up hearing these stories of great injustices and misfortunes has truly influenced my long term goals. I am going to go far because there is no excuse for not doing my best, given all I have been blessed with. When I had trouble speaking Spanish and felt like abandoning my native tongue I remembered my mother and how when she came to the United States she was forced to wash her mouth out with soap and endure beatings with a ruler by the nuns at her school for speaking it. When I couldn't figure out tangents, sines, and cosines I thought about my father and how it took him nearly a year to learn long division because he was forced to teach it to himself after dropping out and starting to work in the 4th grade. And when I wanted to quit swimming because I was tired I remembered my grandfather and how no matter how his muscles ached if he stopped digging, or picking fruit, or plowing he risked not having enough food to feed his family. Pursuing technical fields such as math and engineering first seemed like work for men to me, but the times have changed. All these people, just from my family have been strong role models for me.

I feel that being labeled "underprivileged" does not mean that I am limited in what I can do. There is no reason for me to fail or give up, and like my parents and grandparents have done, I've been able to pull through a great deal. My environment has made me determined, hard working, and high aiming. I would not like it any other way. This is how my Hispanic heritage, family upbringing, and role models have influenced my academic and personal long term goals.

ANALYSIS

This essay, like "All Worth It," (Chapter 7), describes the lessons the author has learned from growing up in an "underprivileged" community of immigrants in LA. The author of "All Worth It" learned from growing up in Brooklyn to "just do it," never accepting failure as an option. This essay similarly shows how the author came to believe that "we should never give up." Both essays are compelling because they provide specific examples from their personal lives to give us a sense of the unique circumstances in which they grew up. However, the author of this essay focuses on the positive elements of her environment: "diversity, opportunity, acceptance, and an abundance of role models." Reading these two essays in conjunction shows that there is no rule for how to write about coming from a disadvantaged background. While "All Worth It" notes more of the negative aspects of the neighborhood and "Lessons from the Immigration Spectrum" focuses on positive lessons, both authors are able to give us a strong sense of their perseverance and strength.

The author of "Lessons from the Immigration Spectrum" cites success stories that are specific to her heritage as a Hispanic immigrant. For example, she describes her father who went "from speaking no English, to excelling in it" and places the story of her grandfather's migrant farm work in a broader historical context by referencing Cesar Chavez. Historical references can be a powerful way to frame one's personal story or family history within a broader ethnic, religious/spiritual, or social community.

This author shares specific examples that provide evidence of her drive to succeed. She states, ". . . there is no excuse for not doing my best, given all I have been blessed with." Her essay shows that she has come to recognize that her circumstances are relatively fortunate compared to the hardships her parents faced. The power of these experiences lies in the stark contrasts they present. We find that the author "felt like abandoning [her] native tongue" while her mother was physically punished for speaking Spanish. Learning about her father's year-long struggle to learn long division helps put her confusion about tangents, sines and cosines into perspective. The contrast between cosines and long division highlights the difference in education levels between the author, who is on track to complete high school, and her father, who did not complete fourth grade. The third example the author provides is a narrative telling about her decision to continue swimming when she is reminded of the hard labor that her grandfather endured. These three examples give us a strong understanding of the lessons the author has learned from growing up with the "immigration spectrum" across multiple generations.

10

HERITAGE AND IDENTITY

"Heritage"

Anonymous
Yale University

"HERITAGE" IS THE FIRST WORD IN my family dictionary, a noun and adverb, for who we are and how we live. My parents taught me that my heritage defines my identity. Through honorific speech towards my elders and adherence to traditional values, I accepted Korean customs as part of the duality that defines my life in America.

Yet, a turbulent disunity stormed under that surface of peaceful co-existence. Though I outwardly represented the model Korean-American son, I loathed fitting this stereotypical mold. My shell was so well-constructed, however, that others mistook me for a successful immigrant. I felt as if I were ripped from the very fabric of my American birthplace, and plunged into a vacuum between my ancestral home and the world I lived in. I felt that my heritage was a short anchor against the relentlessly rising tide: I had to break free—or go under.

While struggling with this chain, however, I came to appreciate what my heritage offered. As a martial arts instructor, I supported students in building discipline and character. As a bilingual tutor, I helped immigrant children adapt to life in America. Soon, I realized that my heritage was an instrument for harmonizing personal development with service to others.

When I was selected to serve in the HOBY World Leadership Congress, my family's financial circumstances did not cover the $1,350 required fee. By infusing my American entrepreneurial energy with Asian medicine, I covered the cost by selling herbal products at my martial arts studio. Though the novelty of my venture brought me to the verge of bankruptcy, I persisted. By researching products, competitors and clientele, I streamlined my inventory to best serve my customers.

Eventually, I created a business aimed at offering others a healthy lifestyle. Sweaty students gulped green tea and chocolate-flavored snacks, dropping dollars for the cause that lay within my cardboard cashbox. Supported by outside donations, I became Greater L.A.'s ambassador in Washington D.C. Infused with new inspiration, I returned with a project grant to spread the martial arts lifestyle of discipline, confidence, and respect.

As my heritage anchored itself to the bedrock of my battles, I integrated Korean tradition with my American identity. Fusing service with civic duty, I entered the L.A. County Sheriff's Explorer Academy. Through the grueling training, I learned to work as part of a team. Appointed as Drill Instructor a year later, I took command of training the older recruits. Through a relationship of mutual respect, I prepared my platoon to dutifully serve the community. Leading this racially mixed group, I empathized beyond the duality of my own identity. I soon discovered that my heritage must transcend my personal struggles to truly embrace diversity.

Heritage is not a mere ethnic label—it is the honor and humanity that I am inspired to uphold. Today, I am grateful to my parents for endowing me with a spirit of dedication and determination. They bestowed a philosophy that speaks through my actions. This inheritance forms the base of my integrity as an individual, and defines my dedication to strengthening the society that I live in.

ANALYSIS

What makes the writer's essay interesting is that he writes about the conflict between his ethnic heritage and his American life. We immediately sense that it is not an easy amalgamation between his Korean and American identities. It might have enhanced his introduction to have provided a specific example of how these two identities clashed. However, his description of this conflict is very powerful and visual, and as the reader, we can tell detect the authenticity of his internal struggle. He writes, "I felt that my heritage was a short anchor against the relentlessly rising tide: I had to break free—or go under."

The writer aptly shows the connection between his achievements and his appreciation for his heritage. When he describes his efforts to raise funds to attend the HOBY World Leadership Congress, he demonstrates ingenuity as a creative entrepreneur. The admissions officers must have admired his self-initiated fundraising efforts and his development of a new market. His experience shows his innovation, persistence and ability to adapt his product line to his customers' needs.

In his example of the L.A. County Sheriff's Explorer Academy, he again addresses his heritage when leading an ethnically diverse group of students. While you may write an essay about a project that you worked on as a team or an experience that you had as a team member, it's always helpful to highlight your individual contribution. In the writer's case, he reveals his full responsibility for selling the Asian medicine and explains his role as a leader of his platoon. You may not be the sole leader of the group, but writing about your personal input makes a more powerful statement than presenting the contributions of the group as a whole.

Throughout his essay, the writer makes connections that are not obvious. At first glance, there doesn't seem to be much that ties together attending a student leadership conference or volunteering with the sheriff's department and ethnic identity. But the writer is able to form links among these topics that result in a single cohesive essay. His writing is engaging because, as readers, we can tell that he truly cares about his topic matter and he shares specific examples of what he has accomplished. But perhaps most importantly, he takes us inside his mind so that at least for a brief time we understand his thoughts, emotions, and reasoning. This is something that admissions officers always desire—to learn something new about the applicant and to understand his or her way of thinking.

"Abuelo"

Angelica
University of Chicago

THE TITLE OF THIS PICTURE IS "Abuelo" which means grandfather in Spanish. At first glance, it seems just a waste of a snapshot. Perhaps just another struggling photographer trying to pay the rent or who simply had one more shot left in a roll of film and took a random picture. It is an 8" by 11" color photograph of a man's neck, more specifically the back of his neck. It is quite wrinkled and brown and white hair has invaded the scalp. At first I questioned why the photographer did not simply take a picture of his grandfather's face. A face would allow viewers to see what the grandfather looks like and tell some kind of story, certainly more than what the back of his neck could possibly tell.

What I came to realize is that this is no random shot. What this picture wants is for me to imagine and to create a story. It does not necessarily wish to be framed but the picture does not want to be overlooked or neglected. It wants to be given a chance to prove itself as equally worthy as any other photograph. I do not need the face of the Abuelo to imagine the story of his life or personality. The back of his neck is just as important as his face.

After spending some time with this Abuelo I learned that the back of his neck is not just brown, it is tanned. Not just a natural tan, that some people are born with, but a particular shade of tan that can only be attained after continuous exposure to the sun. Perhaps this man does a lot of work outside. The distinguished wrinkles are more than just lines. In between them there seems to be some kind of dust. I recognize this dust because it is the kind of dust my father gets when he is working with joint compound.

After examining a little more closely I noticed the multiple scars on his scalp which prevent his hair from growing. The tiny hole in his earlobe reminds me that he was young once and had, like many young teenage boys, pierced his ear. Around his neck I can see a glimpse of a brown necklace. This necklace is very familiar to me because I own one. It is a very thin string with a small rectangular cloth at both ends. Many Catholics believe that it is something sacred.

In this case this picture is not measured by the thousands of words it is worth, but it is measured by what I took from it. It should not be criticized by what it does not have but should be valued for what it does have. I have found something in common with this photograph. All along what this picture wanted from me was to find something familiar. That familiarity sets this particular picture apart from all other photographs I have encountered and what has kept it vividly visible after having come across it years ago. This is exactly what this photograph longed for: to be found familiar and remembered.

ANALYSIS

Angelica takes an unconventional essay prompt, "Describe a picture and explore what it wants," and writes a short and creative essay that not only answers the prompt in an unexpected way but also demonstrates Angelica's dedication to learning more about her history. The essay opens with the surprising sentence, "At first glance, it seems just a waste of a snapshot." The reader immediately wonders, *why write about this photo then*? Angelica goes on to show an aptitude for vivid description, which she uses to illustrate the picture for those of us who aren't able to see it. We are also drawn into the mystery in wondering what meaning a photo of the back of someone's neck, wrinkled with brown and white hair, could possibly have.

Angelica states her answer to the essay prompt directly: "What this picture wants is for me to imagine and to create a story." She goes on to explain why this process of imagining and creating a story is important: the photo will have a chance "to prove itself as equally worthy as any other photograph." Angelica goes on to breathe life into this mysterious photo through a combination of sleuthing and guesswork. The amount of information she is about to extract from small details like the color of Abuelo's skin demonstrates Angelica's impressive imaginative capacity and thoughtful analysis. Even as fine a detail as dust in the wrinkles of the skin does not escape Angelica. She relates this dust to familiar (and familial) knowledge: ". . . it is the kind of dust my father gets when he is working with joint compound." Angelica might have clarified "joint compound" for those who are unfamiliar with the term. Still, her descriptions are intriguing. Angelica's eye for detail leads her to notice a hole in the earlobe from a former ear piercing, and part of a necklace. By linking these details to her father's life as a compound worker and also to her Catholic faith, we learn about Angelica's beliefs and her family life, as well as about her heritage.

Angelica summarizes the point of her essay nicely in her concluding paragraph, when she returns to the original question and answers it in a slightly different way: "All along what this picture wanted from me was to find something familiar . . . to be found familiar and remembered." Angelica's ability to form connections with the photograph are reminiscent of her ability to turn an unfamiliar new place into a "home" for learning and to transform unfamiliar faces into influential friends, things that she described in her other essay (Chapter 7), which chronicled her multiple school transfers.

"Anything Goes"

Jean Gan
Duke University

I HAVE ALWAYS BEEN COMFORTABLE WITH Tae Kwon Do, music, art, and friends. However, as a horse in Chinese astrology, I also need to explore different pursuits, and step outside of my comfort zone. This summer, I ventured beyond the pasture of my comfort zone, and participated onstage in the high school summer musical for the first time.

The biggest challenge of taking this leap was overcoming my own mental barrier—the sign that read, Jean, you have never had a dance lesson; you have no idea how to sing or act. Out of fear that I would feel uncomfortable, I believed that playing violin in the pit orchestra was my calling. However, after three years of pit orchestra experience, I longed to shine in that coveted spotlight. I did not tell my friends about how I wondered what it would feel like to act onstage in front of eight hundred people. When I saw that the title of the musical for this past summer was Anything Goes, I knew that no one would think worse of me for following my aspirations. Confident that my friends would encourage me, I let go of my cautious Chinese approach to life, and let the free-spirited horse within me escape.

Despite my decision to participate in the musical, I was terrified. I wondered whether I would meet any friends and if I would be able to learn to sing and dance well. My fears were intensified because I missed the first week of rehearsals while at a leadership conference in New York City. When I attended my first rehearsal, arriving directly from New York City, my fortitude kept me steady. With confidence and New York City memories in my heart, I joined the rest of the cast and reveled in the excitement. I followed my new friends with a passion for an art form that I hardly knew, but willingly embraced.

From that moment on, I was a horse freely cantering around an open meadow. I had discovered a new point of view, and the grass was greener than it had ever seemed. Some days, I came home with new dance steps to show my parents. On other days, I drew the designs of my costumes when my descriptions at the dinner table would not suffice. The make-up artist tried three times to find the right blush, while the hair team created a different style for me each night. Having to think up a new hairstyle each time was parallel to my shifting opinion of my life and self. Although participating in the musical was initially petrifying, I discovered that taking such a risk was the optimal way to grow and change.

Now, I will not shy away from being in a musical cast because my comfort zone is expanding. Soon it will encompass the grand scope of my interests: from singing and dancing to throwing a sales pitch in front of judges; from learning how to execute precision front-flips to building my favorite piano repertoire; from designing a webpage to arranging chamber music, or developing optics technologies. Such passions will continue to define who I am and what I hope to achieve. My character is being shaped and reshaped by my learning experiences because I am an impressionable human being. As I continue to explore, I know that my interests will solidify into a cohesive whole. Until then, I seek to enrich myself with new opportunities and never look back.

ANALYSIS

Besides being the name of the musical in which she participated, the title of Jean's essay, "Anything Goes," also captures the "free-spirited horse" within her that "ventured beyond the pasture of [her] comfort zone, and participated onstage in the high school musical for the first time." The "horse" metaphor not only captures Jean's adventurous spirit, but also ties to her Chinese heritage, as seen in her reference to the horse in Chinese astrology. Like Angelica's references to her heritage in "No Longer Invisible" (Chapter 7), Jean's mention of her zodiac sign is a creative and subtle way to introduce her culture to readers without her ethnicity becoming the core focus of the paper. Jean alludes to her heritage again at the end of the second paragraph, when she decides to "let go of [her] cautious Chinese approach to life." Some readers might take offense to this cultural stereotype; when writing about culture, it is important to be mindful of distinguishing between personal beliefs and stereotypes.

Jean's second paragraph gives us an excellent sense of her internal debates over whether or not she should take a risk and play in the pit as she swings between fear and confidence. Many successful essays not only relate events but also one's feelings and thoughts regarding the activity. Jean notes that she was "terrified" before the musical but shows her open-minded spirit when she "willingly embraced" the new art form. She refers back to the mentions of horse and freedom when she writes, "I was a horse freely cantering around an open meadow." The specific examples that follow demonstrate the diversity of new activities to which Jean is introduced and the eagerness with which she embraces each one. Jean does a wonderful job of explaining the horse-in-meadow simile with concrete, real-life examples such as these: showing her parents dance steps, drawing costume designs, and experimenting with new hairstyles.

In her concluding paragraph, Jean ties together the many examples she used in her essay to show us how her "comfort zone is expanding." She illustrates some of the contours of this comfort zone, which she calls the "grand scope" of her interests: "from singing and dancing to throwing a sales pitch in front of judges; from learning how to execute precision front-flips to building my favorite piano repertoire; from designing a webpage to arranging chamber music, or developing optics technologies." Illustrations like these can sometimes feel like long lists. Jean might have chosen to list fewer activities so that what she did choose to include could stand out more. The first line, which contrasts singing and dancing with throwing a sales pitch, is most directly relevant to the essay since singing and dancing were new experiences from the musical and throwing a sales pitch may have been part of the leadership conference in New York City that she mentioned briefly. In general, it is most compelling to use examples that are directly relevant to the essay to maintain a sense of focus. Bringing in too many outside references—for instance, Jean's comment on "developing optics technologies"—can seem incongruous and confuse readers. Overall, however, Jean's essay does a nice job of showing the breadth of her interests as well as the depth of energy she is willing to pour into creative pursuits such as the "Anything Goes" musical.

"Strength from Family Struggles"

Anonymous
University of Chicago

EVERY FAMILY HAS THEIR STORY, ALL with aspects that brings them together or drive them apart. I come from a Mexican family, where family is the only thing we know. We share each other's pain and misery and we rejoice for our miracles. We learn and grow through each other.

Even through the darkest days we survive as one. I witnessed those dark days, but I also saw the bright and through it all I evolved into who I am today.

I encountered one of my biggest obstructions when I was a child. I was born into a family that had immigrated to America from Mexico. Although my parents had been in the country for quite some time, they never adapted to the American lifestyle. All I knew was Spanish and my first year of school would soon come. I would sit at the end of my driveway and listen to the variety of sounds that slowly crept into my ear, triggered a reaction and sent confusion running through my mind. Day after day, I would sit there trying to decode this puzzle word by word and the day came when I'd be shipped off to school where I was expected to know English. Kindergarten was one of the hardest years in my life. I struggled tremendously. I was the last one to know my address, I was the last one to know my phone number, and I was the one who almost failed his first year of school. If it wasn't for my father not allowing the school to hold me back, I could have become a completely different person. I struggled throughout my years in elementary school. I went to resource and received help with my schoolwork until fourth grade. I was given a big push forward and since then I have come to realize that I may not be the only one in need. Others will need help and I will be there with a helping hand.

Through the years, my family has undergone a variety of obstacles. I saw my brother completely stumble and fall when he impregnated his girlfriend at the age of sixteen. At the blink of an eye he became a father to be and a husband. Everything came to a halt and he needed to support another person. He worked during the night and finished high school during the day. He struggled even while living at home. As if one example in my house wasn't enough, my sister was expecting a child during her senior year. I remember the day when she told my parents, I was in the room next door crying in pain because she fell into the same trap my brother did. That was the end for her. She graduated from high school and began to work. Now she has two daughters and is trying to make a living. It is hard to see the people you love make mistakes. It is so hard, that it brings tears to my eyes, to know that you wish you could say everything will be ok. They are stuck in a rut and I am putting my best foot forward to give myself the future they don't have.

When my mother was a child she had suffered a great amount. She had become deaf in her teenage years. She lost complete ability to hear in her right ear and partially in the left and to add to all the confusion she was bound by a language. She was living in America with 4 of 5 senses and a tongue that many could not speak. Many would see this as a huge dent in her life, but she managed to start a family. I could not be any more proud of her and thankful for what she has given me. Her "disability" placed a tremendous amount of pressure on my shoulders. She was not able to go to the deli or to place phone calls when she needed to. All of a sudden, all of this had become my responsibility. My father was too busy breaking his back in order to support our family. My mother's personal translator, doesn't sound too shabby? Standing in the middle of the store, making hand jesters, mouthing out words, or even yelling, does attract attention. In those moments I would feel a surge of heat rush from head to toe, goose bumps in every possible crevice of my body, and to top it all off I'd be seven shades darker than a ripe tomato. Shame and embarrassment, how could I feel this way? All this had become routine and the pain and embarrassment finally started to subside, a whole new feeling started to emerge, pride. My mother made me strong. She allowed me to become the man I am today. And after all the pain there are still countless nights that I lie in bed, crying due to the burden that was placed on her and the tremendous lesson I learned. Every sound, every beat, every photon, every little everything has been absorbed into me one way or another, yet these experiences, although insignificant to others, mean to world to me. All these events run through my veins and pump through my heart. I am the passion that is rarely seen. I am the walking story of struggle.

ANALYSIS

This student's essay conveys his devotion to his family as well as his independence from it. He shares honestly about the story of his parents and siblings so that as readers we can catch a glimpse of the "pain and misery" and the "miracles" that he has experienced. This student recounts many adversities, beginning with his memories of being a kindergartener who did not know English. He notes, "I struggled throughout my years in elementary school. I went to resource and received help with my schoolwork until fourth grade." Here, the essay would be clearer had he described what "resource" was and related specific ways in which it gave him that "big push forward." It is important to remember to describe in greater detail those events that represent pivotal life experiences. For him, the support and direction that he received seemed to have inspired him to understand that others would also need help, something that he felt he could provide.

At the end of this first long paragraph, we are curious to learn about how this student was able to manifest this desire to help others. However, he returns to the story of his family and tells about the "mistakes" of his siblings. While the content of this paragraph is certainly compelling, the writer must consider both content *and structure* when designing the flow of an essay. Any content is enhanced by a supportive structure with a logical progression and clear organization. At the end of the second paragraph, he writes, "I am putting my best foot forward to give myself the future [my siblings] don't have." This sentence is enlightening and assists us in understanding the purpose of his prolonged descriptions about his family's suffering. Despite this difficult environment, he maintained his motivation and worked hard to complete his education, believing he must do so to avoid becoming "stuck in a rut."

In the final paragraph of this essay, this student writes about his mother's struggles as a deaf immigrant in America. Recounting his role as his "mother's personal translator," he describes his feelings and thoughts, demonstrating a capacity for astutely recognizing his own emotions. He describes turning the shade of tomato with shame and embarrassment, followed by the emergence of pride. His descriptions about emotions are particularly powerful because he illustrates how they feel in the body. Strong emotions typically elicit a profound bodily reaction, and he captures this beautifully in the scenes at the store where he translated for his mother. The focus on the body makes his final statement, "I am the walking story of struggle," all the more apropos because we see how "all these events run through [his] veins and pump through [his] heart." This student's writing shows us that essay reviewers do not require a perfect grasp of English—English is obviously his second language. What makes this student's essay compelling is his ability to illustrate both vulnerability and strength in confronting the many challenges he and his family have faced as Mexican immigrants.

HUMOR

"Exit Door"

Fareez Giga
Stanford University

I CONSIDER MYSELF TO BE MATURE and focused in my life; I have goals that I strive for and a strong commitment to my education. However, I do have my more humorous moments, just as everyone else. For instance, a few summers ago, my family and I were in Las Vegas on vacation. The over-the-top looking-by-night, eyesore-by-day city was lighted everywhere, and masses of people were walking along the Las Vegas Strip. One night, we went out to dinner and were walking back to our hotel. When we got to the entrance of the hotel, which had automatic sliding doors, there was a huge line waiting to get in, yet there were many other doors to its side unoccupied. So, naturally, I said aloud, "Why don't we just go through those doors," as I pointed towards the unoccupied doors. My family just waited patiently, but I decided to go by myself, so I did, and I walked straight into the EXIT door. I am not sure who was more injured, myself, or my sister who collapsed onto the floor in convulsive laughter. I still have not heard the end of this story, but at least now I can laugh at myself. Many times people get discouraged in their hectic and stress-filled lives, but sometimes you just need a dim-witted accident to occur to put everything in perspective.

ANALYSIS

In this note to his future roommate, Fareez relates a humorous anecdote to reveal the lighthearted side to his personality. This essay prompt gives students the unique opportunity to demonstrate how they would relate to peers of their own age group, rather than an older group of admissions officers. Fareez introduces himself as "mature and focused" with "a strong commitment" to education, which at first glance appears to be a rather hackneyed and unmemorable set of statements. However, he quickly throws in an expected twist by alluding to a humorous moment, thereby piquing our curiosity as he sets up the scene in Las Vegas.

His anecdote not only shows us that Fareez "can laugh at [him]self," but also lets us see that he is close to his family, and especially his sister. Fareez's narrative is enjoyable to read because he includes details to make the story more vivid, like mentioning his feelings towards Las Vegas and describing his sister's "convulsive" collapse from laughter. Though hardly earth shattering, the "blooper" that Fareez shares is nonetheless memorable—he walks headlong into an EXIT door in front of a large crowd of people—and in particular his reaction is noteworthy.

At the end of this short essay, Fareez ties the anecdote back to college life when he alludes to "hectic and stress-filled" times. Fareez's ability to put things in perspective suggests that he will be able to cope with the challenges of college life, and will bring joy and humor to whoever is lucky enough to be his roommate. This essay strikes a nice balance between a casual tone and a deeper analysis. Thus, the topic and style of the essay are reflective of the content, which show us both the silly and serious sides to Fareez's personality. A short essay such as this one is a wonderful opportunity to share a quirky story that makes you stand out in the admissions officer's huge stack of essays.

"Crime Scene Report"

Lauren Sanders
Duke University

CRIME SCENE REPORT
Crime: Missing Person
Location: Duke University, 2138 Campus Drive, Box 90586, Durham, North Carolina 27708-0586
Time: October 2, 2008, 11:00 A.M.
Investigated by: Admissions Officers of Duke University

CASE DESCRIPTION:

On the morning of October 2, 2008, at precisely 7:00 A.M., a Miss Lauren Sanders began to worry. Her future-self entered the gates of a prestigious university in the fall of 2009 and had not returned home. Miss Sanders filed a missing person's report, hoping someone could help her to locate her future-self in a world of possibilities.

The case began with a grueling interrogation of Miss Lauren Sanders, the person who knew most about her future-self. However, the questioning session yielded little information. Miss Sanders could not fully describe herself in the future. Pressured, she stated that "she has the ambition to fulfill all of her goals, is both stubborn and industrious, and wants to experience University life." Miss Sanders lacked a photograph of her future-self, but remarked that "she has brown hair, likes to describe herself as vertically-challenged, and is usually smiling."

NOTE: While unable to describe her future-self, Miss Sanders believed that examination of past experiences could possibly assist the admissions officers in the case. According to Miss Sanders, her future-self has "volunteered in her community and traveled on a global scale."

Physical evidence collected during a thorough search of Miss Sander's bedroom included a Dell laptop, a collection of Jane Austin novels, worn textbooks, and an I-pod. Fingerprinting analysis and DNA processing determined that these items belong to both Miss Sanders and her future-self, and that they use these items frequently. Despite biological traces of the future-self found within the home, laboratory analysis concluded that Miss Sanders' future-self does not reside within her hometown.

With information gathered from the physical search of Miss Sanders' home and Miss Sanders' interrogation, a database search was conducted to determine possible universities in which Miss Sanders' future-self resided. Within minutes, Duke University appeared as a match.

With this lead, authorities conducted numerous searches at Duke University in Durham, North Carolina, probing the dorms, library, and classrooms. All searches yielded nothing, yet the possibility of finding Miss Sanders' future-self remains strong. Professors and students alike, when questioned about Miss Sanders' future-self, strongly believe that many individuals like her come to the University to find their potential paths.

Further examination will be needed to complete this investigation, including a thorough inspection of Miss Sanders' resume and letters of recommendation. Hopefully, the leads that we have will direct us to the whereabouts of her future-self.

NOTE: According to Miss Sanders, the future-self plans to travel on a foreign-exchange student program and hopes to conduct research in one of the many labs available to undergraduates. At present, these areas have not been searched by professionals.

On the morning of October 2, 2009, at precisely 7:04 A.M., the admissions officers found Miss Lauren Sanders' future-self at Duke University. She had hidden in the incoming student body.

ANALYSIS

Lauren's "Crime Scene Report" proves that there is no "standard" format for a college admissions essay. This essay's creative structure completely breaks the mold. Not only is it written in letter format, it also includes quirky NOTES in the body of the letter. While Lauren takes a big risk in deviating from the standard introduction-body paragraphs-conclusion structure, her essay is undeniably memorable. Lauren successfully pulls off her caper—both in the fictional mystery story she tells, and in her playful writing style.

The creativity of the "Crime Scene Report" probably attests to Lauren's personality. We see that she is not afraid to take bold risks in her writing and stand out in a crowd. This unabashed attitude can be seen in her audacious and hilarious ending: "She had hidden in the incoming student body." This is a completely unexpected yet confident way to assert her strong belief that she deserves to be admitted to Duke.

The clever way that Lauren infuses details about her interests throughout her writing helps add more "serious" elements to the mischievous format of her essay. For example, under the guise of an "interrogation," we learn that she is ambitious, "stubborn and industrious" and curious about university life. Later on, we find more specific data that is relevant to Lauren—that she hopes to study abroad and conduct research in a lab. Perhaps Lauren could narrow the scope of this research by describing the lab she sees in her future, as this lab might be in biology, psychology, robotics, and endless other possibilities. In addition to sharing her goals, Lauren reveals past experiences that have shaped her life, specifically volunteerism and international travel. This note piques our curiosity about these experiences; ideally, Lauren would discuss these in more detail in another essay. Lauren creatively uses this format to present not just her future goals and past experiences, but also her appearance (we envision a "vertically-challenged" smiling brunette) and some of the things around her that hint at her interests (her laptop, Jane Austen novels, textbooks, and I-Pod).

All these details present Lauren from a number of perspectives. Overall, the specifics provide content to what would otherwise be a fun and humorous, but perhaps not terribly substantial, piece of writing. Lauren may have considered combining the paragraphs that begin "With this lead . . . " and "Further examination . . . " Though these two paragraphs help move along the "plot" of the crime scene, they don't give us substantially more information about Lauren herself. Since space is so precious in college essays, it is important to edit carefully. Eliminating redundancy creates more space to add enriching and edifying details that will more fully present the complex person that you are.

12

AN INFLUENTIAL PERSON

"John Nash"

Jonathan Cross
Duke University

AFTER SPENDING A WEEK WITH JOHN Nash, I may have stumbled upon a central purpose of my life. Well, not Nobel Laureate John Nash himself, but whenever I describe Fred, their characteristics seem quite parallel. Fred is unique, possessing an indomitable spirit to fulfill his dreams without fear of failure. Not only is he the most brilliant young man I have ever met, he exhibits a genuinely compassionate heart. Sadly, many people may never recognize Fred as the beautiful individual that he is, or what he has to offer. While our society may call him "challenged," I have come to recognize him as an unexpected role model. For Fred, you see, is autistic. He does not interact well with people, and is often unable to express his thoughts clearly or articulately. He doesn't understand why people laugh at him. Yet even so, Fred is blessed with an acute sense of purpose and caring that is unmatched by most—including perhaps even the most altruistic among us.

Several years ago I traveled with a small group of Fairfax County high school students to Portland, Oregon to compete as a Finalist in the Intel International Science and Engineering Fair. I was excited at what was certain to be an experience of a lifetime—having no clue that the most valuable lesson would come not from the Science Fair itself, but from Fred. Because of my prior experiences in working with special needs children, the school administrators asked me to room with Fred during the trip. I distinctly recall my initial anxiety and reluctance about the prospect of taking care of another individual during the stressful, high-pressure atmosphere of the competition. In retrospect, though, this was the beginning of an incredible journey for both of us—but especially for me.

Fred's passion—actually more of an obsession—is theoretical mathematics. He eats, breathes, talks, and probably sleeps mathematics, to the point where he annoys others by his constant chatter about it. His idea of fun is solving differential equations on a napkin in a fancy restaurant, oblivious to others wanting to socialize or relax. That Fred is brilliant is unquestioned, a fact that was clearly evidenced in his science project where he solved a math problem previously believed by experts to be insolvable. Yet in his own mind Fred firmly believed his entire raison d'etre in life was the pursuit of math—and that he was destined to use his incredible mathematical ability to help make the world better.

However, Fred's disabilities were only a fraction of the challenges that faced him. Growing up in a dysfunctional home, he suffered from a lack of love and patient understanding. Still, Fred's life revolved around his relationships and mathematics. Although he has few close friends, people are indescribably important to him, and he always treated them with sensitivity and compassion. Unfortunately, some people—including but not limited to his peers (who can sometimes be quite cruel)—are unable to set aside their prejudices long enough to see his uniqueness as the incredible gift that it is. His enthusiasm and his indomitable spirit in the face of adversity taught me valuable lessons—lessons I will carry with me for the rest of my life. He taught me to live for what you truly cherish, to be passionate about your dreams, and to always smile in both the service of others and adversity. He has shown me the truest meaning of love for others, and the ability to understand and always live for what is important. A trip that started with me "taking care of him" turned into a trip of substantial personal discovery.

Children with special needs have powerful talents, and if we could only open our hearts to hear their voices, we would learn what it means to live without conventional boundaries. I have lived a week with a genius, not only of the mind, but more importantly, of the heart—and my life has been permanently changed because of Fred.

ANALYSIS

Jonathan begins his essay with a reference to a famous figure, John Nash, but wisely doesn't assume we know who he is and mentions that he is a Nobel laureate. Then, the essay hooks in the reader by throwing in a twist: this essay is not about John Nash at all, but about someone named Fred. It's obvious that Jonathan holds Fred in high esteem, but it is initially unclear just who Fred is. However, as we read about Fred, we not only meet someone who has influenced Jonathan, but we are also introduced to Jonathan's admirable ability to be open-minded towards an individual even when others might be dismissive. As Jonathan notes, "While our society may call him 'challenged,' I have come to recognize him as an unexpected role model." This is certainly not the typical role model story, where one might name a family member or famous person. The parallel between Fred and John Nash underscores Jonathan's respect for Fred, and this unusual and unexpected comparison show us how Jonathan stands out from the rest of society.

Note that Jonathan is careful not to get on a "high horse," making much over himself. Instead, he writes, "Fred is blessed with an acute sense of purpose and caring that is unmatched by most—including perhaps even the most altruistic among us." The last part of this statement adds a sense of humility so that Jonathan does not seem to be judgmental toward us for not accepting people with autism or other disabilities in the way that he is able to do. Generally, taking a moralizing or condescending tone is alienating for readers, who want to be *invited* into your story, not estranged from it. Indeed, Jonathan further avoids a high-minded tone by describing his "initial anxiety and reluctance" at rooming with Fred, even in spite of his previous experience in working with special needs children. Jonathan's honesty is impressive: many people might not admit to such seemingly taboo or even discriminatory thoughts of not wanting to spend time with special needs children, even if these thoughts are true. However, Jonathan's honesty helps us understand why he sums up his time in Portland as "an incredible journey . . . especially for me."

Jonathan takes a risk in devoting the third paragraph and much of the fourth paragraph of his essay to describing Fred's story. However, because we know that Fred does not interact easily with others, we can surmise that Fred felt comfortable enough with Jonathan to share so much of his life with him. We can also see that Jonathan is an astute observer and compassionate listener. Though Jonathan may have chosen to present fewer details about Fred, he does a good job of bringing it back to himself when he writes, "[Fred's] enthusiasm and indomitable spirit in the face of adversity taught me valuable lessons—lessons I will carry with me for the rest of my life . . . A trip that started with me 'taking care of him' turned into a trip of substantial personal discovery.'" In essays about personal role models, it can be tempting to write about the role model and lose sight of oneself. For a college admissions essay, however, it is important to remember that admissions officers ultimately want to learn more about you. If you are writing about someone else, it is important to make explicit how this person has influenced *you*, something that Jonathan does well in the last sentences of his fourth paragraph.

The strength of Jonathan's essay lies in its many unexpected elements. Though attending the Intel International Science and Engineering Fair is clearly a huge honor, the essay tells us about a person. And this individual is hardly a famous person, but he is spoken about with the highest reverence and respect. Thus, Jonathan demonstrates the strength of his character; he is likely to be an asset to the student body of any college because of his exemplary acceptance of people from all backgrounds.

"Then and Now: How the Perseverance of a Working, Single Mother Molded the Persona of her Chinese-American Daughter"

Lisa Kapp
University of Pennsylvania

I GREW UP IN A FOUR-ROOM apartment in the middle of Beijing at the turn of the twentieth century. Common household features such as the existence of stairs within a house were thought of as decadent luxuries representative of the incredibly wealthy. My life was simple. At five years old, it was differentiated by two things, the times I was with my mother and the times I was not.

My single mother was a chemist and professor at the University of Beijing. Even at a young age, she distinguished herself from her peers with her remarkable ambition and intense passion for learning. From growing up in the frigid winds of Northern Mongolia, to becoming one of three students to earn a full scholarship to China's most competitive university, to working as a government-sponsored chemist in Goslar, Germany, my mother accomplished more before I was born than most people achieved in a lifetime.

Unfortunately, I would not learn of the fabulous successes and arduous trials of my mother until much, much later. All I could understand or not understand at five years old was why my mother was rarely home, why I did not see her for three months during the summer when I lived with my grandparents, and why I was forced to go to a daycare owned by a tyrannical monster who would tell ghost stories to make me cry. Even now, much of my knowledge about my mother's early life is something I am still piecing together. As was the case then, my full understanding of her brilliant yet ill-tempered persona is continually hindered by the simple troubles of life. Although now, they are the issues of an eighteen-year old teenager rather than those of a five-year old child.

I remember nights we would spend together when she was busy with her research and classes; I would sit in a desk next to her, drawing pictures and imagine that I was her personal assistant. I also remember times when I had to stay home alone because she had a lecture to give or errands to run; I would lean against the window sill staring down into the bleak, concrete streets waiting and watching for the return of a petite form in a bright red jacket. Yet despite the forlorn days and the lonely nights, I feel neither regret nor resentment towards those early years or my mother. On the contrary, I am incredibly proud and grateful for all the difficulties she endured in order to raise me properly. Had it not been for my childhood experiences, I would not have matured at such an early age or developed such a strong sense of independence.

We moved to America in the spring of 1997. The transition of cultures was daunting yet it failed to dishearten my mother. Like every other experience in her life, she treated the move as an opportunity. However, even my mother was not immune to the overwhelming cultural shock, and despite her perseverance and accomplishments, she continually struggled with the language barrier and the difference in societal values.

While my mother was forced to labor against such changes, my young age enabled me to adapt quickly to the new environment. Unfortunately, my "Americanization" has caused a great deal of mystification and incomprehension in my mother. Not only do our manners of speaking differ, but we no longer view traditional beliefs the same way. Her lack of encouragement for my participation in athletics and her excessive emphasis on my grades have been both frustrating and upsetting. From my gregarious nature and social outings to my obdurate refusals to comply with her every long-established demand, she has been forced to accept the evolution of her daughter from that of Chinese doll to American teenager.

Nevertheless, despite our various differences and my acute assimilation into another culture, I have never lost sight of what mattered most to me, nor forgotten the roots of my heritage and rigorous upbringing. My mother's persistence and endurance are qualities which I have proudly assumed and carried with me in every activity of my life. From facing the ignorant racisms of elementary classmates to the malicious jealousies of middle school peers, I have never doubted or second guessed the work ethic and moral code that she instilled in me. Her resourcefulness has also been highly influential and taught me of the importance of seeking opportunities. Whether it was working along side *Philadelphia Inquirer* journalists or researching marketing strategies for a startup company, I have learned and developed with each success and letdown encountered throughout my middle and high school years.

The difficulties of my mother and the difficulties that I faced in two countries on two continents continue to define and shape my personality and character. As mother and daughter continue along the journey of life, I hope that she can come to accept and embrace the daughter whom she has so diligently raised while I hope to slowly unravel the full mystery that is my mother and, one day, finally comprehend and appreciate the entirety of her effect on my life.

ANALYSIS

With an impressive vocabulary and keen sense of reflection, Lisa has written an essay that conveys the story of her unique upbringing across two very different cultures. This essay weaves together Lisa's history and personality with that of her mother. Like Timothy's essay "Self Mind," (Chapter 7), Lisa balances information about herself with that of descriptions about her mother. Lisa's essay is particularly memorable because she traces the evolution of her thoughts and feelings toward her mother as she grows up. Rather than being a typical "role model" story, Lisa explains the difficulties and challenges she has faced in America with her "brilliant yet ill-tempered" mother. Writing about both strengths and weaknesses—whether about yourself or other people—helps to humanize people in essays. This also contributes to a tone of honesty and authenticity. However, overemphasizing weaknesses or negative emotions *isn't* desirable since these essays are first and foremost ways to present yourself and argue why you should be accepted to a college. Essays are not forums for whining or complaining.

Lisa exemplifies this non-complaining attitude in the first half of her essay. One interpretation of her personal history is that she was left home alone and neglected. However, Lisa asserts, ". . . despite the forlorn days and the lonely nights, I feel neither regret nor resentment towards those early years or my mother." The concrete, evocative images that Lisa shares with us—pretending she is her mom's personal assistant, searching the "bleak, concrete streets" for a glimpse of "a petite form in a bright red jacket"—help explain what "forlorn days" and "lonely nights" looked like for Lisa. These images convey a powerful mood without the distraction of harsh judgments.

In the second half of her essay, Lisa explains the tensions brought about by her immigration and "Americanization" to the U.S. Lisa is frank in her feelings towards her mother, noting, "Her lack of encouragement for my participation in athletics and her excessive emphasis on my grades have been both frustrating and upsetting." However, rather than dwelling on the negative aspects of such emotional issues, Lisa presents the bigger lessons that these feelings represent: her independence as well as her respect and appreciation for her "heritage and rigorous upbringing." Lisa's essay nicely weaves together her past experiences in Beijing, present activities in America, and future hopes of unraveling the mysteries presented by the tensions between American and Chinese culture.

13

ISSUES

"Sustainable Development in South Africa"

Steve Schwartz
Columbia University

AS I SAT AT A TABLE in the corner of a cafe, hunched over a press release I was writing, I asked myself, "Why is a youth advocate from Long Island, halfway around the world in South Africa this summer, debating issues of sustainable development at a United Nations conference?" I needed to meet a deadline for the Youth Caucus at the World Summit on Sustainable Development (WSSD) after an exhausting but exhilarating day of lobbying. My goal was to help persuade world leaders at the largest United Nations conference in history that pursuing sustainable development is essential for the future of our planet. Because I had attended a previous UN conference about children's rights, I understood the importance of sustainable development in this context. Then, I was chosen to represent SustainUS, a national network of American youth, at the WSSD. I raised all of the money needed for my trip. I was thrilled to witness the human spirit in its purest sense, taking collective action to care for the less fortunate around the globe.

It was one thing to debate language in the conference document about goals set to provide people in developing nations with access to water. It was quite another to visit Soweto, only a few kilometers away from the conference, and to meet poor Africans living in shanties with limited access to water. This observation embedded in my mind the seriousness of my work in a way that no statistic could describe. The challenge on paper seemed quite different from the harshness of Soweto and Alexandria and the long-suffering faces and pleading eyes of the beggars there. I reminded myself that I needed to work around the clock while I was in South Africa to help these impoverished people.

After arriving in Johannesburg this past August, I traveled to the International Youth Summit. I drafted the youth declaration which was used for lobbying, and I helped to write a statement from the youth delegates for government representatives to read and consider while negotiating. While at the WSSD, aside from writing daily press releases that became Associated Press and Reuters articles, I drafted speeches which were presented to the delegates, including over one hundred heads of state. I experienced an adrenaline rush when I fielded questions from reporters during a press conference. These challenging situations were new learning opportunities for me and provided me with knowledge much different from what one learns in high school. I want to learn more about the histories of international financial institutions and the ways they interact with national governments.

As a result of my attending the World Summit, I have gained a new perspective on global politics and its effects on people's lives. The thought that people from around the world can join together to solve a global issue never fails to impress and inspire me.

My participation in the WSSD has taught me more about the convergence of politics, international relations and the environment than I have learned in any other activity or in the classroom. Working with others to reveal the crucial need for sustainable development is essential to our world's successful future. All of my experiences have helped me to understand how international meetings operate and to accept the responsibility that comes with the privilege to attend and contribute to the solution.

ANALYSIS

Steve's essay gives us insight into his experiences as a youth advocate in South Africa and youth representative for the WSSD. This unique opportunity is obviously a great honor. Steve does a good job presenting specific examples of his summer experiences and relating the larger lessons he learned from them.

In his introduction, Steve might have helped contextualize the situation by explaining what it means to be a "youth delegate," how long the WSSD was going to last, why he needed to write a press release, and what kind of lobbying he was doing. While impressive, the first paragraph in this essay is almost overwhelming because it contains so much information with limited explanation. Additionally, the reference to the SustainUS conference is confusing. It is unclear whether the next two sentences about fundraising for the trip and witnessing "the human spirit in its purest sense" refer to the SustainUS conference or the South Africa conference. Avoid the temptation to inundate readers with information and make sure that what you do write is clear and concise. Think of your college application as a package where you can include information about yourself through many different avenues—the essays are just one channel for introducing yourself to the admissions officers.

The second paragraph of the essay is strong because it focuses specifically on Steve's experiences in Soweto. The contrast between the conference and the shantytowns is striking. Steve might have elaborated more on his experiences of meeting "poor Africans living in shanties with limited access to water" to further demonstrate why "this observation embedded in [his] mind the seriousness of [his] work in a way that no statistic could describe." Steve demonstrates his commitment to helping others in his assertion, "I needed to work around the clock while I was in South Africa to help these impoverished people." His essay would be even stronger if he could more explicitly relate this lesson to what he learned from the International Youth Summit. Clarifying the distinctions between the Youth Caucus at the WSSD, the International Youth Summit, and the World Summit would help readers be on the same page as Steve. The ease with which Steve uses these terms clearly demonstrates his familiarity with government and politics. However, it is important to remember that college admissions essays are typically written for the general reader, rather than a specialist reader. Exceptions to this include essays that ask about specific career paths.

The conclusion of the essay cleanly ties together Steve's diverse experiences and looks towards the future, where one suspects that Steve will consider working towards sustainable development, both in and out of the classroom. Had Steve applied to a school with a strong international development or political science program, he might have also referenced these specific university assets to tailor his essay for that specific university.

"A Young Voice for Seniors"

Ariela Koehler
MIT

NOVEMBER 23, TWO YEARS AGO: THANKSGIVING. My mom and I celebrated the holiday as we had done for the last three years—by delivering turkey dinners to homebound senior citizens. After carrying the food to their kitchens, our brief visits with them were filled with laughter, hugs, and the sharing of family photo albums. In the midst of all the warmth and vitality, though, I couldn't help noticing the signs of loneliness and isolation: the windows with dust suggesting they hadn't been open in ages, the faded Christmas cards from 1995, and the tables with a single place setting. It was during these visits that I committed to find a way to better connect with the seniors in my community.

I discussed my desire with the mayor of Fremont in December two years ago. He agreed that a younger voice could prove to be beneficial and mentioned the Senior Citizen Commission for the City of Fremont (an advisory board to City Council that worked to directly address the needs of local seniors). I formally applied to the Commission and was unanimously appointed by City Council in February last year, becoming the youngest Commissioner in Fremont's history.

Although I was initially met with skepticism from my fellow Senior Citizen Commissioners, I was committed to sharing my vision of the benefits of intergenerational interactions. For the next two months, my after-school hours were devoted to calling nursing homes, negotiating with movie theater managers, and recruiting teen volunteers. The resulting event was the Senior Movie Outing, which paired teenagers with wheelchair-bound seniors for a fun afternoon at the movies.

As a result of my hard work on the successful outing and the rave reviews from all who participated, my fellow Commissioners became more respectful of my contributions and open to my input. During the annual grant-reviewing period (when the Commission decides which non-profit organizations will receive City funding), I advocated to fund Lavender Seniors, an organization which supports gay and lesbian seniors. While it had not previously been funded by the City, I strongly believed it fell within the Commission's charter of "serving the needs of all seniors." After sharing my rationale for proposing to fund Lavender Seniors, I was proud that the Commissioners kept an open mind and the majority voted to grant the organization funding.

In the two years since my appointment, I have cherished the unique opportunities I have had to learn from people with different perspectives and backgrounds. My time on the Commission has taught me to be more confident when expressing my ideas, and to be more open to hearing others' thoughts. I am proud to be a trusted voice for seniors in my community.

ANALYSIS

Ariela takes advantage of this optional essay to illustrate a unique perspective on her life. While her other two essays focused on her passion for science, this essay helps create a "thorough impression" of other aspects of Ariela's life, namely her commitment to public service and experiences in local government leadership. This essay is reminiscent of Anastasia's "Cuddle Buddies" (Chapter 8) in presenting an example of going above and beyond an assigned service task. In Ariela's case, she is delivering turkey dinners to homebound senior citizens. Her compassion shines through when she notes, ". . . our brief visits with them were filled with laughter, hugs, and the sharing of family photo albums." However, it is Ariela's keen sense of observation that helps her to notice "signs of loneliness and isolation": dusty windows, faded Christmas cards, single place settings. These evocative details show that she recognizes a community need—"a way to better connect with the seniors." The contrast to the joy and laughter and the indications of loneliness make this first paragraph emotionally compelling and clearly demonstrate the issue that Ariela hopes to address.

What makes Ariela's story unique is that she is not content to rest with this observation. Instead, she takes her concern to someone who can help facilitate the change she envisions. By providing the dates in her essay, Ariela shows us the compressed time frame in which all of the actions and changes she created took place. This highlights her ability to act quickly and suggests that she will be a mover and a shaker in her college setting.

Ariela's essay also stands out because she describes the challenges she encounters in the process of creating change. First, she faces skepticism from fellow Senior Citizen Commissioners. However, she overcomes this resistance by staying committed to a shared "vision of the benefits of intergenerational interactions." Ariela's ability to work on a team is all the more remarkable because the team isn't comprised of her peers at school. Thus, her position on the Senior Citizen Commission shows us that she is diplomatic in her ability to work with others. Through her hard work, the Senior Movie Outing was created, a success that helped garner her more respect from her fellow commissioners.

Not only did Ariela help create more opportunities for intergenerational interaction, but her efforts also facilitated progressive social change by convincing the commissioners to fund Lavender Seniors. As the end of Ariela's essay makes clear, her two-year personal involvement on the commission is more than just an impressive title; it is a role that has helped her learn confidence and hone listening skills in representing her community.

14

LEADERSHIP

"Birthing a Business"

Jason Y. Shah
Harvard University

AT MY AGE, FEW PEOPLE CAN genuinely claim that they have had a life-changing experience. After attending Leadership in the Business World (LBW) at the Wharton School last summer, I became one of those fortunate people to have experienced a life-changing academic program. Four weeks of meeting business executives, working with teammates through the night perfecting our professional business plan, experiencing the independence and responsibility that will come with college . . . none of this was advertised in the brochure for LBW, but all of this is what made it uniquely meaningful to me.

The business leadership program centered on one culminating activity: the prestigious LBW Business Plan Competition. As we prepared for this, we heard from Wharton faculty members and many corporate heavyweights including Brian Roberts, CEO of Comcast Corporation. Meeting educators, executives and entrepreneurs broadened my knowledge of business, created a strategic network of connections and proved profoundly inspiring; nothing motivates me more than seeing hard work and sharp thinking reach fruition. I vividly remember when a managing director of a venture capital firm singled me out for a networking demonstration. Expecting me merely to pretend to hand him a fake business card, he was dumbfounded by impressed when he glanced back as he accepted an actual business card from my tutoring business. As my business card now rested in Mr. Kimmel's Rolodex next to elegant cards from established businesspeople, a lesson was ingrained in my mind about acting uniquely in order to distinguish myself in a field of equally qualified and eager peers.

Despite the inherently competitive nature of LBW, I established enduring friendships with students from far-reaching places, such as Shanghai and Accra. We shared stories over meals in Houston Hall about life at home and engaged in heated discussions about business ethics. Regardless of the origin of our passports, we became a family while learning about each other's cultures and future business aspirations. The lessons of compassion and hard work from the business plan competition also heightened my experience. Once when a fellow marketing officer was struggling with determining channels of distribution for our product, I disregarded trying to seem individually superior, and we cooperatively tackled the problem. Putting the team before the individual was a concept that materialized itself during my experience. The bonds between all of the students and advisors spurred my entrepreneurial spirit as I experienced how friendship supports business.

I knew this experience had changed me forever when I triumphantly concluded our team's business presentation, confidently promoting our product and connecting with a crowd of peers and venture capitalists. During the evening following the presentations, my fellow teammates and I beamed with boundless relief and pride when the VCs announced our team, EnTECH LLC, as the first place winners of the competition. Exploring and honing my business and entrepreneurial skills was intimidating initially, yet with creativity, hard work and an unparalleled group dynamic of cooperation, this experience cemented my passion for business and opened grand doors of opportunity.

ANALYSIS

This essay of Jason's helps us appreciate the "entrepreneurial and philanthropic endeavors" that Jason refers to at the end of his Common Application personal essay "Hurricane Transformations," (Chapter 15). This type of cross-referencing or linking can be an excellent strategy for presenting yourself as well rounded without trying to cram too much information into a single essay. After reading "Hurricane Transformations," college admissions officers are likely to be curious about what Jason's projects as a community leader are; and this essay is the perfect answer to that question.

While the first sentence of this essay, "At my age, few people can genuinely claim that they have had a life-changing experience" may sound slightly patronizing and condescending, it does succeed in piquing our curiosity as readers and hints at Jason's maturity and confidence. It is important to think about the tone that the overall essay communicates. Jason conveys a confident tone in his writing by telling us about the "uniquely meaningful" experience he had through the LBW program, one he clearly fashioned for himself. This contrasts to the more contemplative tone in "Hurricane Transformations." Varying the tone between essays is a method to show different sides of your personality.

Jason gave a brief description of the highlights of LBW's event-packed four weeks ("meeting business executives, working with teammates through the night perfecting our professional business plan, experiencing the independence and responsibility that will come with college") without reading like a brochure. Then he wisely chose to focus on the culminating activity. Indeed, Jason shares how he learned the lesson to act "uniquely in order to distinguish [him]self in a field of equally qualified and eager peers." This sentence shows us that Jason is willing to go above and beyond what is expected and to leave his comfort zone in the process, yet also demonstrates consideration and respect for his peers. The anecdote about meeting Mr. Kimmel is also an artful way to let us know that Jason has started a tutoring business for which he even has a business card, a testament to his thoughtfulness and professionalism.

This mix of pride and humility is particularly fitting in the teamwork that Jason describes: "we became a family," "we cooperatively tackled the problem." Jason is probably interested in studying business and entrepreneurship in college, and the story of EnTECH LLC's creation through dedicated hard work demonstrates his ability to be both a leader and a team member, highly valued traits when working on a business team. What is striking about Jason's essay is that it lets us in on the journey that created EnTECH; indeed, even if his team hadn't won first place in the competition, we would still be impressed. Jason's story could have looked like "1st place in LBW business competition" and "works well on a team" in a resume; but the tone of the essay helped the award/trait come alive and stick vividly in the reader's mind.

Jason Y. Shah is the founder of INeedAPencil.com, a free online SAT preparation program. The site has 60 lessons and two free practice tests.

"Beyond Dictionary Definitions of Leadership"

Victoria Tomaka
University of Chicago

"All I know about leadership I learned from . . ." What items could a person use to describe leadership qualities?

Inspired by the student council advisors at my high school.

STUDENT COUNCIL WAS A BIG PART of my life in high school. I have participated in it since my first year of high school. When I first joined, I was quiet, naïve, and unwilling to participate in many activities. I was scared to meet new people and afraid to apply myself. This all began to change. Half way through my first year in student council, one of the advisors can up to me and asked why I did not participate that much. I did not have an answer for her and did not know how to respond. After this, I began to think of an answer. I became frustrated and decided to change. I started to show up at events and had a great time. I realized I loved this and wanted to start leading these activities. In my sophomore, junior, and now my senior year of high school, I asserted myself and took on a strong leadership role in student council. I did not figure out the answer to why I was so reserved until this year with the help of this question.

When I looked up leadership in the dictionary, it said that it was the capacity to lead and the act or instance of leading. These are two very broad definitions of leadership. Many people have different notions of what this word actually means. When I was challenged to use different items to describe what leadership actually is, I thought this was going to be a hard and obnoxious task. What could I learn from comparing leadership to a stuffed animal or a rubber chicken? But when I sat down to come up with a couple of answers, I realized that leadership could be compared to almost anything a person wants.

All I know about leadership I learned from a calculator. A calculator can add everything together to come up with the best answer. It can delete what is unnecessary and only include what is important. It can solve any type of problem. These are all important equalities a leader has to have. A leader has to be able to add all of the ideas together to make the best possible plan. Leaders have to know how to decipher the good and the bad out of an idea. They have to be versatile and know how to deal with different types of issues.

All I know about leadership I learned from a ball. A ball is able to bounce back up after it is dropped. It is round and has no creases. A ball can be thrown back and forth to different people. All of these qualities are also leadership qualities. A leader has to be ready for every situation that is thrown at him or her. He or she has to be able to bounce back from any setbacks and never dwell on the past. Leaders have to exhibit many qualities and never be closed-minded about a situation. A leader must be able to delegate when he or she cannot get the work done. They have to trust everyone they lead to be able to "catch the ball" and keep a project rolling.

This activity made me realize that being a leader is so much more than just having authority and having the ability to take control of a situation. A leader has to be trusting of all the people he or she leads and, leaders must be able to combine ideas into one encompassing idea. They cannot sit in the background and watch events happen; they have to jump in and be involved. They should not delegate all their responsibilities away.

Leadership is more than what the dictionary says it is.

I learned through all of this that I have many of these qualities. I have the ability to solve problems, lead through adversity, and be versatile. From answering this question, I realized that I could lead effectively, even if my leadership style is different from other individuals. When I joined student council in my first year of high school, I did not have these qualities because I was never put into a situation where I had to lead. I was too reserved to try. When I tried, I learned that I could succeed in this. I did not realize until I answered this question about leadership. I was never able to see that being a leader is not just about taking control of a group and telling everyone what to do. When

I was a freshman, I thought leadership was this. I did not know that I did not have to be forceful and strict. I stereotyped a leader then. This is where I went wrong. A leader is about being yourself and never letting anyone change you. I thought I had to change to be a good leader. Only when I expanded my comfort zone did I realize this was not true. It only took three years and a silly question/game to figure this out.

ANALYSIS

Vicky's essay combines both playful metaphors and an honest appraisal of her experiences in Student Council to demonstrate the evolution of her thinking about leadership. Vicky begins by revealing some of her weaknesses in Student Council: "I was quiet, naïve, and unwilling to participate in many activities. I was scared to meet new people and afraid to apply myself." Vicky takes a similar tactic to Angelica in "No Longer Invisible" (Chapter 7) by presenting an image of herself before her transformative decision to take on "a strong leadership role in student council." This first paragraph could be strengthened by a more detailed description of what Student Council is and what students' roles are. It's best not to assume that admissions officers will know about the groups and activities you reference in your essay, so contextualizing clues are always helpful. Vicky could have explained how many people were members of student council.

The most memorable part of Vicky's essay is her act of looking up leadership in the dictionary and not feeling satisfied with the definition she found: "the capacity to lead and the act or instance of leading." This unclear definition, combined with a challenging question/game to compare leadership to things like stuffed animals and rubber chickens, compelled Vicky to discover that "leadership could be compared to almost anything a person wants." Another contextualizing clue that could provide more clarity for this essay is to know the origin of this game. Who assigned Vicky this "hard and obnoxious task"? One of the key strengths in Vicky's essay is her honesty about her thoughts and emotions. You may be tempted to romanticize the truth in an admissions essay, but writing honestly is not only ethical, it also allows your authentic voice to shine through.

The third and four paragraphs provide creative comparisons between leadership and two unexpected objects: a calculator and a ball. Vicky writes clearly how attributes of calculators and balls are also qualities of effective leaders. Vicky does a good job of summarizing the lessons she learned from this comparative exercise: "This activity made me realize that being a leader is so much more than just having authority and having the ability to take control of a situation . . . Leadership is more than what the dictionary says it is." In the final paragraph, Vicky relates the conversation about leadership qualities in general to her own leadership duties. This is an effective way to demonstrate her ability to apply abstract principles directly to her life and it makes the essay feel relevant. It is important to keep in mind that these essays are ultimately personal statements, not philosophical treatises. It is always prudent to reveal enough about yourself that your essay reader will know more about you—not just a philosophy or an idea—after reading your essay. In Vicky's case, we understand more about her thoughts on leadership as well as her own responsible, but not overly strict, leadership style.

15

PERSONAL GROWTH

"Beauty"

Anonymous
Yale University

PEOPLE SAY THAT INNER BEAUTY MATTERS more than outer beauty. But when I looked into the mirror and saw my face covered with unsightly blemishes, it was hard to tell myself that and believe it. By the time I entered high school, my acne had gotten worse, and my self-esteem was at an all-time low. So in the summer of ninth grade, I embarked on an unexpectedly difficult and emotionally trying quest for clear skin, an experience that culminated in one of my proudest achievements.

My typical daily diet consisted of sugary cereal for breakfast; salty turkey sandwiches, soda, and chips for lunch; a candy bar for snack; and rice and fried noodles for dinner. I never thought that my diet would be a cause of my acne, but the possibility first came to me when I was reading a skincare article. Desperate for a cure, I searched "clear skin diet" on the Internet. The websites that turned up all echoed the same message: a balanced and healthy diet is crucial for beautiful skin. The recommended foods listed included large portions of fruits, vegetables, grains, nuts, and fish; 8 glasses of water daily and only small amounts of high-sodium, high-fat, and high-sugar foods. I researched further and found out that the expensive chemical cleansers that I had been using were not the answer—gentle face washes and a coat of sunblock were inexpensive products that could reduce breakouts. I knew that changing my entire diet and skincare routine would require a tremendous amount of commitment and willpower. But determined to improve my skin and my self-confidence, I began to transform my lifestyle. I started by incorporating fruits and vegetables into my meals and replacing sugary cereal with whole grains, chips with carrots, and fried noodles with salmon. For a long, painful week, I stuck to this diet and restrained myself from any junk food. My skin condition changed gradually but substantially. By the end of the week, my skin was noticeably smoother, clearer, and brighter. Yet I found myself relapsing, unable to continue for long without indulging myself, unable to swallow the horribly plain salads and chewy carrots. Every time I stopped, the acne came back. It came to the point where I despised the acne and coveted the clear skin enough to force myself back on track. It became an excruciating pattern of cravings and self-restraint. I struggled with these two impulses until I became used to healthy eating, even enjoying it. Now, two years later, my skin is better than ever and I have never gone back to eating the way I had before.

I have no awards or medals to show for my particular achievement. But no academic distinction in the world can match what I gained from my experience with changing my diet: healthier skin, self-confidence, and newfound mental strength. Above all, I realized that by improving my outer appearance, I had enriched my inner appearance.

ANALYSIS

"Beauty" provides an intimate portrayal of the author's struggle against acne. Most admissions essays tend to focus on resume-worthy activities. As the author admits, "I have no awards or medals to show for my particular achievement." But this essay shows that accomplishments in one's personal life can also be just as successful as essays focused on more prominent or recognizable activities. Other essays in this book also use personal topics not obviously related to academics or typical extracurriculars to give us a stronger sense of the author's personality, such as Alex's "Box of Chocolates" (Chapter 9).

This essay stands out for its candor about the author's feelings of low self-esteem when she saw the "unsightly blemishes" she faced each time that she looked in the mirror. The exacting details of the essay help show us the ups and downs in the author's "unexpectedly difficult and emotionally trying quest for clear skin." After sharing the results of her extensive research, the author concludes, "I knew that changing my entire diet and skincare routine would require a tremendous amount of commitment and willpower." The essay then goes on to show the waxing and waning of the strength of this commitment. Like other essays that share about weaknesses and strengths, this account humanizes the experience, allowing us as readers to relate to the process. For instance, we can admire the author for her restraint during "a long, painful week" of a completely different diet. Anyone who has ever failed to keep a New Year's Resolution or other lifestyle transformation vow can sympathize with the statement, "I found myself relapsing, unable to continue for long without indulging myself." The author's unsavory descriptions of "horribly plain salads and chewy carrots" add a humorous touch of detail to the essay while also underscoring the difficulty the author experienced in changing her diet. Rather than present an easy problem-solution setup, the author frankly shows us the cyclical nature of this journey by sharing such statements as this one: "It became an excruciating pattern of cravings and self-restraint." This essay shows that essays need not describe rapid changes and eureka moments; stories about gradual transformations and processes with many setbacks or retrogressions can also be quite compelling. In the case of this author, she struggled with cravings and self-restraint until she "became used to healthy eating, even enjoying it."

The conclusion nicely sums up the key lessons found in this essay. Besides the obvious benefit of healthy skin, the author also gained "self-confidence, and newfound mental strength." The reference to the classic expression about inner and outer beauty helps introduce and conclude the essay. This creates a nice wrapped-up effect. The author's changing attitudes towards the belief that "inner beauty matters more than outer beauty" shows her transformation. At first, she doubted both her outer and inner beauty; but after her two years of determined lifestyle modification, she found her inner life enriched by her improved outer appearance.

"Keeping up with the Beat of the Drum"

Shreyans C. Parekh
University of Pennsylvania

THE HINDU GOD, BRAHMA, SEEING THE plight of a society tainted by envy and greed, presents a boy with a drum that he can only hear, not see. This instrument, which is supposed to bring patience and discipline to humanity, is the foundation of Indian classical music. The boy has yet to discover that musicians use this tool to speak, allowing their minds to transmit messages through the vibrant pulsations of their notes.

My guru told me this story when I began learning the tabla, a North Indian classical drum. Though he never revealed the ending, he offered one clue. "It doesn't matter how fast your hands can beat the drum if your mind cannot keep up with them."

A typical American teenager, I had always yearned for raw strength and speed on the tabla. I thought those were the qualities that made the perfect percussionist. During concerts, I saw musicians' fingers gliding across the head of the drum producing the extraordinary impression of force, immediacy of genius and intensity of passion that left audiences spellbound. I knew that to become the best at tabla, I needed to display my talent in a similar way. I wanted to play equally as fast and forcefully, even if it meant sacrificing precision for power.

I asked my guru to train me to play like the maestros, but he said I lacked mental focus; I didn't listen to or enjoy my music. He believed the mind and body must be in sync in order to master the instrument. I never fully understood this concept until the imagination of one visually handicapped child attuned my mind to the beat of the drum.

As a summer volunteer at the Braille Institute in Anaheim, I developed the musical talents of blind elementary school children through teaching the tabla. My friends and I bought instruments and music with the money that we made during a summer recycling program in our neighborhood. During our first class, the children jumped into action, thumping erratically on their instruments. I chuckled at the sight of nine jubilant youngsters producing musical mayhem.

Chaandni was different. Shy and reserved, she felt the drum's smooth texture and stroked the soft middle portion of the drum head. I stood astonished as she performed her ritual. Tap. Listen. Smile. Tap.

Listen. Smile. I could see her contemplating the emerging rhythm and resonance of each successive pulse. Watching a budding musician feel the delicate timbre of each drumbeat is a thrilling sensation.

I learned more from observing than I did through years of erratic practice. Chaandni would eagerly listen to a musical piece, then strike incessantly until she produced a matching pitch. When she stumbled, she would sit patiently pinpointing her mistake. She didn't speak; her insight and emotion glowed through her music. For the first time in my life I felt the depth of the drums. For the first time, I truly comprehended and loved the instrument.

She was indeed a special soul. Her curiosity was insatiable; her regard for the drum was incomparable; her smile was inspiring. Her joyful progress inspired me to perform in London this summer with my guru. Driven by the spirit of a young girl who never let her disability impede her innate talent, I played gracefully in front of hundreds of spectators and cherished the inner triumph.

I am a living example of Brahma's story. The combination of grace and force on the tabla is my channel for communicating emotions. My tale ends with the appreciation that the mind is a beautiful vehicle for the drum.

ANALYSIS

Using the drum story as an introduction, the writer draws in his reader. Shreyans provides just enough detail to pique our curiosity as we strive to understand the message; yet the plot is simple enough that the story doesn't overwhelm us. Many students make the mistake of focusing too much on a related story and not enough on the main purpose of the essay. Shreyans has just the right balance, ensnaring the interest of the reader right from the beginning and then moving quickly to the main body of the essay.

In the next three paragraphs, Shreyans sets up the main conflict in the essay. The clever quote from his guru, "It doesn't matter how fast your hands can beat the drum if your mind cannot keep up with them," foreshadows the importance of thought as a part of musicianship. Shreyans explains that at first, he wanted to just play the tabla with as much force as possible, without regard to the contemplation that should empower the performance. By introducing us to the beginning point of his process, he is able to set up the rest of the essay to show us his growth.

The visual description of those playing the tabla in concert is very powerful and helps us understand the instrument better even if we aren't quite sure what it looks like or how it sounds. We can almost see the performers' fingers "gliding" and the "spellbound" audience members. Details like these bring the essay to life and help the admissions officers relate to the story being told.

Using the purchase of instruments to transition from the musical part of the essay to the volunteer work at the Braille Institute provides a nice connection between the stories. This is a great way to work in how he and his friend raised funds to buy the instruments and then took the initiative to volunteer at the institute. Again, the details that he provides about Chaandni help us to see what he sees. We can visualize her tapping, listening and smiling. We can feel his thrill from watching her.

Through his observations of Chaandni and her contemplative playing of the tabla, Shreyans demonstrates that he has undergone a transformation. We can see that he is now ready both physically and intellectually to perform. The conclusion has a meaningful tie to the introductory story.

When you write an essay about an activity, it's more powerful to describe the thinking that goes into the event rather than just the activity itself. This will allow the admissions officers to understand why you have committed yourself to the activity and what you gain from it. The essay that Shreyans wrote wouldn't have been nearly as effective had he just described his playing. What makes it compelling is that he tells a story through his learning to play the instrument and that he describes the mental aspect of playing. He also demonstrates how he evolved in his attitude toward playing the tabla.

Shreyans C. Parekh is an MBA student at The Wharton School of the University of Pennsylvania. He is the vice president of Koyal Wholesale, an online wholesale discount supplier of wedding, party, and event supplies (www.koyal.com). He can be reached at shreyans.c.parekh@gmail.com.

"Hurricane Transformations"

Jason Y. Shah
Harvard University

I USED TO SPEND ENDLESS NIGHTS wide-eyed, anxiously dreading a high school life teeming with harsh peers and hollow hallways, immersed in a cold atmosphere eternally void of familiarity's warm embrace. I'll admit that this is not a hopeful vision; nevertheless, I certainly risked accepting this ugly reality when I supported my family's decision to uproot itself and move from New Jersey to Florida after my freshman year.

Somewhat flexible, my parents gave me a significant voice in the decision as I would be most profoundly affected. Yet, I had spent my entire life in the same cozy center-hall colonial in the same New Jersey suburb. I had known my friends since youth, when we had snowball fights during the icy winter and ran through lawn sprinklers during the summer. Teachers knew my family and cordially greeted me in the halls. I could never move. In my mind, I was set!

Or was I? Instinct tugged at my heart, something was missing in my life because life is not about being "set." Lured by the concept of a fresh start, I yearned for the chance to write my own story. As the son of Indian immigrants, I had adventure in my blood; the time had come to venture beyond my comfort zone and stake a unique claim in Florida.

The first few months were trying; only birds joined me during lunch and I spend weekends alone writing introspective poetry. My fifteenth birthday centered on a family discussion about our affection for our new home while Hurricane Charley pounded the life out of Florida. I regretted moving. By fortuitous research, however, I learned more about innovative entrepreneurs who were shaping our world. I have not looked back since.

My self-inflicted adversity finally evoked personal growth. I constantly introduced myself to strangers and pursued my passions in different activities. By launching and supporting community organizations, I transformed into a proactive leader as I overcame difficulties in varied contexts. Continuously seeking challenges in the community and IB Program, I teamed up with other motivated citizens and students to thrive and contribute to my new home.

Today I am highly involved in my community with many friends and mentors. Nobody knows me for my family or childhood, just for who I am today. The results of my own decisions and actions mean much more than what has been bestowed upon me. I would risk it all again because I know that I can only enjoy what I have earned. Breaking away from the risk-averse crowd that holds an exaggerated fear for what can be lost has been refreshing. I have gained trust in myself to defy odds because I never would have dreamt of the happiness and accomplishments that I have been honored to achieve in Florida.

College will certainly thrust a fiercer Hurricane Charley at me, but I will stare it straight in the eye and exceed expectations, eventually leaving an enduring legacy for the world through my entrepreneurial and philanthropic endeavors.

ANALYSIS

Jason's essay provides a powerful story of self-transformation from an introverted person to a community leader. The metaphor of the hurricane—a catastrophic event that requires rebuilding afterwards—makes this essay memorable, as we see how hurricanes related both literally and metaphorically to Jason's life. The hurricane provides a vivid image that reminds us of the force of the challenges Jason faced, both in witnessing Hurricane Charley and also in shouldering the "self-inflicted adversity" of moving to Florida.

Self-transformation is an ambitious topic to write a single essay on—after all, this is often the topic of entire biographies. Jason does a good job of reigning in the vastness of this topic by providing specific details and identifying concrete events. For example, he paints the image of a "cozy center-hall colonial" and shows us the "snowball fights" and "lawn sprinklers" of his youth. Descriptions like these create an evocative sense of the comfort and familiarity of Jason's suburban New Jersey home. This is much more memorable than simply stating that he has an emotional attachment to New Jersey. The contrast between the cheerful scene in New Jersey and the "hollow hallways" Jason imagines in his new school help us appreciate how challenging the prospect of moving was to Jason.

In the third paragraph, Jason reveals an adventurous and risk-taking part of his personality that he connects to his heritage as the son of Indian immigrants. As the narrative unfolds, Jason shows us how his decision to move is hardly easy at first, but that his willingness to confront a challenge in order to generate personal growth demonstrates courage and a commitment to learning. "I yearned for the chance to write my own story," writes Jason, who goes on to demonstrate how he steps into that bold dream. "By fortuitous research," he continues, ". . . I learned more about innovative entrepreneurs who were shaping our world. I have not looked back since." Jason may have chosen to elaborate more on what the nature of the "fortuitous research" was and who some of these "innovative entrepreneurs" were, especially since he refers back to entrepreneurship and philanthropy at the end of his essay. While descriptions are helpful to set the context and scene, it is important to spend time elaborating in pivotal moments, since these are so critical to a narrative essay.

In his last paragraph, Jason reflects on what he has learned. Particularly relevant for a college admissions essay, he anticipates even fiercer challenges in college, but makes it clear that he is willing to embrace these. As readers, we are impressed by his willingness to rise up to meet challenges, while also appreciative of the vulnerabilities Jason has shared by telling us his fears before moving to Florida and his lonely lunches before he began to transform into a proactive leader.

"The House on Wellington Avenue"

Jackie Liao
Stanford University

A THIN SHARD OF SUNLIGHT SLICED through the vent of the windowless, cold, and cramped one bedroom basement apartment. The apartment stood three stories high with its weight suffocating the basement. I sat on the stained carpet, alone, playing with my one and only prized Hot Wheels car. My mother was working her ten-hour shift as a minimum wage waitress and my father was nowhere to be found. My father left our family when I turned three-years old. He also left the burden of his reckless gambling debt to my mother and left us to fend for ourselves. At the time, my mother barely spoke any English, yet she had to find work in order to support us. She became occupied with work, so I was frequently isolated at home. The house on Wellington Avenue in Daly City evolved to represent all the suppression my mother and I endured. As a child, wherever I could go to be away from the cell, I went.

A few days after my eleventh birthday, I trudged home on an afternoon to discover our house robbed again, this time of my mother's savings for the following month's rent and my new "Stingray 5000" water gun. I burst into tears and cried in my mother's fragile arms. It was that moment I vowed to do something about our situation. I was tired living in that horrid house, being deprived of my mother because of her demanding work schedule, and feeling like the whole world was constantly against us. Early in my childhood, I realized that our family was financially poor, because of that, I wanted to be rich in knowledge. Every day after school, I would take the transit to the Daly City Public Library where I could be away from the miserable house and focus on my studies. It was there that I would max out my library card to read Harry Potter novels and sit at the wide tables with my head in textbooks and magazines, searching for a better life. My mother knew the anger I had for the house, as a result, she would indirectly encourage me to channel out my negative feelings for the house into positive ones for learning by dropping by the library after work with apple juice for me. My appreciation for my mother is great because she still managed to set time aside from her work to attend to my needs. My objective was to gain all the knowledge I could, in hope of devising a plan to get us out of the Wellington Black Hole. At one point, I spent a whole Saturday looking for some sort of mathematical equation that would cure our blight. Enriching my knowledge was my naïve way of trying to improve and control our bleak situation. Fortunately, my mother's relentless effort for work allowed us to move to a better part of Daly City.

When I finally got my driver's license at the age of sixteen, after a vigorous curriculum of driver's education, driving lessons, and a driving test, the first place I drove my mother's old Toyota Camry was to the house on Wellington Avenue. The freedom of driving allowed me to explore a place where I had been trapped in for so long. Crouched on the warm cement, I glanced pass the faded wooden walls and peered through the constricting vent to see the three year old that once sat on the cold floor. As I stood with the sun shining on my back, I acknowledged that my mother and I were given a situation that we did not choose, but we ultimately became the ones who changed the course of our lives. A photo of the Wellington house sits on my bedroom window edge, casting a small shadow when sun light beams in. It serves as a painful reminder of my background, and an inspiration to continue excelling in life, even when unfavorable conditions dominate.

ANALYSIS

Jackie's essay is similar to Sarah's "Unshakable Worth," (Chapter 7) and Timothy's "Self Mind," (Chapter 7) in that it takes a family difficulty—growing up in poverty with an absentee father—and transforms it into a story of growth and personal strength. The beginning of the essay conveys an oppressive and stifling mood with its description of "The House on Wellington Avenue," a title that in itself alludes to the rich themes of immigration, coming of age, and poverty present in Sandra Cisneros' famous *The House on Mango Street*. Jackie's details are vivid and carefully chosen to evoke a sense of loneliness: the "thin shard of sunlight," the "windowless, cold, and cramped" room, the "suffocating" basement, the "stained carpet," her single toy as she is home alone. The comparison of this room to a "cell," as in a prison cell, is the pinnacle of this austere representation of her childhood life. Jackie continues this sense of darkness when she later describes the apartment as the "Wellington Black Hole." These differing but consistent descriptions bolster our understanding of Jackie's feelings towards her childhood home.

However, Jackie doesn't spend the rest of her essay complaining about this dire situation. Instead, in the second paragraph, we learn about a moment where she makes a vow to improve her situation after being robbed. Her mom's "fragile arms" contrasted with Jackie's determination make such a vow all the more impressive when the reader realizes that it is an 11-year-old child who decides to become "rich in knowledge" as an antidote to her family's poverty.

In describing this quest for knowledge, Jackie demonstrates a gift for choosing small but evocative details: Harry Potter, the apple juice her mother brought her, a day spent "looking for some sort of mathematical equation to cure [her family's] blight." Jackie writes, "Fortunately, my mother's relentless effort for work allowed us to move to a better part of Daly City," but she might also have given herself more credit for supporting her mother.

The final paragraph strikes a balance between the victory of having moved away from Wellington Avenue and the emotional scars that remain in Jackie's mind. Again, her keen eye for description evokes a haunting, nostalgic mood when she writes, "Crouched on the warm cement, I glanced past the faded wooden walls and peered through the constricting vent to see the three year old that once sat on the cold floor." The sentence alludes to Jackie's indomitable spirit, one that will undoubtedly serve her well when she faces new challenges in college.

16

TALENT

"A Dramatic Coup"

Fareez Giga
Stanford University

I SAT THERE, STUNNED FOR AN instant, and then jumped as high as I could and screamed as loud as my voice would allow. Blood rushed through my entire body, while the butterflies in my stomach finally flew away. I had just received my LAMDA Diploma with Honors, a task that has only been done by one person before me. LAMDA, the London Academy of Music and Dramatic Arts, comes to my high school, as well as others in the states, and gives what are essentially acting exams. In these exams, you must perform a series of monologues, and to receive the Diploma you must perform four five-minute monologues, one pre-1910, one post-1980, one Shakespearean, and one of your choice. I had worked for weeks on my monologues, perfecting them as much as I could, staying after school, working at lunch, even at home, despite the shouting by my sister for me to stop. When it came time to perform, I was incredibly nervous; however, after I came out of my performance, I lingered outside the theater, waiting upon my results, and when they came, I was astounded. Not only was I able to pass my exam, but also I came out of it with greater knowledge of theater than I had when I started. I learned a great deal from taking these various exams, most notably the age old lesson that hard work does pay off. The personal splendor I felt was one that I had never felt before, and I live to feel it again.

ANALYSIS

Fareez shares a meaningful accomplishment in a small space. He effectively explains the significance of the LAMDA Diploma with Honors—an award that only one other person had received before him—and portrays a sense of jubilation which reveals to the reader his excitement. Fareez then describes how much work went into preparing the four monologues, each from different time periods. Plus he adds detail on how much he worked to perfect them, even humorously revealing that his sister begged him to stop. He concludes with the greater meaning that he learned from the experience, that hard work pays off.

In this limited part of the application, Fareez accomplishes a lot and touches on all the elements that highlight the achievement as well as positive aspects of his personality. It's important to remember that admissions officers will not know the significance of most awards unless you tell them. Describe how few people receive the award or how selective the competition is. Briefly explain the amount of work that was involved or how difficult it was to prepare. Then, put the award into perspective. What did you learn from winning? How can you apply what you learned to your future endeavors? Why was winning important to you? If you write about receiving an award, it's important to do more than just state that you did. You should also give context to the honor.

"Music as My Second Language"

Jean Gan
Duke University

MUSIC HAS SHAPED MY PERSONAL AND intellectual life in many ways. Music is a common language that connects me to others who share my enthusiasm for creating it. Furthermore, I learn about my own preferences and personality through the pieces that intrigue me. As I expose myself to a wider array of styles and eras, my musical tastes grow more complex. Through music, I welcome opportunities to expand my friendships as well as my instrumental horizons.

I began studying piano at age six. For the next five years, my mother lived vicariously through my musical education, which her family had not been able to afford. In fifth grade, as I was becoming an earnest piano student, I was selected to commence violin lessons and play in my elementary school orchestra. From that day on, I saw life from a violinist's point of view.

Although I am a seasoned pianist, an ambitious solo violinist, and a fledgling cellist, I am, above all, a passionate chamber musician. My experience in a chamber quartet has had a strong impact on my character. When I was the second violinist, I simply enjoyed making music with my friends. Only after I became the first violinist did I feel the responsibility of leadership settling uncomfortably on my shoulders. However, the burden soon became a part of me and transformed into enthusiasm. Now, as the quartet leader, I use the small group setting to channel each of our individual creative instincts. Each member of the quartet shares her musical interests, bringing favorite repertoire to the table, so that we each participate in the learning and playing experience. The quartet is also an outlet for my musical fancy. Ever since I discovered the Finale music writing software, I have delighted in arranging works for our quartet to play and perform. This year, my goal is to arrange and perform the Ferrante and Teicher version of the love theme from *The Godfather* for a piano duet and orchestra.

As my aspirations grow, I aim to arrange music for a greater variety of instruments and to explore jazz, pop, and other styles of music on the piano. I desire to join others with similar talent and passion at Duke. However, before I leave my high school, I hope my appreciation for music will leave a mark on my community.

ANALYSIS

In "Music as My Second Language," Jean writes about how "music is a common language that connects [her] to others who share [her] enthusiasm for creating it." Jean packs a lot of information into a short essay while keeping the topic tightly focused. The language metaphor helps tie this essay together: Jean's assertion that "musical tastes grow more complex" parallels the growth of someone learning new vocabulary when studying a foreign language. And just as learning a language expands ones possibilities for connecting with people, so too does Jean note that music helps her connect with others and expand her friendships.

In relating her childhood history of exploring "instrumental horizons," Jean not only tells about her lessons in piano and violin but also draws in the history of her parents, who were not able to afford a musical education. Jean demonstrates a nice balance between her personal history and the story of those who shaped this history—in this case, her parents. When writing about past events, focusing solely on oneself can create a distorted sense of self-as-center-of-the-universe. Of course, it is appropriate to focus mainly on oneself—these are, after all, *personal* statements—but it can be useful to describe the people around you in setting the stage for telling your story. This not only helps readers contextualize your situation but also shows your ability to connect your own experience to the experiences of people with whom you interact.

This short essay connects to Jean's longer essay, "Anything Goes" (Chapter 10) in continuing the theme of expanding horizons and building upon her current knowledge. In both essays, Jean does an excellent job of balancing descriptions of her personal drive and motivation with illustrations of her ability to work collaboratively. For example, in this essay, we see that though she is "a seasoned pianist, an ambitious solo violinist, and a fledgling cellist," Jean is "above all, a passionate chamber musician." Throughout the panoply of her musical experiences, Jean wisely chooses to hone in on her experience as the leader of her chamber quartet. She demonstrates her egalitarian leadership style when she notes, "I use the small group setting to channel each of our individual creative instincts." Her passion for acquiring new skills can be seen by her discovery of Finale music writing software. Jean's creativity and motivation can be defined in her very goals, for example, her desire "to arrange and perform the Ferrante and Teicher version of the love theme from *The Godfather* for a piano duet and orchestra." Writing about these future aspirations gives Jean an excellent segue into discussing why she hopes to join Duke's musical community. Here, Jean might have chosen to write a little more about "why Duke" specifically. When writing reasons you want to attend a college, it is important to do research on the school and to write in a way that the college name is not interchangeable with that of any other university. Jean could have made her ending even stronger, had she mentioned a specific group at Duke so that this essay would have been noticeably specific to that university.

"My Bedroom"

Fareez Giga
Stanford University

I RAN AROUND NERVOUSLY, YELLING AT my parents to wait downstairs; I did not want them to see anything that was going on. I rushed as fast as I could to make my bed, something most teenagers do not usually do. I made sure everything was in proper order as I called my parents up to my room. As I placed the last pillow on the bed, I acquired a sense of completion and achievement. I had done it; I designed and redecorated my bedroom. It was at this point when I, in my heart, became an interior designer.

This picture represents more than just a bedroom to me; it is my first step on a path that I hope directs me to fulfillment. Designing my bedroom allowed me to explore the creative aspect of my life, and I was, and still am, able to appreciate the amount of creative talent I possess. It has become an intense passion in my life and I value this a great deal. This process illustrated the creative potential that I possess within myself, and I know that I can apply this promise in any aspect of my life.

One of the greatest features of this project I took on is that I was able to see the results of my actions immediately. It was a hands-on experience that I enjoyed to its fullest, and I was exultant with the outcome. Overall, this project was a great success in my eyes, and even in the eyes of my family and friends who are amazed at my capabilities with design. However, as the designer, I do get frustrated with infinitesimal flaws. On the wall to the left of my bed there are two shelves and framed artwork that I created myself. In the process of the installation, I centered these shelves and artwork on the wall; however, the palm tree that I placed in the corner covers up one of the frames. I now know that it probably would have been better if I moved the shelves and artwork to the left of the wall. The importance of this is not the flaw itself, but in the fact that I learned from what I had done and know how to improve myself the next time. Overall, I feel the room came out beautifully and it symbolizes my first true triumph with design.

Though this project meant a great deal to me emblematically, I also just had fun with it. Utilizing my imagination, and figuring out how I was going to make things work within the room was simply enjoyable. Not only was the design process pleasurable, but also the actual painting, nailing, and organizing itself was satisfying. I was also able to bond with my father through the project. He joined me in my most successful achievement of the room—the design and creation of the headboard. This venture and this picture epitomize my success. I consider my bedroom to be an elegant, contemporary work of art, and this picture embodies all the work I put into my design as well as the sense of achievement I received after its completion.

ANALYSIS

Fareez's introduction creates mystery in the very first of his sentences that draws the reader in. We want answers. Why is he making the bed? Why is he in such a rush? What is he hiding from his parents? We want to find out what engages him in such totality.

In the second paragraph, Fareez explains the point of the essay—his creativity. This paragraph is a little general, and it could have been strengthened with the use of details. He might have shared more about the roots of his creativity, how he discovered and developed his talent, or how he hopes to use his inventive nature and unique ideas in the future. Still, we learn about a meaningful talent that he has, and we can tell that he is incredibly passionate about having a creative outlet.

In the third paragraph, Fareez shares a specific example of how he gets frustrated by a small defect. By describing how the palm tree covers one of the pictures, he gives us a visual image and shows how meticulous he is with his work. He keeps the tone positive by explaining how he will use this as a lesson "the next time." It is always best to use a specific example rather than general terms.

In the last paragraph, Fareez illustrates the strong connection he has with his father and how he enjoyed the physical work that went into the project. This gives an additional dimension to Fareez's work by pointing out his ability to work with another person as well as his obvious enjoyment in actually implementing his designs in a hands-on way.

The strength of Fareez's essay is that it presents an aspect of his personality that is not easily shown in the rest of the application. There is no place on the application to detail that he is creative, and he did not receive any honors or awards for this project. His essay shows that you can write about a topic that is not connected to an *official* activity, award, or honor. Sharing something that you've done on your personal time can give the admissions officers a glimpse into who you are.

"A Special Performance"

Anonymous
Harvard University

I STOOD BEHIND THE CURTAINS LISTENING to the applause to the previous act. I exhaled, realizing that this was a moment that fulfilled my childhood wish. Tonight was special because instead of an alto aria or a jazz lick, I had prepared a song unique to my identity. I curled my fingers around the microphone and waited impatiently as the curtains opened.

My love for performance stemmed from my appreciation of music as a child. In the city in China where I spent the first ten years of my life, I never found a choir to join and never laid eyes on a grand piano. Nonetheless, I treasured my passion for song and sought ways to bring music into my life. I sang with our old record player when I was barely tall enough to reach it. On certain afternoons, my best friend and I would tape bed sheets to the ceiling as curtains and invite neighbors to come listen. There, we sang in duet, danced, and bowed while clasping each other's hands. Captured in our own musical sanctuary, we never noticed the hours that passed by.

Music evokes in me the emotions that words and pictures cannot. I also revel in the intellectual challenges that music offers. I find it thrilling to tackle difficult, delicious repertoire, and I enjoy composing my own melodies. Through music, I can share and celebrate my past. When I was asked to share my cultural talents at my high school, I looked for a song that my mother sang when I was young, but I could not find the sheet music. A week before tonight, I sat down by the old piano in the practice room at school. With only the old tune ringing faintly in my mind, my hands soon took a life of their own and experimented with chords, arpeggios, and trills. I superimposed these on the original melody and composed variations. My voice, too, frolicked with the piano as I sang the tune repeatedly. I was lost in another musical paradise. I felt like a child again, tucked under the covers, listening to my mother's song as I drifted away to dreams.

Now, dressed in an old Chinese dress that my mother had worn in her youth, I stepped onto the empty stage illuminated by pale blue light. I held the microphone up to my lips and smiled before starting. Then, I brought to life the beautiful ballad that had brightened my childhood in China. My mind overflowed with warm memories of that faraway city as I lulled the audience with my melody. When I caught my mother's face in the audience, I knew she nestled in the same air of nostalgia.

Music allows me to present my native culture and contribute to the diversity in my community. It has stimulated my mind and provided an outlet for my creativity. To me, nothing is more pleasurable than being imaginative. Carrying my childhood love of music through my teenage years has been a gratifying experience, and I look forward to continuing in my undergraduate years.

ANALYSIS

The beauty of this student's essay is that she opens herself up to us, the readers. She starts with a catchy opening, explaining in rich detail how she is standing behind the curtain and why the night is especially meaningful to her. We can feel what she feels as she stands there. She gives a detailed visual description and explains her thoughts as well.

The author then explains the roots of her interest in music. By sharing her childhood experience, she demonstrates how this has been a lifelong passion for her. We can imagine her as a child with her friend, putting on performances for the neighbors. Knowing how an author's interest in a given field of study began can add depth and dimension to the reader's overall characterization of the student.

In the third paragraph, our musician shares what goes through her mind. This is valuable to admissions officers because they can see her ability to analyze her thoughts and her level of self awareness. Self reflection demonstrates maturity and the capability to take a step back from a situation and see the deeper meaning of it. She explains why she is so tied to music and why it is an intellectual experience for her to recall her childhood song from memory and slowly piece it together.

Through her essay, we understand why this specific performance holds such great meaning. We see the connection to her past and to her mother. She makes several accomplishments through her writing—sharing an extracurricular interest, touching on her childhood growing up in China, revealing the intellectual side of her talent, and showing the connection that she has to her heritage and her family. After reading this essay, the admissions officers probably felt that they had a deeper understanding of who this student was and that she was someone they'd like to get to know better.

17

TRAVEL

"Extra Page"

Lauren Horton
Stanford University

YOU'VE GIVEN ME ONE MORE PAGE to tell you about myself. Just one. There are only eight boxes for extra-curricular activities, only three lines to tell about my summers, just over two inches to write a note to my future roommate, and only one page to fill in all the holes, to color in all the blank space. Unfortunately both for me and for you, entire lives don't fit into boxes and personalities can't be completely sketched on paper. I have to do my best to show you who I am, and you have to do your best to find me in all this black ink. So, best of luck to you. As for me, I will write just one more page and hope it gives you a clearer image of who I really am.

You have noticed, I'm sure, my list of extra-curricular activities. What you can't see is the struggle that went into compiling that list. For one thing, my practice list was comprised of far more than eight activities, so I was forced to group things together and to leave things out. Every summer and winter, I travel with my youth group on a service trip, sometimes within this country, other times around the world.

The summer before my freshman year and again two years later, we spent two weeks in Costa Rica, living with families there and working both helping build a renovation on a church there and playing with children in a refugee settlement called Pavas. The year in between, we ran a day camp for underprivileged children in San Antonio, Texas, and the summer before my junior year, we did various kinds of service in Columbus, Ohio. For our winter trips, we have done urban outreach in New York City and in Miami, trying to use those experiences to help our downtown church improve its outreach ministries. My service experience with church goes beyond these trips twice a year, though. I spend several evenings each year volunteering in the homeless shelter in my church's gym both with youth group and with my family. We also go as a family each year early on Christmas morning to serve breakfast at the shelter and celebrate the holiday with the guests. These are pieces of the categories I call "Central Presbyterian Church youth group" and "Community Service" that I didn't have space for in the box, but that mean a lot to me and play huge roles in my life.

Another experience that I haven't found a space for is the Maine Coast Semester, the four months I spent on Chewonki Neck in Maine during the fall of my junior year. Although my essay provides one snapshot of the experience, it cannot possibly speak to everything the semester meant to me. Moving out of my family's house and into a cabin with six girls my own age was extremely exciting for me, and what I found when I got there was even better than what I had expected. It was a place I could relate to. In science class, we would learn to identify the trees and wildlife that were living just outside our cabins. In the afternoon, working on the farm, we would lovingly tend the animals and plants that we would then harvest, prepare in the kitchen, and eat. Each of us realized our connection to every other member of the Chewonki community and to the land itself, and learned to be responsible with that connection. When I was assigned to collect recyclables before breakfast for my morning chore, I showed up just as promptly and with just as much energy as when my chore was to milk the cows or to clean the bathrooms. Similarly, when a teacher asked me to read an assignment for homework, I got it done, not simply because I wanted to keep a good grade, but because the entire class depended on each person's individual preparation in order to have rich, meaningful discussion.

Coming home, I realized that here, too, I was connected to my community. Although it is larger than the one in Maine, I still have the same responsibility to those around me, and will have that responsibility to whatever community I am part of for the rest of my life. In my daily life, just like on my service trips, I try to look for chances to benefit something greater than myself. In college, I look forward to becoming part of a new community, and figuring out how to find my niche, so that I can serve that community as well as be served by it.

ANALYSIS

Lauren makes perfect use of the extra page offered on the Stanford application by addressing topics that weren't fully fleshed out elsewhere. The first paragraph is a little risky because there is such limited space and often it doesn't work to write about something not related to the main topic of the essay. For many students, a seemingly unrelated topic can become a tangent that doesn't add much and that consumes valuable real estate. However, because Lauren is a skilled writer, she pulls it off, and she demonstrates her personality through the introduction. She uses creative phrasing such as, "Entire lives don't fit into boxes and personalities can't be completely sketched on paper." She also demonstrates her sense of humor writing, "So, best of luck to you." The humor isn't over the top but comes across as a friendly, slightly irreverent challenge.

As Lauren progresses into describing her activities, she smartly focuses on those that she was not able to fully explain elsewhere in the application. In her synopsis of the Central Presbyterian Church youth group, she writes about specific contributions she made with the homeless shelter. It always helps to give examples with details of defined individual contributions. This fills out her experiences and gives context to what she's done. Another approach might have been to provide greater detail about one specific activity rather than list the many community service projects that she worked on through the church.

When writing about living on Chewonki Neck in Maine, Lauren describes not just what she did, but the greater knowledge she gained from the experience. As the reader, you can easily detect her genuine interest in learning and you can almost feel her excitement in studying the wildlife and trees outside their cabins or growing her own food. This authentic passion for learning is one that admissions officers admire and want to see in students who are admitted, and the way that Lauren presents this seems natural and not forced.

Finally, Lauren draws a connection between her experience with the church and the Chewonki community by explaining how one allowed her to serve the community and the other allowed her to form a bond with it. She then applies this connection to her future plans. This is an effective way to conclude the essay because Lauren illustrates her ability to analyze her accomplishments and further explains how she will apply what she's learned to future opportunities.

"Looking Beyond the Castle"

Brian Aguado
Stanford University

One of Stanford's essay prompts is to provide a photo and explain its significance.

I ONCE BELONGED TO ROYALTY, STROLLING along the lush pastures of grass and enormous spires of Renaissance structure. Unfortunately, I was not given a crown on my voyage, even though I felt the crown when visiting the grand castle in Spain. The picture shown is important to me not only because of the spectacular view, but it also represents my passions for the study of Spain's cul-tural history and literature as well as how those subjects offer clues to discovering my individuality.

Traveling to Spain gave me the chance of a lifetime to explore its history with respect to my personality. In the photograph, the castle in the background once belonged to the great royal unifiers of Spain named Ferdinand and Isabella. With their process of unification came the exploration of the Americas. Explorers such as Christopher Columbus established Spanish territories in the New World, such as Colombia, which is the country my parents are from, and I was born. From this chain of causality, Spain's history essentially created my existence. Pondering about my historical background from Spain, perhaps I would have never been born if the king and queen never unified Spain. I could be speaking Arabic if the expulsion of the Moors never occurred under the hands of the Spanish monarchs. Curiously,

I could have been born as an Indian native, because the New World would have never been explored. Perhaps, I wouldn't be looking at the same photo, explaining its significance! Frankly, exploring Spain's history has enabled me to discover my origins. When viewing the picture through my point of view, I see myself returning the roots of my creation.

Spain also offers a vibrant history of literary works and significant innovations in Hispanic literature. Similar to the exploration of history leading to a clue for learning about myself, I have the ability to explore the literature the Hispanic culture has to offer. Knowing two languages allows me to discover the essence of ideas authors such as Gabriel García Márquez, Jorge Luis Borges, and Cervantes wanted to convey to their audience. Since language is to a code for ideas, I can decipher two different kinds of codes, English and Spanish, to understand the author's emotions placed into his or her literature. Spanish literature also enhances Hispanic culture as a positive influence in the world. Reading literature in Spanish and English consequently has allowed me to further search for clues about my cultural origins, since Spanish literature is considered a voice among the people.

Perhaps my interest in these two subjects came from knowing I come from a Colombian family. I am the first in our family to be born in the United States, and as a result, I represent two different cultures. Knowing I come from a culturally different family, I feel passionate about exploring my family's cultural roots because it is a method to discover clues about my individuality, as well as the origins of my family. In the USA, the last names of Aguado or Granados are rarely found among common Americans. When I traveled to Spain, I purchased wooden plaques showing the coat of arms from my ancestors bearing the Aguado and Granados names. When I found these plaques commemorating my family, I had felt I found yet another clue to my personality, since my last names were found from Spain (similar to finding a needle in a haystack). Finding my coat of arms on my trip proves my origins lie within the history and culture of Spain. The trip to Spain gave me the opportunity to explore my existence as a human being, as well as knowing from where I came.

Based on my perceptions, my picture represents to me the complex evolution of my personality, since I am constantly finding new clues leading to the understanding of who I am. This picture is a part of my constant search for my individuality and is a reminder of the beginning of my personal exploration. This is my crown.

ANALYSIS

Brian's essay opens with a sentence that piques our curiosity, a trend seen in several other essays, including Oana's "A Different Kind of Love" (Chapter 3) and Sarah's "Unshakable Worth" (Chapter 7). A first sentence that invokes a question in the reader—in Brian's case, the question is "How does Brian belong to royalty?"—is an effective way to engage your audience right from the beginning.

Brian reveals the key to this mystery in the second paragraph by tracing the history of Spain back to his family's origins. As he explores the "chain of causality," Brian demonstrates his "passion for the study of Spain's cultural history" by making references to Christopher Columbus and the expulsion of the Moors. He also shows his skills in imaging: "I could be speaking Arabic . . . I could have been born as an Indian native" and, playfully, "Perhaps I wouldn't be looking at the same photo, explaining its significance!"

These details also relate to Brian's interest in finding "clues to discovering [his own] individuality." The term *individuality* can have several possible meanings. Brian might have shared his personal interpretation of the term in order to give us a better sense of what the "constant search for [his] individuality" means to him. Remember to define the key terms in essays if they are potentially ambiguous. Clarifying important terms brings personal interpretation to the written words and also helps reduce redundancy. For example, Brian writes several sentences that seem related to discovering his individuality and heritage. "Frankly," he explains, "exploring Spain's history has enabled me to discover my origins." We gain other clues in these sentences: "Reading literature in Spanish and English consequently has allowed me to further search for clues about my cultural origins" and "I feel passionate about exploring my family's cultural roots because it is a method to discover clues about my individuality, as well as the origins of my family." These might be more powerfully condensed into one concise statement placed at the beginning of the essay.

Brian's essay provides strong examples of his passion for Spanish history and literature using the memorable metaphor of royalty, finding his coat of arms, and discovering his metaphorical "crown." Using a single photograph, Brian was able to share about his heritage and his personal passions. Many strong essays highlight one's individual interests and talents within the broader framing of a group. In Brian's case, his passion is Spanish history and literature, and the "group" is comprised of his ancestors and the Spanish culture they represent.

18

VIGNETTE

"Polar Bears"

Lauren Horton
Stanford University

THE BUZZING OF THE ALARM CLOCK suddenly stops and, to my surprise, I am awakened not by the noise but by the silence, rudely jerked from my sleep. Six forty-five, the numbers read. I pull my comforter tighter under my chin and close my eyes, fully intending to get up in a few minutes. I'm sure I'll wake back up in a few minutes, but not yet. I can't do it yet.

"Lolo!" someone's whispering to me, in my dreams I'm sure. "Lolo, get up! Aren't you coming?" Coming where? One instant of confusion. Only one blissful instant, and then it all makes sense. It's Saturday.

"Yeah, I'm coming." The listlessness of my voice surprises me. I groan and fold the thick layers of blankets off of me. The frigid December air pounces. As I watch, thousands of tiny bumps germinate on my arms, and the fine hairs stand alarmingly straight. After getting out of bed and pulling on my bathing suit, I eagerly throw my winter coat around my arms and shoulders. I debate crawling back in my bed. No one said I had to do it.

I look at my cabinmates, and I push that thought from my mind. Although Lucy and Tuna stay nestled in their beds, Cara is pulling a sweatshirt over her head. Emily and Constanza are standing quietly, fully dressed, and Sarah is duct-taping a pair of flip-flops on her bare feet. Shoes. I had almost forgotten. I open the door, and look down at our tiny porch. My tennis shoes are indeed there, frozen solid. I force the unyielding layers of ice around my feet, wincing. The laces crunch, and small crystals of ice fall gently to the floor as I tie a bow on each shoe. Everyone is ready. It's time to go.

I wrap my arm through Constanza's as we step off the last wooden step from the cabin. The air isn't so bad out here--probably a few degrees above zero. My feet begin to tingle and then to burn. We trudge through the snow as quickly as possible, and I'm sure my excitement is visible on my face.

Soon, we can see the water of the Sheepscot River, stained with thin sheets of ice. Most people would say we're out of our minds. My friends back in Atlanta will call me crazy. I grin. Squeezing Constanza's hand on one side and Emily's on the other, I stumble through the mud left by the receding tide.

"One, two, three!" We count together and sprint into the icy water, diving under the surface just for an instant. As we clamber out of the water and toward our chilled towels, our semester-mates cheer wildly. The next threesome heads toward the water.

Later in the morning, the thirty-six students at Maine Coast Semester file into the dining hall for breakfast, about twenty of us dripping wet and beaming. Five of us sport shorts and sunglasses in a foolish attempt to defy the cold. I follow my friends to a table where a large book stands open, and sign my name under the heading "Polar Bears: December 7." As I sit eating my bagel, I catch the eye of a wet-headed polar bear across the room and we smile together.

ANALYSIS

Many students think that their essays need to be about a serious topic such as a current event, revelation about themselves or remarkable achievement. Lauren takes a different route. While she describes an accomplishment, it's not a traditional one that culminates with a trophy or hours of community service and not one with an easy-to-summarize lesson learned. What makes her essay work, rather, is that she presents an experience with memorable details that allows us as the readers to draw our own conclusions about what she's gained from it.

The introduction attracts attention and is very relatable, as we've all had mornings in which we've ignored the beeping alarm clock and pulled the covers tighter. Lauren summons a little bit of mystery with the introduction because we don't know what's ahead of her. When she reveals that it is a Saturday morning, we wonder why she would want to wake up so early on a weekend.

The descriptions are extremely vivid, from the goosebumps ("Thousands of tiny bumps germinate on my arms, and the fine hairs stand alarmingly straight") to putting on her shoes (". . . small crystals of ice fall gently to the floor as I tie a bow on each shoe"). We can almost feel the chill of the air, see her tired cabinmates getting ready and hear the crunch of her shoe laces. Details such as these draw us as the readers into the essay and make us feel like we're not just witnesses but active participants.

Then Lauren builds on the mystery of the story. Why would she put her winter coat on top of her bathing suit? When she writes, "No one said I had to do it," we as the reader wonder what "it" is.

After the plunge, it is notable that Lauren doesn't conclude with a moral or overriding message, but we've still discovered much about her. We've learned that she is a writer who can describe a scene vibrantly, a storyteller who can draw us in with details that touch our senses and develop a mystery and a person who forms meaningful friendships through actions not words. Lauren's essay is memorable and gives the admissions officers something to latch onto. They'll remember her as the student who took the frigid plunge in the water.

It's not a requirement to write an essay about a serious topic or one with a serious lesson learned. Sometimes it's just right to write a story in a memorable way. After reading this essay, the admissions officers probably felt that Lauren was a student they wanted to meet, one who had something to add to the prospective class.

"Moving"

Laura V. Mesa
Stanford University

THE QUICK RIPPING OF THICK TAPE and the heavy thuds of cardboard boxes echo throughout an empty, unfamiliar, and lonely house. As the heavy boxes are slowly opened and their contents revealed, my young heart jumps for joy. There, within that scant and unexpectedly durable shell of cardboard, lie my invaluable possessions. After removing the bubbly layer of protection from my valuables, I begin to place them, one by one, onto my familiar, yet strangely new shelf.

I first lift out my ragged and faithful stuffed animal Mr. Teddy. Though torn, dirty and missing his left eye, he reminds me of my youth and the one constant friendship in my life. He has traveled with me thousands upon thousands of miles to and from each of the seven vastly different living experiences that have defined my life. Mr. Teddy has been there with me throughout the difficulty of every one of the transitions in my life.

Next, I pull out a small, fragile lamp decorated with blue and white pinstripes. A small yellow duck lives at the bottom of the glass compartment. As I fumble with the rotating switch, I see that only two of the three different settings are properly working. Now, after years of travel, only the nightlight and brightest setting work. I leave the light on at its brightest setting and place it on my night table. The brightness comforts me.

I return to the box to pull out my thick, denim blue journal and my favorite ink pen. I flip through the pages, pausing to glance at my informal collection of favorite pictures of friends, articles, and tidbits of memories that I have compiled through the stages in my life. I open to the last section of the book and glance at my favorite quotations alphabetically sorted by subject and author. I look up Woody Allen and smile at his ridiculously funny honesty and place my journal on the ledge next to my window.

After refueling my ink pen I scoop up my carefully packaged Rosary and Bible. As I crack open the case, the pearl white beads of my Rosary glint in the sunlight and my ivory covered Bible, given to me on my First Communion, opens to the front page. There, written in my aunt's handwriting, is a greeting written in Spanish and signed by my now deceased grandparents. These two items represent one of my only connections to my relatives and the history of my family in Colombia: a common religion and a belief in Providence.

After saying a quick prayer of thanksgiving I pull out my final and most necessary possession. The dust flies off the glass as I blow across the surface. There, under the grime of travel, lies my own face fixed in time. Enclosed within a light maple frame, a color photograph captures my eleven year old self clothed in bright purple soccer shorts and a white sleeveless uniform shirt. My hair is tightly pulled back in the quintessential ponytail, sweat dripping off my skin and dirt covering my socks. My face is frozen in an expression of relief, domination, and triumph after scoring the game-winning goal in the merciless sun of a Houston summer. I study the image and wipe a single tear from my eye. My knee aches sympathetically, and I prepare to hang the picture. As I pick up the hammer, I realize that although soccer is no longer a part of my life, I have filled the vacancy in my heart with other challenging and significant activities that I have grown to love with the same fervor. That picture, though simple, encompasses the passion that is my life. It will forever symbolize for me the love and dedication I have for everything I do.

With a last glance, I hang the heavy frame on the wall. The box is empty, unlike the room. Although the room is only filled by a few items, it is occupied by the only items I will ever need for the rest of my life: friendship, humility, self-expression, family, God, and passion.

ANALYSIS

The framework for this essay provides a way to tie together a number of things that are important to Laura. She covers five different sets of objects; and through each of these, she reveals a part of herself.

What makes this essay especially effective is that Laura works her thoughts into the descriptions of the items. For example, she writes, "I begin to place them, one by one, onto my familiar, yet strangely new shelf." By describing the shelf as "strangely new," she reflects her apprehension about having her possessions in a new setting.

Through Mr. Teddy we learn that Laura has moved many times. Relocating is always difficult and requires acclimating to new surroundings, choosing different friends, and perhaps even adjusting to an unfamiliar culture. The admissions officers can conclude that Laura is probably someone who is flexible in new situations, adept at making friends, and willing to establish roots.

Laura shows her sentimentality when describing the lamp. We can imagine that at one point, all the settings worked. Her description makes us wonder for what adventures the lamp has provided light as Laura worked to see her way through them.

As someone who keeps a journal, Laura shows that she is self reflective. She is a person who is introspective and has a sense of humor, mentioning Woody Allen. These are qualities that probably piqued the interest of the admissions officers. They like to see students who can take a step back to reflect on their actions and who can laugh about life.

Through the Rosary and Bible, Laura shows her connection to religion and her family. We learn about her family ties to Colombia.

The heart of the essay is the soccer photo. Through the photo, she introduces her background with the sport and how an injury stopped her from playing. But she also reveals that when she did play, she played hard and was good at it. Laura then shares that other activities have filled the void of soccer. What makes this part of the essay work is that she shares her feelings in an unguarded and honest way.

The flow of Laura's writing is just right. She covers many aspects of herself and highlights her values by providing enough detail in her description of each item that it emphasizes its meaning.

Through this essay, the admissions officers learned a lot about Laura—that she has made many transitions throughout her life, she is sentimental about her past, she is introspective, she has strong connections to her family and religion, and she is a person who commits herself with passion. As you are writing your essay, keep in mind that you have a similar goal—to reveal something about yourself or your values to the admissions officers. They want to know what makes you the person who you are.

WHY OUR COLLEGE

"Exploring Life's Intricacies"

Mathew Griffin
Brown University

BECAUSE I FIND LIFE'S INTRICACY SO amazing, biology and its related subjects are the most enjoyable topics for me. Within biology our brains interest me the most, which—with their countless neurons and chemicals—give us unmatched emotion, uniqueness, and potential. Due to the possibilities of understanding emotions and mental problems from their source, I'd like to develop a great understanding of neuroscience, and use it to help people overcome diseases and mental barriers as a doctor, allowing them to achieve the highest possible quality of life.

Brown University would also give me the greatest ability to help people. With their deep community involvement and famous neuroscience department, I would have an outstanding opportunity to help people as I develop the utmost understanding of neurology. The open curriculum will also bring me more benefits. The ability to study multiple languages and social sciences will help me interact and exchange ideas with fewer limits. Moreover, the curriculum will allow me to become an outstanding scientist. The way in which this could help me scientifically is best summarized in the words of my biology professor at Kent State University: "One of our major inhibiting factors in addressing more complicated issues of science is that scientists need to have a sweeping grasp of multiple disciplines such as psychology, biology, convention physics, and quantum physics. And if that wasn't bad enough, you're going to need amazing writing skills to convey your ideas to other people and seem credible." I don't necessarily expect to achieve full mastery in the four or five years I spend as an undergraduate, but I believe Brown is where I'll have the best opportunity to advance in these areas. To expand even more, the open curriculum would allow me to surround myself with individuals that are just as passionate about languages and sciences as I am. With these classmates I would love to have great conversations and even participate in research. Attending Brown University will bring me all of these things, which will aid me in becoming the best doctor and scientist I can possibly be.

ANALYSIS

Mathew's short essay directly addresses the proposed question in a way that provides plenty of supporting evidence without extraneous details. The opening paragraph shows Mathew's curiosity and knowledge about neuroscience. He describes his higher goal for studying neuroscience: "to help people overcome diseases and mental barriers as a doctor, allowing them to achieve the highest possible quality of life." This sentence shows that Mathew is not only interested in acquiring knowledge, but applying it as well.

The second paragraph begins with the comment, "Brown University would also give me the greatest ability to help people." It is not clear what the "also" refers to in this sentence; a better transition sentence might have provided a tighter logical structure. However, the subsequent sentence does an excellent job of conveying a specific reason and explanation for choosing Brown. "With their deep community involvement and famous neuroscience department, I would have an outstanding opportunity to help people as I develop the utmost understanding of neurology." To demonstrate greater familiarity with the program, Mathew might have included names of particular faculty from whom he was interested to learn, or aspects of the famous department. Since most Ivy Leagues are high profile, it is usually a good idea to cite more than just fame in explaining one's reasons for applying to a school. Mathew's description of the "open curriculum" is an excellent example of a more specific aspect of Brown University. Being able to use the university's terminology demonstrates a level of familiarity with the school that admissions officers are likely to appreciate.

Mathew quotes his biology professor at Kent State University in support of the benefits of the interdisciplinary opportunities that Brown's open curriculum offers. This quote is one of the most compelling aspects of Mathew's essay. Not only does the quote convey a strong opinion, but it also tells us that Mathew is a precocious high school student who is already attending classes at the university level, and that he has listened carefully to his professor, whose words have served a mentoring role. Mathew might have chosen to explain his relationship to this professor in greater depth—especially if he knew the professor on a personal level—since this would also demonstrate that he listens during lectures and also takes the initiative to meet his teachers.

Mathew's hope that the open curriculum would allow him to surround himself with "individuals that are just as passionate about languages and sciences as [he is]" clearly highlights two aspects of the open curriculum he is particularly interested in: languages and science. Though his enthusiasm for science is evident from his opening paragraph, he might elaborate on why languages interest him. In general, it is best not to introduce major interests or themes at the end of essays, since this may leave readers with lingering questions and a sense of dissatisfaction that these were not answered.

"Leveraging Potential"

Cameron McConkey
Cornell University

THE FAMOUS GREEK MATHEMATICIAN ARCHIMEDES ONCE said, "Give me a lever long enough and a fulcrum on which to place it, and I shall move the world." The basic principle of a lever is that as the length of a lever increases, the effort needed to be exerted to accomplish a task decreases. This fundamental law can also apply to life. Life's levers are experiences and opportunities that combine to motivate the individual to succeed. However, a lever is useless when forced upon an incorrectly placed fulcrum. Fulfilling oneself with passion and values is to build and place a strong and stable fulcrum. Without a passion for success, these opportunities and experiences become obsolete. Few find the correct balance between these variables and thus fail to reach their full potential. I, however, plan to be someone who finds that balance.

In an effort to build a successful lever for myself, I have searched for these experiences and opportunities all of my life. I have always had a passion for learning and a natural drive to succeed. At the beginning of my sophomore year in high school, I began to volunteer at a local, family owned zoo. This idea came from an innate passion for animals and an ongoing interest in science. At first, it was simply to complete a community service graduation requirement, but soon thereafter, I realized it was so much more. Work there was not like what most zoo volunteers experience. When other volunteers were following zookeepers and watching animals through cages at larger commercial zoos, I was spending nights "monkeysitting" my supervisor's newborn Japanese snow macaque. However, calling it work solely alludes to labor. It was more of a life-altering, unique opportunity and provided me with the experience that clenched my decision to major in animal science.

Along with my passion for animals, I am also always looking for ways to challenge myself intellectually. I am an active member of my school's Envirothon and Math teams and a Science Olympiad competitor. After high school, it has always been a goal of mine to attend an academically competitive university. A few years of researching brought me to Cornell's College of Agriculture and Life Sciences (CALS). After attending the CALS open house and information lecture on the animal science department, I knew it was the perfect fit. One of the reoccurring themes of my conversations with students and professors alike was CALS dedication to shaping students into leaders.

With the experience I have gained in working at the zoo, I see myself emerging as a natural leader. Leaders are those few who do manage to balance the use of their "lever and fulcrum." In high school, I also have worked my way to positions such as; NHS President, Steel Drums Ensemble President, and Student Representative to the School Board. Leadership roles like these are not something I plan to make the past after high school. In a school like CALS that has so many extracurricular activities to get involved in, I am sure obtaining positions similar to the ones I hold now would not be difficult. One of the clubs that I have seriously explored is the Pre-Vet Society. Veterinary School is something that I plan to pursue after college and hope to get involved in at the undergraduate level.

The building of a successful lever has only just begun for me. There is still so much that I have not seen or done. Life is full of opportunities that can lead to great experiences, one of my greatest being volunteering at the Woodland Zoo. With all of the opportunities CALS has to offer, if given the chance to attend, I am certain that I would utilize every one; becoming not only an active member of the university, but a leader of tomorrow.

ANALYSIS

Cameron's essay revolves around the theme of a lever and fulcrum, which he references numerous times in order to demonstrate the balance that he strives to find in building a successful life. He introduces the lever and fulcrum with a memorable quote by Archimedes and then goes on to explain it in his own words. When using quotes from famous people in an essay, it is best to explicate the quote using one's own words, or explain why this quote is personally meaningful. Cameron does an excellent job of clearly explaining how the lever and fulcrum provide a metaphor for his life: "Fulfilling oneself with passion and values is to build and place a strong and stable fulcrum."

This metaphor makes for a clear life vision, which Cameron captures in his statement, "In an effort to build a successful lever for myself, I have searched for these experiences and opportunities all of my life." He then describes a number of these experiences and opportunities. The transition between the fulcrum/lever metaphor to the second paragraph in which he describes his experiences volunteering at a local zoo may seem a bit abrupt. Even so, Cameron's description of the zoo and his "monkeysitting" story are unusual and memorable, and they show us that Cameron is passionate about animal science.

The third paragraph begins to list numerous experiences in which Cameron has participated. This is appropriate for a resume or CV; but in essays, it is best not to list activities unless they are crucial to illustrating a bigger point. Compared to bullet-point lists, it is much harder in the essay narrative to remember activities when they lack the tie to a story line. In Cameron's essay, the Japanese snow macaque is more memorable than the list of accomplishments such as "NHS President, Steel Drums Ensemble President, and Student Representative to the School Board" because it is presented in a story-like way so that you can almost visualize Cameron as he "monkeysits" for his boss.

One theme that appears throughout Cameron's activities is his dedication to science; however, he unexpectedly emphasizes the leadership aspect of these experiences. The penultimate paragraph lists examples of Cameron's leadership experience, where again, highlighting a single activity might have been more effective. As a tie-in, Cameron refers back to his original metaphor in noting, "Leaders are those few who do manage to balance the use of their 'lever and fulcrum'." He skillfully weaves in his experience at CALS, which shows Cornell University specifically why he has chosen their university.

The last paragraph in particular brings together the lever metaphor, the zoo experience, and Cameron's experience at CALS to show his commitment to Cornell. Cameron's essay could have been strengthened by using the lever/fulcrum metaphor less and introducing leadership earlier on. Though it may be tempting to save big revelations for the end of an essay, often mentioning or at least alluding to these points will help readers frame your topic. One challenge for short essays is to fight the temptation to write everything you can about yourself. As Lauren notes in her essay (Chapter 17), we can hardly fit ourselves into one measly page! It is more effective to highlight specific aspects of your life.

"Inspiration from an Energy Conversion Machine"

Anonymous
Caltech

EVERYONE KNOWS THAT IT TAKES BOTH hard work and a good understanding of the subject in order to complete a project. However, I never appreciated the other academic strengths and personal qualities needed until my 11th grade physics final. The task was to create an energy conversion machine that would undergo a minimum of five energy conversions. The construction of the machine piqued my interest in pursuing an engineering career and later became the pivotal factor in my decision to apply to Caltech.

I knew from the beginning that it would be a challenge to complete just the minimum requirements for the project. Believing that my teammates and I had the ability and potential to do better, as the team leader, I made it our goal to cover the conversions of all eight energy types that were taught in class. I also strived to add into the machine a bonus feature of breaking an egg. Struggling to find a solution for breaking the egg, I reflected upon the force of gravity we had learned. This idea led to a trap-door mechanism that would allow the egg to fall under gravity and break upon impact.

In addition to excelling in math and the sciences, I am also a strong visual art student. Enjoying drawing and designing, I gained a different perspective that I may not have had as just a science student. The creativity and imagination from the visual arts allowed me to use toilet paper rolls, Styrofoam, and Popsicle sticks as the primary materials to construct the machine in a limited space within limited time. Together with good planning, coordination, and the ability to work in a team, my innovative perspective from visual arts made this project a success.

On the due date, I watched with a prideful glee as the machine operated smoothly. For going beyond the minimum requirements, the machine was very well received. Beyond earning an excellent grade, the challenge of completing this project intrigued my increasing interest in engineering. My expectations and goals as a future college student were also evolved during the process.

Certain that I wanted to become a professional in the engineering field, I began searching for a college that would provide me with an excellent academic and hands-on experience. While I knew that Caltech is a prestigious science and engineering school, it wasn't until I received the Caltech Signature Award that I developed a stronger interest in becoming a Techer. Upon further research, I realized that Caltech is the college for me.

At Caltech, my engineering aspirations will be realized in this challenging, research-integrated environment. The rigorous coursework and the generous research opportunities at Caltech will provide the challenge I need to achieve my goal of becoming an engineer. In return, I believe the combination of my academic strength and creative personal characteristics will definitely contribute to Caltech and help to add to the interdisciplinary atmosphere of the school.

It takes more than just hard work to succeed as an engineering professional. However, it can be achieved with the outstanding educational opportunity at Caltech and with my other academic strengths and personal qualities.

ANALYSIS

When writing an essay about why a college is a fit for any given student, it's tempting to just regurgitate the information found on the college's website, discussed in its catalog or heard during a campus tour. A greater challenge is to address specific reasons that the college is a fit for you, and what many students omit—*why* you are a fit for the college. This student's essay succeeds on both fronts.

She begins by explaining her academic and professional interest in engineering with a clear, concrete example. An example or anecdote is always welcome to readers because it is stronger to show than it is to tell. In this case, the student's actions strongly support her desire to become an engineer. This story demonstrates that the writer is the type of person who goes above and beyond, not just meeting the minimum requirements, but far exceeding them. The admissions officers could tell that this student does not merely do her class assignments to get a grade, but that she actually enjoys the process of learning and then applying that knowledge to real life. Genuine academic pursuit is one of the key factors that admissions officers want to see in applications. They want to see that you are not just studying because you have to or because your parents tell you to, but that you actually enjoy exploring an academic field.

This student also showcases a unique talent that many other applicants to the university probably don't possess—an artistic ability. Admissions officers are always seeking students who have an out-of-the-ordinary trait or skill to enhance the entering class. They could easily envision how her artistic eye could help her develop creative solutions that other engineering students without her talent might not see.

This writer makes a connection between the project and her interest in engineering, which eventually leads to her desire to attend Caltech. This evolution makes sense, and the admissions officers can easily see how her academic interest led to her professional interest in engineering and her ultimate interest in Caltech. She also manages to mention that she received the Caltech Signature Award—an award from the Caltech alumni association—for her science performance as a high school junior.

Overall, she addresses two critical questions: 1) what she will gain from Caltech and 2) what Caltech will gain from her attendance there. She does so in a way that also highlights her academic passion, visual arts talent, and even leadership. The essay is very specific about her inspiration and individual reasons for wanting to attend Caltech.

WAIT LIST LETTER

Pen-Yuan Hsing
Duke University

This is not an application essay, but it is a letter that Pen-Yuan wrote after being placed on the wait list. Pen-Yuan tried to address topics not covered in the Common Application and was ultimately accepted to Duke.

Mr. _____, Dean
Duke University Office of Undergraduate Admissions
2138 Campus Drive Box 90586
Durham, NC, USA 27708-0586

Dear Mr. _____,

Boy! Was I disappointed to receive your letter! However, I do welcome the chance to explain more clearly my values, passions and reasons why I think Duke is my first choice.

My application and recommendation letters stated my scientific accomplishments. The passive thermoacoustic cooling device we presented at the Intel International Science and Engineering Fair (Intel

177

ISEF) won the Best of Team Category and First Award, among numerous other special prizes. We patented this device and are working with Taiwan's Compal Corporation, your computer could very well be using parts built by them, to iron out a few more problems and to eventually share this revolutionary product with the world. Now I would like to talk about more about just who Pen-Yuan Hsing is.

My education started in the US when I was 7. Having come from Taiwan, faced with enormous cultural and language barriers, I had to learn to adapt. Overcoming loneliness and self-conflict, I made lifelong friends and English became in many ways my mother tongue. Returning to Taiwan in fourth grade mirrored this difficult transition. Some may find me quiet and reserved, it's because I learned to listen, and understand. Yet when the time comes, I do take the initiative and let my voice be heard, as my friends, teachers and parents can so often attest.

Years later, I was unanimously elected as the head of Taipei WetNet, a student-run organization that promotes environmental education and awareness. We hold seasonal conferences on environmental matters for students from all over northern Taiwan to participate. One story really struck a chord in me.

For many years the Waimushan coastline was littered with thousands of plastic beads used in the fabrication of plastic products. Wildlife there mistook the beads as food and stuffed themselves to death. One can see many half-decomposed animals filled with plastic beads in their bodies. Our organization filed a report to local authorities requesting an investigation. The mayor learned of this and bought truckloads of sand to cover up the beach. This successful "cleanup" of the coast got him re-elected a second term in office. Two months later, the extra layer of sand was washed away by tides, re-exposing the plastic beads and animals started dying again. We weren't willing to settle for that. People do not realize that *whatever harm we do to the environment is ultimately done on ourselves.* This is what Taipei WetNet tries to convey in all of our activities. We started as just a few friends taking an excursion to the beach, but now Taipei WetNet has impact on the national level. We had meetings on environmental policy and education with officials from the presidential level. I am grateful to have been the head of Taipei WetNet during this extraordinary time. Of course, *all my accomplishments, science projects and environmental activities, do have their share of difficulties and setbacks. It is through them that I learned the most.*

For a student to do these things in Taiwan's test-score-oriented culture is considered a highly risky venture. My science project didn't win for several years in a row; I was warned to either stick to the traditional path of cramming and testing, or "face the consequences." Under tremendous social pressure, I persisted, having faith that the skills I gained are more important. I like the apprehension of waiting for data to collect and the eventual thrill of seeing things finally turn out right, especially an experiment you labored on for countless nights. I like the satisfaction that what you are doing is making a difference in the world, such as the life changing experience of participating in Taipei WetNet's activities. Last year, my work was finally recognized in the world's largest scientific gathering, the Intel ISEF. They even named a celestial object after me, the "minor planet" *Hsingpenyuan*, with others like *Einstein* and *Cleopatra*. While gratifying, this experience only made me more humble and dedicated. The average lifespan of a Taiwanese male is around 70 years. Almost through one-third of it, *I do not want to waste the rest trying to be someone else*. This is why my first choice is Duke.

What first caught my eye was the Focus Program, with its interdisciplinary education and service learning opportunities. In fact, the first paper I co-authored and presented was about Taipei WetNet's experience in environmental service learning. A course in Duke's special Research Service-Learning program will definitely be one I plan to take. I am also very interested in Duke's environmental science major. In many schools, it would be great if it even has a minor in environmental science or policy. In that case, they often lack actual hands-on training and accumulation of field experience. However, the Nicholas School's course and curriculum not only offers a solid education in basic science, it also provides ample opportunity for field study through unique facilities such as the Marine Lab and the Duke Forest. This is exactly what I think how we should learn about the environment, by actually doing something and seeing change. With Duke's unique opportunities, I can continue to do research starting from my first year. (Also worth mentioning is the mild weather, definitely a plus for a Taiwanese student like me!)

I look forward to becoming a Blue Devils fan, and perhaps even get a Kville experience. I also love reading science fiction and playing the piano. One great story I read was *The Days Between* by Allen Steele, it's about a man who suddenly woke up alone on a spacecraft that is still 200 years from its destination. Steele's vivid description of how the character coped with loneliness and his determination to survive resonated within me. This also happens when I listen to Chopin. I try to rush home before 10 each night, the unofficial time limit for playing music in our apartment, to play the piano. Chopin's music, torn with great strife and conflict, yet with a romantically optimistic touch, is something I could relate to, that I can share my feelings with. I would love to take a Piano Course if I may come to Duke.

My unique qualities and experiences, so diverse yet intrinsically intertwined, allowed me to become the first Taiwanese student ever to receive the Ministry of Education's full scholarship award to study abroad. With full backing of this scholarship, I strongly believe that armed with a strong Duke education, I will be able to make a difference in the world.

Finally, I would like to express my deepest thanks for all the time and effort you have placed in the application process. My mother is a professor at the National Taiwan University who is agonizing right now over their undergraduate applications. This, along with my own background and experience helped me understand how difficult it must be to make an admission decision, as it has the potential to change the future of the world.

Sincerely yours,
Pen-Yuan Hsing

cc: Ms. _____
Coordinator of International Admissions

21

ADVICE ON TOPICS FROM IVY LEAGUE STUDENTS

A Risky Approach That Worked

"My Stanford admissions essay topic asked me to write about an experience when I had to take a risk. I wrote about my very first time in a long time eating peanuts even though I was very allergic. For a long time, my allergy to peanuts controlled my life as I had to live in perpetual fear of it whenever I went out to eat. I wrote about how I finally took a stand against it one day during a big family dinner since I did not want to make a big fuss and ruin the mood. So I didn't care if the Kung Pao Chicken had peanuts. We ordered it, and I ate it anyways. Apparently, I was still quite allergic to peanuts, but I'm glad I did it just to see if all that avoidance was warranted."

"Thinking back about my essay, I realize I took a risk on how I wrote that essay. I personified peanuts as a real living enemy that I despised. I started off my essay with the line: "I looked at the peanut and the peanut looked back at me." It was a little quirky, and I tried to inject as much humor as I could into it."

—*Dan Tran, Stanford University*

An Education Inside and Outside of the Classroom

"I wrote about two topics: the first was about my experience as part of a delegation that traveled to Tahiti and Easter Island, and the second was about my boarding experience in high school. I selected the former topic because the education I received as a delegation member (history and cultural lessons, singing and dance classes, etc.) and the cultural exchanges that took place on the trip opened my mind about my Polynesian ancestry even further than the run-of-the-mill history and performing arts classes at school. I wrote about the latter topic because the dorm was my home in high school and had a special place in my heart."

—*Anonymous, Yale University*

Showing a Personal Connection with the University

"I remember distinctly the topic for Stanford, which was pretty open and flexible. It was to send in a picture and write about its significance for you. I sent in a picture of my sister and her son. She had gone through Stanford while raising a kid. I picked this because it related to Stanford, but also because I was able to talk about how I want to get the chance to experience Stanford in a different way...a way my sister was never able to."

—*Selina Cardoza, Stanford University*

The Mother-Daughter Bond

"I wrote about the topic, 'A picture is worth a thousand words. Select a picture or photo of your choice, and elaborate on its significance to you.' Ultimately, it worked because I had something to say—I chose a photo of my mother and me; just before applying to college, my mom had survived cancer treatment. Her strength during this time showed me just how amazing she was and how strong our mother-daughter bond was."

—*Jessica S. Yu, Stanford University*

Exemplifying a Different Kind of Diversity

"I wrote a bunch and got help from my favorite English professor who helped tell me which ones were complete garbage and which ones made me look like an all-star.

"I chose ones that either identified me as a really unique individual or instances in which I learned a life lesson in a rather unconventional way. The key is making yourself stand out. For the former I wrote about the fact that I come from a diverse background but that it is more interesting than the normal diversity. I'm half black half white and I wrote about the fact that my Italian parent took over making the corn bread while my African-American parent took over making the pizza and what it was like to grow up in a surprisingly diverse neighborhood.

"For the latter I chose to write about the fact that I did NOT read *Great Expectations* for freshman year English even though it was required. In the end

I came to regret this decision because I SparkNoted it, and it sounded really awesome by chapter 24. I made an oath to myself after that to read every assigned book no matter what kind of hard work it took, even if the other kids were getting better grades than me by reading synopses."

—*Colin Adamo, Yale University*

My Family and Heritage

"Since I applied to numerous colleges, several of which had different applications, I had to write a lot of different admissions essays. My favorite one, (the one I think of when someone asks me about my personal statement), was written about my family and my heritage. I have always been proud of my heritage and grew up with a very supportive family which influenced me a great deal through my childhood. I had been told that it was ideal to write about something you are passionate about and that is important to you, and as my love for my own culture had always given me a great appreciation for all other cultures and had opened my eyes to the world in a different way, I felt that it was the perfect topic. I used the concrete idea of a Lebanese game I learned as a child from my cousins to show how my heritage impacted me."

—*Maya Ayoub, Harvard University*

A Confession about Anime

"I chose to write about an unusual interest, my attendance at anime conventions and my love for all things Japanese animation-related. I approached it from an entirely humorous perspective, as a confession/testimonial about my 'addiction.' I have a lot of personality, and I like to write a little more informally in order to showcase that, which is why I picked that topic. Also, our prompt included submitting a picture, and I had a photo of me in costume that fit just perfectly with the scenario. It really just came to me; I am very grateful to my subconscious for working with me on that one."

—*Magali Ferare, Stanford University*

Highlighting an Activity

"For my main admissions essay for Penn, I wrote about my experience at the International Space Settlement finalist competition after my junior year. The reason I chose this was because it was something that I could tell in an interesting story format, and it wasn't something that many people could say. Also it was my main activity outside of school curriculum."

—*Mark Su, University of Pennsylvania*

Inspiration at All Times of the Day and Night

"My essay was for the 'free theme' section of the common application. As a child, I never did like to be told what to write, and I didn't like even further to be told to write something that would 'sell' myself like a commodity to the reader. I imagined myself in the reader's shoes: does he or she really want to read a chronological tale of every award I have won since kindergarten no matter how cleverly disguised the tale is in the shape of an essay? If I was the college admissions officer, I would run away screaming after the fifth such essay.

"There was no constraint on the topic or style for the free essay, as long as I kept under 500 words. I found the freedom invigorating but at the same time a little scary. It was like being handed the wreckage of a typhoon and being told, 'Here, sort this out.' There were so many phrases, images, and ideas floating around that it felt like trying to catch water.

"The essay was written in four or five different installments. The theme was beauty, in my eyes. I always had a habit of collecting pictures and phrases I find particularly beautiful or inspiring in my journal. Using those as a basis, I carried my essay around in a notebook. Whenever I had time, felt particularly happy, or just when inspiration hit, I sat down and scribbled something. I really wrote my essay in some bizarre places! I wrote while stargazing at the beach; I wrote at 3 a.m. after a school dance (late nights are very good for creative writing!); I wrote in AP Physics class; I even wrote after coming home from a drag race.

"I don't feel, by any means, that because of my method, I wrote the most convincing or self-flattering essay ever. Even now, I don't know if my essays were the reason I got into Wharton or the reason I DIDN'T get into MIT (dream school), but I know for sure, that my essays represented me (as I was then), as honestly as a mirror."

—Susan Sun, University of Pennsylvania

Tying an Event from the Past to the Present

"My essay was about a presentation I helped to give to the Cerritos City Council about a book that my elementary school had written about the city. I chose this event because I felt that it showcased all the qualities that I was proud of—my flexibility, my ability to communicate well with others, my ease at public speaking, and my ability to work well on a team. I was able to weave these qualities into my telling of this story very well. My one concern was that the event took place too long before that time--so I was careful to emphasize the importance that this event had in the shaping of these qualities in me, and I also emphasized the fact that these qualities are still present and an important part of my life."

—Michael Ayoub, Harvard University

Passion for Design

"For my admissions essay topic, I chose one aspect that I was extremely passionate about—design. Starting in high school I began to gain an interest in design—interior, architectural, etc. My admissions essay was about the process I went through in designing my own bedroom at home. The reason I chose this as a topic was because I knew I would be able to write about it fairly easy. It represents a concrete experience and manifestation of my passion for design, so I knew I would be able to reveal who I was, who I wanted to be, in that essay."

—*Fareez Giga, Stanford University*

Balancing Activities and Responsibilities

"My essay topic was the way I balanced being on the basketball team with my responsibilities to my family at home. As my father was constantly gone working and my brother left home, I was the 'man of the house' so to speak. The topic developed after I wrote and scrapped several essays."

—*Robert Lee, Columbia University*

Starting the School's Newspaper

"My essay focused on starting my high school's newspaper. I spoke of my family publishing business and my summer internships in the media industry and how those led me to start this newspaper. I discussed the challenges associated with starting the newspaper, the actions/steps that I took and the sacrifices that I made... and I related a lot of the situations back to growing up in a publishing family."

—*Zachary Richner, Harvard University*

Zachary Richner is on the management team of Carter Admissions (www. carteradmissions.com), a college admissions mentoring and essay editing service.

International Travel

"Penn had an option asking to describe a time when you had a new experience. I couldn't deal with the open-endedness so I decided to choose something. I wrote about going to India my sophomore year and meeting my great uncle. His children were wealthy but he still chose to live on a farm. I wrote about being able to understand it. It was the first time I had visited the country in 10 years. India had changed a lot over those 10 years from the early '90s to early 2000s. In Bangalore the IT industry blossomed and bloomed, and it became overpopulated."

—*Ravi Patna, University of Pennsylvania*

Showing Creativity with a Photo

"The topic I chose was to attach a picture to the application and to write about that picture. I chose that topic because I was looking for something that would allow me to be creative and original. I think it's so important to write an essay that no other student possibly could have written. I didn't want to feel stuck giving a 'cookie-cutter' answer, and I wanted to let my silly side show, to complement my very serious academic/extracurricular record. I chose a picture of myself and a group of friends in shorts next to a 10-foot tall snowman we had built. I wrote about the experience of swimming in the ice-cold ocean in Maine in December. It was definitely not your typical essay, but I think it rounded out the rest of my application well."

—*Lauren Horton, Stanford University*

Writing about My Heritage

"I wrote about my heritage as a Korean American because it spoke about who I was, who I am and who I want to become. It came naturally to me because it was something that had been a recurring theme in my life."

—*Anonymous, Yale University*

Showcasing Leadership and Community Service

"When I was applying for Caltech, there were two long essays. One of the prompts was on how you discovered Caltech, the reasons why you decided to apply, and what you would contribute to the school. The second prompt gave a choice of writing on an event that changed your life or on an activity outside of math and science that is meaningful to you. The prompts have changed, and Caltech now uses the Common Application.

"In general, there were two topics that I decided to use for my personal statements. One was on a team project for a physics class, and the other was on playing the piano at a senior home. So for Caltech, I decided to use the team project as the topic for the first prompt and piano playing for the second prompt. I used the team project to exhibit skills such as leadership and creativity. I also weaved into the essay about how my interest in engineering developed from the project, leading me to search and find Caltech. For the second prompt, I incorporated playing the piano and volunteer work, combining passion with giving back to the community."

—*Anonymous, Caltech*

Describing Personal Items and Their Signficance

"I was given three essay choices in my admissions application. Although I do not recall the actual text of the question, it basically asked me to name and describe a couple of personal items and how they related to my life. I ended up choosing this question because I felt that it gave me the most creative flexibility in trying to get my story across. I also chose it because as I was brainstorming all three questions, it was the only question in which most of my ideas seemed to flow together seamlessly."

—*Laura V. Mesa, Stanford University*

Passions for a Musical Instrument and Language Study

"Two key themes that I chose for my admissions essay topics were: my interest in the tabla, a North Indian percussion drum and my interest in learning languages and specifically taking a Korean language class offered in my high school. I chose these because they conveyed my desire to really develop the few activities that I was MOST passionate about. A concern of mine is that students feel that they have to do anything and everything offered within their school and community in order to get into a top college, and I often found myself falling into this trap in high school. I wanted to convey in my college applications, that I would only dedicate time and energy to the activities that I was MOST passionate about, and this passion radiated through the right mix of sensory details and analysis of the emotional ties to the activities that I was engaging in."

—*Shreyans C. Parekh, University of Pennsylvania*

Presenting a Brand as an Entrepreneur

"I wrote a Common Application essay that prompted me to 'Evaluate a significant experience, achievement, risk you have taken or ethical dilemma you have faced and its impact on you.' I chose to focus on a risk that I had taken for my essay because in my application I wanted to portray myself as a risk taking, self-starting entrepreneur. I framed my family's move to Florida in the middle of my high school years as a personal risk; generally 'My family moved.' is not interesting enough, so I had to spice it up a little bit.

"For my Harvard-specific supplemental essay, I described an 'academic experience (course, project, paper or research topic) that has meant the most to [me].' instead of 'unusual circumstances, a list of books I have read recently or travel experiences in another country.' Again, trying to craft myself as unique from the other 20,000 applicants and create a personal brand, I wanted to do something that would make me look like a daring businessman. That was risky because Harvard and academia are not pro-business from my understanding and I would be pursuing a liberal arts degree. However, I knew this set me apart and I could make a compelling case. I described a summer program that taught entrepreneurship after 11th grade, which transformed my personality and career interests."

—*Jason Y. Shah, Harvard University*

Conveying Intellectual Curiosities

"The process of selecting an appropriate admissions essay topic was a challenging task and not one that I took lightly. I had to sort through a variety of considerations before deciding on a specific idea or experience. How can I convey my passions, abilities, and reflections in a genuine and humble fashion? How can I possibly weave all of my divergent interests into a smooth, cogent essay? Finding that common thread was the challenge, for I needed an effective vehicle for expressing a complex amalgam of thoughts in less than 750 words.

"Eventually, I settled on the experience that I thought best captured my essential characteristics, my intellectual curiosities, and my fundamental passions. I chose an experience that truly illustrated the ideas I wanted to convey—instead of just telling the reader about the event, I showed them what had happened and drew them into the story. By establishing a relationship with the audience I could make my message more potent and much more compelling."

—*Jonathan Cross, Duke University*

Connecting Jigsaw Puzzles to Medical Research

"I wrote my admissions essay about how I used to do jigsaw puzzles when I was younger as a metaphor for how I look at the world and my interest into going into medical research. I arrived at this by thinking a lot about habits/interests of mine and trying to find something at least slightly distinct and relevant to why I was a strong candidate. I really wanted to highlight my interest in science and the labwork that I had done and basically was looking for some sort of common thread about my personality that I could tie it to. I did a lot of initial brainstorming, outlined a couple ideas that seemed to fit this criteria and ended up going with this. Even though I changed my mind about going into science before I even got here, I think the metaphor still is a pretty good way of describing determination and interest in problem-solving."

—*Anonymous, Harvard University*

A True Reflection

"With all my college essays, I wanted to give the reader a true reflection of myself. I conveyed what lessons really stuck with me throughout high school as well as showcased my activities and personality strengths. Even when I read my essays four years later, I can still say with certainty that my essay is a reflection of me as a senior in high school."

—*Anonymous, Princeton University*

Dealing with a Loss through the Essay

"I chose to write about how the death of one of my closest friends changed my view of the world. I also incorporated how a recent trip to Nigeria reinforced my newly found appreciation for life after my friend's death. I chose this topic initially as an outlet for my pain. While writing this essay I was still dealing with my loss and was able to come to terms with the ordeal after I wrote out my emotions."

—*Nnenna Ene, Duke University*

Not Afraid to Be Cheesy

"My admissions essay topic was...well (as conceited as it sounds) a slightly humorous essay about me, with a play on words. But really the essays are supposed to showcase you in a way that might not show through in the rest of your application materials. It was really over-the-top cheesy, but that was what I was going for. I wanted my essay to stand out as someone who didn't take themselves too seriously since I'm sure they get a million essays about triumphing over adversity or a life changing event. Those topics are fine, but really they just want to know about you as a person, and your essay doesn't have to portray you as someone who will solve world poverty or be the next president. Really you just need to show that you will be an interesting and valuable addition to their network. A teacher asked me a great question when I was brainstorming for my essay: What makes me different from the other thousand people that are applying?"

—Anonymous, Harvard University

A Personal Topic

"I selected a personal topic because I thought it would have the most force and leave the strongest memory possible in the admissions officers' minds. I chose a topic that I thought was unique and very personal to me and am confident that no one could have said what I said in the exact same way—I knew what I was sending would be powerful in its own right."

—Sarah Langberg, Princeton University

Growing into Leadership

"My admissions essay topic was based on my experiences as the leader (drum major) of my high school's award winning marching band. This was the extracurricular activity that I felt was most significant in my personal development, as I evolved from a freshman band prodigy who was both distant and a bit arrogant, to a senior who emerged as an engaged leader and had built lasting friendships with my peers. It explored the fact that although I was always a standout member in high school music programs, I did not until my later years develop an 'emotional stake' in the success of these programs and discussed the event that initiated my shift in attitude."

—Devin Nambiar, Columbia University

Shaking Hands with the President

"When I applied, there were two essays—an optional one and a 500-word one. I wanted to communicate a lot, and having an optional essay was great. For the 500-word essay, the topic was to describe the world you come from. I wrote about being from Egypt, the macro perspective of the current situation in Egypt, my vision for where I wanted Egypt to be and how that it could be accomplished. In the last paragraph, I said that the issues require a lot of problem solving and leadership skills. I couldn't think of a better place than MIT to prepare me for that. I think the end of the essay, the punchline, is very important. That's the last thing the reader is going to see.

"The first line is also very important to attract them, to get them to pay extra attention. The admissions officers read tons of applications each day. If you make them enjoy your essay, it will definitely pay back.

"For the optional essay I wrote about a camp I attended, the Seeds of Peace. The program brings together youth from regions of conflict such as

India, Pakistan, the Middle East and the Balkans. Through the program, I met Israelis for the first time. It was a very moving experience.

"For the first line of the essay, I wrote that I still remembered when I shook hands with the most powerful man in the world. The admissions officers were probably thinking, 'Why is he meeting the President?' They probably wanted to read more. I linked the experience with my grandfather who had a strong role in my development and passed away after a 13 years struggle with cancer. The last paragraph was about learning I had won a scholarship from Egypt that would allow me to apply to top colleges in the U.S. I ended with visiting my grandfather's grave and realizing that he was smiling from up above. It's important to make the essay as personal as possible. Really be yourself."

—Anonymous, MIT

Showing What Makes You Different

"There were four options to choose from and a fifth option to write your own prompt. I chose the first essay option: 'Chicago professor W. J. T. entitled his 2005 book *What Do Pictures Want?* Describe a picture and explore what it wants.' I chose this topic because I thought it was pretty interesting, and I felt this option would allow me to express my creativity the best and perhaps show why I too was uncommon. The other options were also pretty interesting but I chose the one I felt I could write the most about.

"For the personal statement I struggled a lot more to find a topic. My counselor and college advisor always told us to write about what makes us 'different' from all other students. At first I thought that piece of advice was not helpful but looking back on it now, I think it's the best way to start brainstorming. I had to reflect on my high school years and recall the experiences that impacted me the most and contributed to the person who I had become."

—Angelica, University of Chicago

Choosing the Topic that Flows

"I wrote about my volunteer work, reading with children at our local library. I expanded the topic to reflect on my love for working with kids and the traits of children that I admire and hope to embody. This topic matched the requirements of a good topic—it was something I was passionate about and had a firsthand experience with. But ultimately I chose this topic because it was the one that worked the best. I made a list of many different possible topics. I started writing on a couple of them, and ultimately this was the topic that flowed the easiest for me."

—Manika, University of Pennsylvania

A Blank Slate

"I chose the question that allowed me to pick my own topic. I thought this was the best way for me to express my true self, and I thought it was what UChicago was looking for based on their reputation."

—Ashley Mitchell, University of Chicago

Balancing an Out There Topic with a More Conservative One

"I wrote two primary admissions essays because I used the Common Application, and most schools had supplements that asked for another piece of writing. This worked to my advantage because the topic of my 'first pick' essay was a little out there, and I had the chance to give colleges a funky essay as well as a more normal one. I am a quirky person and wanted to reflect that in my admissions essay, so I pretty randomly decided to write an essay comparing my love of bacon to my love of learning. I don't even like bacon, but I certainly wrote about it as though I did it in that essay!"

—Mariam Nassiri, Duke University

Sharing the Kind of Person You Are

"I used the Common Application and selected the third topic, 'Indicate a person who has had a significant influence on you, and describe that influence.' The reasons were: (1) I think one of the best ways to communicate is through stories, (2) I think a very personal essay has great potential to touch people and (3) I happen to have a personal story that is suitable for this purpose.

"Topic 2 about an issue of personal, local, national or international concern is an opportunity for one to express their thinking and make an argument. However, it could be a lot less personal. I believe it is more important to show what kind of person you are, rather than your intelligence. If I were an admissions officer, I would be much more interested in accepting a passionate student that has a lot more to learn, than a smart jerk."

—Pen-Yuan Hsing, Duke University

An Inspirational Teacher

"My Common Application essay and the one that Duke received was about my ninth grade English teacher, a former Black Panther who introduced me to spoken word poetry and socially conscious music. Those two subjects pretty much define who I am, so it was an easy choice."

—Anthony Gouw, Duke University

Analyzing a Character

"Most of the schools to which I applied were on the Common Application, so from the list of possible topics, I chose to create my own. The summer before senior year, I had performed for the first time as a cast member in my school's production of 'Anything Goes' by Cole Porter. I used this eye-opening experience as a starting block for my essay, which turned into an exposure of my own character and emotions."

—Jean Gan, Duke University

Reflecting on Your Upbringing

"I chose to write about my upbringing in a low-income single parent household. When choosing the topic to write about, I thought about what shaped and defined me as a person."

—Jackie Liao, Stanford University

A Love of Languages

"When I began writing my admissions essay, the first thing I asked my-self was: what makes me different from all of the other thousands of people applying to Stanford? Surely, they all had amazing grades and a full load of extracurricular activities, so I needed something that was unique, something that made me stand out in the crowd.

"From a very young age, while still living in my native country of Romania, I had developed an exceptional passion for the Spanish language. I thought it would be pretty rare to find another applicant who had grown up half-way around the world in Eastern Europe speaking one language, fallen in love with another language from watching TV at age four, and immigrated to the U.S. where yet another language was spoken, in a matter of less than nine years. So I decided to write my essay on my love for Spanish and the different hard-ships that I had to endure in order to make sure that Spanish would always be in my life."

—Oana Emilia Butnareanu, Stanford University

Selling Yourself

"For the Common Application essay, I decided to choose the prompt: 'A range of academic interests, personal perspectives, and life experiences adds much to the educational mix. Given your personal background, describe an experience that illustrates what you would bring to the diversity in a college community or an encounter that demonstrated the importance of diversity to you.'

"By choosing this topic, I was able to sell myself to the admissions officers. The main question that people want to know is 'What are you going to con-tribute if we admit you?' This prompt allows the readers to see who you truly are. I really enjoyed this prompt because I was able to write about my personal experiences. One of the easiest things to write about is yourself."

—Enrique Vazquez, University of Chicago

An Informal Education at Home

"For the two admissions essays, I wrote about my gymnastics career and my family. The first essay was about the valuable skills I gained from dedicating 11 years of my life to the sport of competitive gymnastics. I pulled out specific skills (i.e. discipline, time management, team work, etc) and highlighted how I developed those skills from training and competing as a gymnast and then described how I would apply those skills as a student-athlete at Yale."

"My second essay described my family. As the youngest of six children, in addition to having many other friends and family constantly moving in and out of our house, I had a very interesting and stimulating upbringing. My father was the headmaster of a boys' school in Potomac, Maryland and would provide housing to some of the international exchange students who attended his school for as long as they needed (a year, two, ten!). Growing up, I had several semi-big brothers from Bulgaria, Mexico, and Spain and even an African-American boy from inner city Washington, D.C. whom my father took in after befriending his family through his work in Anacostia with Mother Theresa and the Missionaries of Charity. I always thought he was my brother since he lived at our house from the day I was born. This allowed me to be exposed to several different cultures without even leaving my own home!"

"My blood siblings were also a part of my informal education at home. Each of them is extremely bright but in very different ways. I learned through them every day. James, the eldest, was a Classics major at Hopkins who went on to receive his master's at U.T. and is currently pursuing an M.B.A. at Duke. Liz went to the University of Pennsylvania and received a B.S. and master's in nursing, and later an M.B.A from Wharton. Catherine received her B.S. in mechanical engineering at Princeton and J.D. at Suffolk. Joey went to the Coast Guard Academy and received his B.S. in civil engineering, then went to Virginia Tech for a master's in civil engineering and is currently pursuing his M.B.A. at Berkeley. Mary went to the University of Maryland where she received a B.A. and master's in special education."

"Both my parents value education above all else and truly instilled a passion for learning in all of their children. My father (Harvard and Georgetown Law grad) encouraged poetry recitation and constant reading. In addition to my formal education, this informal education I received at home was what really prepared me for Yale and the world beyond!"

—*Anne McPherson, Yale University*

Writing about a Picture

"I answered the question, 'A picture is worth a thousand words, as the adage goes. Include a photograph or picture that represents something important to you, and explain its significance.'"

"I thought this essay question was unique in the sense that the admissions committee wanted to see more than just text. Stanford was the only university that I applied to that asked for something other than an essay."

"I ended up choosing a picture of myself standing in front of a castle in Segovia, Spain, named El Alcazar. I was fortunate enough to win a scholarship trip to Spain through the Spanish Honor Society. My essay topic resulted in a description of how my life changed after the trip, realizing I was a more independent individual. The picture represented my personal exploration of my individuality and how my personality evolves through important events in life. The essay topic essentially chose itself; I found it easy to write about such a huge event in my life."

—*Brian Aguado, Stanford University*

A Business to Help People

"My admissions essay was about a computer repair business that I had started while in high school. While this business was not especially successful by any stretch of the imagination, when I worked on it I really enjoyed it, and I felt it showed how much I wanted to help people. I focused a lot of my application about how I would like to use my knowledge to help people, so it only seemed reasonable I talk about how I have helped people."

—*Mathew Griffin, Brown University*

On Diversity

"I applied using the Common Application. I picked the essay on diversity because I thought that would be the one I would be able to say the most on. I talked about my experience as an Indian American. I thought that would be the most effective thing to write on and would demonstrate what I'd be able to bring to the university community."

—*Aditya Kumar, Brown University*

Leadership

"I selected my own topic for my essay for University of Chicago. My topic was, 'All I know about leadership I learned from...' I was having a lot of trouble expressing myself with the suggestions the university gave so I decided to create my own to highlight my strengths. I had been in student council all four years of high school and have held leadership roles, so I thought this would be perfect to write about. The idea was actually given to me by one of my student council advisors as a joke. But after seeing that leadership could be compared to almost anything, I saw this as a perfect topic to demonstrate my creative ability and my student council experience."

—*Victoria Tomaka, University of Chicago*

A Crime-Scene Report

"I applied with the Common Application, and I chose to write on a topic of my choice. I spent weeks last year trying to come up with a good essay. My junior English teacher told us that we needed to make our essays stand out.

The admissions officers read hundreds of applications every day, and our essays needed to be unique. I wasn't sure how to do this. I wrote one about a car wreck, but my English teacher quickly rejected it as bland and uninteresting (lots of people write about car wrecks apparently). A friend advised me to write my essay about something I enjoy doing. At the time, I was taking a forensics class which fascinated me. So, for my admissions essay, I wrote a crime-scene report in which I am searching for my future self at Duke University."

—Lauren Sanders, Duke University

An Influential Person

"My essay was about my childhood and the difficulties I faced growing up in China with a single mother as well as the profound influence she had in my life. I chose this essay topic because I wanted to write something 'beautiful', something that I really absolutely cared about and could pour my heart into. At first glance, you could say the essay topic is generic because it's simply about an influential person in my life, but I made it mine because I meant every single word I wrote."

—Lisa Kapp, University of Pennsylvania

Bringing Together Multiple Facets of Your Life

"I selected the theme of 'the power of people' as my essay topic, and related two life events and my career aspirations to that theme. First, I related my experience while riding in the MS150 bike ride and explained that I felt a deep connection with the event and the other participants because my father has multiple sclerosis, and their help may help find a cure for it.

"Then, I described the selfless acts of kindness experienced by many people from the Houston-Galveston area during Hurricane Ike, specifically in my own family.

"Finally, I displayed my true belief in the theme by showing the essay reader how my career aspirations (public health) relate to it.

"I chose a semi-broad topic to write about because I knew I could relate many different facets of my life to it and would not feel the need to repeat information in my essay. In addition, I could relay information about my personal beliefs, my family, my background, and my goals all in one concise, two-page paper. It was the easiest way to make all of these aspects of myself cohesive and interesting for the reader."

—Suzanne Arrington, Columbia University

An International Conference

"I wrote about my experience as a youth delegate to the United Nations World Summit on Sustainable Development in Johannesburg, South Africa. My participation in this conference was my most impressive achievement at the time, and the conference happened to fall immediately prior to the start of my senior year of high school. As such, making it my admissions essay topic was a no-brainer."

—*Steve Schwartz, Columbia University*

Showing Initiative through a Foundation

"I talked about a foundation I started when I was in 7th grade. It's called Cuddle Buddies, and we collect new and slightly used stuffed animals for abused and underprivileged children. I chose it because it has been such a large part of my life, and it is something that I have worked hard on for so long. I also felt like it reflected my personality and values."

—*Anastasia Fullerton, Stanford, Brown*

A Love of Music

"I wrote on music, specifically about my experiences in composition. Seeing as music was my primary activity in high school (I was in band and choir for four years, was the lead in the school musical, was a drum major of the marching band, sang in the select vocal ensembles, was in all-state band and choir) and music was what I planned to study in college, it was a fairly easy choice. It was basically about how much I loved music and why it meant so much to me; in retrospect, it was pretty cliché."

—*Samuel Linden, Harvard University*

Family Responsibilities

"My general essay was about the struggles I have in Brooklyn which are a bit out of the ordinary when juxtaposed next to someone across the country. It comically mocked the 'normal' teenage life of working hard and discussed the major role I have as the biggest sister to my ten month old brother, two year old brother, and seven year old sister. I actually had no idea that I would talk about how mature I am and chaotic my life is while juggling the work I have to do with my siblings and the ton of work I have at Brooklyn Tech. My most influential teacher told me I should write about my struggles because she felt it would get at my essence. I did-and managed to keep a down-to-earth comedy that kept my story light hearted yet significantly strong."

—*Anonymous, Cornell University*

The Importance of Motivation

"I actually had six admissions essays for MIT. Most of them were about science since I had to keep in mind the school for which I was applying, which is a very science-oriented school. At the same time though, I did include essays which had nothing to do with science that I thought were unique. Besides talking about what I have accomplished, I also explained why I accomplished it—what my motivation was. Anyone can do things, but what really sets you apart from the crowd is your journey—the steps and reasons for why you do what you do."

—*Ariela Koehler, MIT*

Tying a Tragic Event to Family History

"I chose to write about my older brother's death, while also tying in pieces of my family history. My brother's death changed my life—I had to write about it."

—*Timothy Nguyen Le, Yale University*

From Environmental Issues to Halloween Costumes

"I was really into environmental issues so I wrote about how I came to join different groups and what I liked about them. I also did AP environmental science as an independent study. I just talked about why I liked the environment, what fueled me to work on that area. I remember one essay asked about something I created and I talked about how I always made really intense Halloween costumes. I made a Gumby, a Chiquita banana lady, mermaid, etc. Some essays I talked about being a Mexican American and what it meant to me as a teenager in a Los Angeles public school."

—*Anonymous, MIT*

On Challenges

"I selected the essay that revolved around my life experiences and the challenges I faced because I felt that this question really helped connect me to the admissions officers. They would get to read into my personal life and see how hard I had worked to make it where I was. It would also a way to let them know about me and sell myself, because every challenge was a chance for failure, and maybe I did fail at times, but I managed to work hard and endure. This meant that regardless of the challenge I would face, that Stanford would be the place for me, because no challenge was hard enough that I could not work though, as my life was a time of much challenge so far."

Andres Cantero, Stanford University

Self-Improvement

"The first topic was about a risk you have taken. I wrote about my decision to try out for We the People, a competition civics team. I talked about how even though the program involved a lot of public speaking and I was very shy, I wanted to be on the team to improve my speaking skills.

"The second topic was a free-choice one. I wrote about how I was eating very unhealthily and it was having a bad effect on my complexion (A bit shallow, right? but it gets more than skin-deep. Pun intended). I completely changed my eating habits and discovered that I could achieve something that was extremely difficult (staying on a healthy diet) if I was determined enough.

"Both of my essays have a theme of self-improvement, which was very important to me. I chose these topics for this reason: because they show how I have taken it upon myself to grow in ways outside of academics."

—Anonymous, Yale University

Inspiration from Robert Frost

"My essay was based on my love for the woods that surrounded my home and my experiences within them as a child. For the conclusion of my essay I used the last line of Robert Frost's well known poem 'Stopping by Woods on a Snowy Evening.' I grew up on the New Hampshire border MA, so you can imagine that the area was similar to what Robert Frost was actually writing about!"

—Mollie Mattuchio, Brown University

ADVICE ON WRITING FROM IVY LEAGUE STUDENTS

Communicate Your Personal Voice

"Speak. Do not simply record your thoughts on paper, but use your words as a conduit for expressing yourself. The essay is the only opportunity you have to communicate your personal voice. While the resume and the questionnaire may be unique in the sense that no one has the exact skill set or range of experiences that you have, the language is dry and static. The essay, on the other hand, is a dynamic narrative that has the potential to explicate a personality. Your essay should capture some facet of your character, perhaps through an experience or a philosophy on some issue or event. The presentation of your voice is delivered in a language unique to you.

"Do not assume that your essay should follow some model or structure. Yes, it is important to have structure and a coherent flow (and be grammatically flawless), but never feel that you have to copy another's style to be successful. The essay is a vehicle for your voice—and it should be in your own language. Think of the admissions essay as a live interview with someone hard of hearing. Instead of speaking, you must resort to writing. The degree to which you activate your language, guide the reader along the contours of your narrative, and deliver the raw electricity of your experiences will determine your essay's success."

                    —Jonathan Cross, Duke University

Be Genuine

"Be confident and authentic about yourself; don't try to be someone you're not or try to fashion yourself into someone you think the admissions committee will like. Ultimately the committee is looking to build a class, and you never know if they're looking for someone who is exactly like the genuine you."

                    —Anonymous, Yale University

Not Trying to Be Profound

"I went through many different drafts of my college essay and tried to go in different directions with it. I tried to be introspective and serious in my essay but realized that at the age of 17, I didn't have much to be profound about. I felt my strength was in my humor and wanted that aspect to show. After finding a more genuine voice, writing that essay became much easier and faster.

"When citing something specific like a personality trait or an event that significantly characterizes the student, I think it's important to think hard about how to stand out from the crowd. I don't intend this to mean sensationalize or create a fictional story, but I do think everybody is unique or has something unique in their life to write about."

                    —Dan Tran, Stanford University

Focus on One Aspect

"The essay is your chance to give them a taste of who you are. Select something that will embody you. But don't try to describe all of yourself. That would be hard to do in 500 words. Instead focus on one experience and go in depth, describe it in detail. You are an interesting person just for wanting to apply to these colleges. Your story is worth reading, so tell it!"

                    —Selina Cardoza, Stanford University

Write about What You Want to Write about

"Write candidly, freely, and truly. Don't worry about impressing admissions counselors with the 'perfect' essay. The more you write about the things you want to write about, as opposed to the things you think you should be writing about, the more natural and eloquently it comes out.

                    —Jessica S. Yu, Stanford University

Demonstrate How You're Different

"Why are you different, really different, from all the other kids who are just as qualified? Don't portray yourself so that any other student could fill the same spot you're asking for."

—*Colin Adamo, Yale University*

Start Early

"Start early so you have enough time to brainstorm an idea that will be enjoyable to write about. It's very important to write about something that has either made a big impact on you, that you love, or that shows your personality. That way, it will be less of a chore, and it will really show through if the essay is meaningful to you. Also, (a piece of advice I was given my junior year), if you start early, you can write up the essay early enough to go back and look at it after some time, returning with a fresh new perspective. This will help a great deal. Finally, be fully aware of all the essay topics, due dates, and any important announcements or changes, so that nothing stresses you out at the last minute. The college application process is a stressful chore, so it is best to be organized and have a good attitude from the beginning. Essay writing and editing is a lot of tedious work, but if you give yourself enough time for it, it can be a fun and transformative process as well."

—*Maya Ayoub, Harvard University*

It's Okay to Describe Yourself Like a Crazy Person

"For advice, I really can only say what Stanford, the UC system, and every other school I applied to encouraged me to do. Be yourself. Speak as you are, not as you think you want them to see you. I talked about myself like a crazy person but with a lot of humor and self-awareness. That's my style—I observe, I criticize, and I satirize.

"My friend went a more 'traditional' route and wrote about her time spent working with an after-school children's program, but I doubt it was the content that got her noticed. Her love for the kids and her hopes for helping them in a greater capacity in the future shone through the page. Just be yourself. Write about something that impassions or allows you to express you, and that will translate to any reader.

"Also, don't be afraid to let lots and lots of people look at it. Don't compromise on anything you're set on doing, but listen to constructive criticism."

—*Magali Ferare, Stanford University*

Explaining Why You're Not the Same

"I would say one of the most important things is to identify something that sets you apart from all the other applicants. In the end, at the top schools you are going to get many students who have done similarly extraordinary things, so choose something that tells the admissions officer why you're better, not just the same as, the next guy/girl. Also, it's much easier to write with impact when it is about something that you have a very genuine interest in."

—*Mark Su, University of Pennsylvania*

Write When You're Fed, Warm, and Loquacious

"Write when you are in a good mood. Don't write when it's 11:30 PM, and the essay is due in 30 minutes at 12 midnight. Don't write when you just failed a test. Don't write when you just had a fight with your parents (presumably about why you haven't finished your college applications yet).

"Write when you are feeling fed, warm, and loquacious. Write when a sudden idea makes you go Ooooohhh!! This may mean you have to resort to my dorky method of carrying a notebook around for a week or so (Yes, I know it's weird; I've been told many times it is weird) but it is definitely worth the effort."

—*Susan Sun, University of Pennsylvania*

The Importance of Freewriting

"I think the best piece of advice is to start early. The earlier you start, the more relaxed and satisfied you can be. I'd say start off by free-writing, that's always how I get my best ideas. Start off with a blank sheet of paper (or a blank word document)—then write for five or ten minutes straight, without erasing anything and without ever stopping the flow of words. Once you find a topic, write a draft—then put it aside for a couple days. Only with the perspective of time (which is a luxury you'll want to have, so start early) can you truly edit well."

—*Michael Ayoub, Harvard University*

Think before Writing

"Sit down and think about yourself to figure out what specific qualities you like about yourself, and think of a story (symbolic or real, or both) that really exemplifies or shows those qualities."

—*Robert Lee, Columbia University*

You Don't Need an Extraordinary Story

"Write about something you are passionate about. Do not feel you have to show off your awards... but you shouldn't be modest either. You want the essay's focus to be something that the reader will remember. You want the reader to label you (e.g. 'the girl who likes to bake chocolate cookies' or 'the gymnast who won an Olympic medal') so that s/he can remember you throughout the process. Remember that everyday events can be—and often are—best to write about... it is not necessary to have an 'extraordinary story' to tell... you are aiming for the reader to get a sense of your personality and of what drives you."

—*Zachary Richner, Harvard University*

Remember That Your Readers Are Adults

"I remember sitting on my bed, I didn't know what they wanted me to do. Did they want me to encapsulate my life? At 15 you haven't had much of a life. What I ended up doing is taking the Penn prompt to answer the open-ended prompt. If you're faced with an open-ended prompt, find a prompt that you have relevant experience with. Make the essay entertaining with a nice story. If you have an essay already written, you can spin the conclusion, manipulating the essay to answer the prompt.

"My high school, Whitney High School, helped a lot. They had a two-week writing workshop. It made me get started early. By having to start in July or August, you're constantly thinking about the essay. It only gets better as you get closer to the deadline.

"Not everyone has that resource, but you can get started early and have many people read your essay. You want it to have wide appeal because you don't know who will ultimately read it. You never want to sound so serious that an adult would laugh at your writing. An admissions officer has to read 1,000 essays, and he doesn't want to be bogged down with a very serious piece. Put yourself in the place of the reader."

—*Ravi Patna, University of Pennsylvania*

Showcase What's Not Elsewhere in the Application

"I really think the most important thing is to let yourself shine through... and especially the parts of yourself that aren't listed anywhere else in the application. Be creative and make sure to tell a story. I knew that what was really missing from my application was my sense of fun and adventure, and my willingness to try just about anything. I think my essay captured that, and I hope that it caught the attention of the admissions officers!"

—*Lauren Horton, Stanford University*

Tell a Story

"Tell a story, and tell it well. I believe that telling a story is the most direct way of sharing a piece of yourself with someone else. I believe, however, that the story should also be able to express growth over time rather than a moment of self-realization (ex. climbing a mountain)."

—*Anonymous, Yale University*

Focus on Your Fit with the School

"Keep in mind the purpose of your essays! Sometimes people forget the purpose of the essay is to demonstrate how they are compatible with a school; instead, they just write a story that fits the prompt. However, admissions committees read hundreds of essays. They don't have time to sit and guess what you're trying to tell them. As a result, keep flowering unnecessary story details to the minimum. You want enough details to make your essays vivid and interesting, but you're not trying to write a novel.

"Furthermore, you are trying to convince the admissions committee why you would fit in with the school. Something I found useful was to look up the mission statements of schools and demonstrate how I would fit in. For Caltech, they have a big emphasis on integrating research and education, an interdisciplinary atmosphere, and helping students develop into creative members of society. As a result, I tried to incorporate those details into my essays.

"Finally, please make sure you don't submit essays about why you want to attend MIT! My roommate is part of the undergraduate team on the admissions committee, and she tells me that unfortunately, there are a number of applications with MIT in the essays. Obviously, the admissions committee doesn't smile upon that—it's one of the reasons why you should really put an effort to making the essays for each school unique. Just as you want to stand out to the admissions committees through your essays, the admissions committees want to see how their schools stand out to you and why you should belong there."

—*Anonymous, Caltech*

Target One Idea

"At least when it comes to writing admissions essays, try to focus on one idea. This type of essay is difficult to write because it can feel like you're trying to squeeze your entire life into a few paragraphs—which generally results in too many underdeveloped ideas that all fail to do you justice. Pick one idea and stick to it. Doing so will give you the flexibility to be creative and will help you feel as though you are in control of your writing."

—*Laura V. Mesa, Stanford University*

Get Feedback from Current College Students

"First, reach out to as many high school alumni and friends who are attending the colleges that you are applying to and ask them if they would be willing to spend some time to critique and offer feedback for your essays. Ask for feedback early in the college admissions process to give them plenty of time to get back to you in case they are pressed for time as your college application deadlines approach.

"Second, read as many college essay samples as you can before your essays are due to help you get a feel for the key points that admissions essays touch upon, help you generate ideas and to get your creative juices flowing.

"Third, try to stand out when writing your essays in as many ways as you can: choose original essay topics, let your unique writing style shine, and depict unique reasons why you want to be admitted to a specific college.

"Lastly, write about activities that you are most passionate about. Only then, will the essay display your true energy and interest in the activity. This passion will speak for itself in your essays."

—*Shreyans C. Parekh, University of Pennsylvania*

Write What You Know

"My best piece of advice when writing a college admissions essay is to be honest and reveal who you truly are. Admissions committees will see so many of the same essays, people describing their achievements and extracurricular activities. Choose something that makes you different, that makes you stand out from the rest of the crowd. It is refreshing to hear something new and exciting. More importantly, whatever makes you different, makes you stand out, is probably the thing that will be easiest for you to write about. Write what you know, reveal who you are, and make a statement."

—*Fareez Giga, Stanford University*

Don't Rely on Your SAT Vocabulary

"Be yourself. It is cliche and might not be as reassuring as other things, but with thousands of essays written, your SAT vocabulary and generic experiences that 'changed your life' won't get you as far as a starkly genuine voice."

—*Jason Y. Shah, Harvard University*

Anything Is Possible

"First of all, remember anything is possible. When I told my advisors that I wanted to apply to Wharton with a 3.5 GPA, I got laughed at. I worked all summer on my application and my essay, and in the end, I was the one laughing. That being said, you really want your essay to be unique, not just creative. You want to have a story that NO ONE else can possibly have. This means don't talk about being the president of a club, or about playing a sport. Although I had a pretty impressive resume (I started a nonprofit to raise money for children's hospitals and did research with Caltech affiliated Jisan Research Institute), I still knew that there were hundreds of other candidates out there who had done research and had been involved with non-profits. So, I decided to write about a movie I made for my dad's 50th birthday that was a parody of *Forrest Gump*. I knew that even though this was completely irrelevant to anything on my application, it would make me memorable and give the readers a glimpse into Alex Volodarsky the person, not the student. When writing your essay, just remember: is it possible that there's someone out there who can just change the name of the sport/club/organization and turn in the same essay? If the answer is yes, choose another topic."

—*Alex Volodarsky, University of Pennsylvania*

An Everyday Experience Can Work

"My major advice in selecting a topic is that the essay doesn't have to be about some sort of epiphany or life-changing moment—sometimes it's easier to write about the everyday things that separate you from everyone else. You want to show who you are as a person - if there is one defining event that shows this, great, but if not, don't try to force one. Instead do some introspection, and try to highlight something about your personality or experience that stands out. Also, keep a fairly narrow focus—don't try to write about everything that you've done in high school. Instead pick one thing that really highlights what you can bring to that college."

—Anonymous, Harvard University

Recycle and Choose Wisely

"Start early! I started writing my essays in the summer, and all the essays I wrote during that time, I ended up throwing away. Also, recycle your essays for different schools and scholarships—it's usually easy to modify your essays a little bit to fit various prompts. Also, choose your essays wisely. The combination of your long and short essays should give different perspectives of who you are."

—Anonymous, Princeton University

Presenting Your Unique Qualities

"Write an essay that demonstrates your true self. I think that it is important to reiterate and to clearly show a school the positive and unique qualities that you can bring to their institution. I would also suggest staying away from stories that seem 'cliché' and trying to focus on a topic that is idiosyncratic such as a trip oversees or a unique volunteering experience."

—Nnenna Ene, Duke University

Get Help from Your Teachers

"Ask your high school teachers to look over your essay. They are usually happy to help, and when you get into a top choice school they like to feel like they contributed to your success."

—Anonymous, Harvard University

Be Unguarded

"Write about something that you know is unique, maybe a bit personal, and powerful—either positively or negatively—to anyone who reads it. I think it's helpful to remember that your essay is quite personal and that no one will ever put your face to your writing later on if you do choose to attend that college. Share as much as you want and don't have fear that others will judge you for it or remember you for it later on in the game—they won't. Think of your essay as a powerful tool that you can use to get you in, but not something that you have to be guarded about in the least—it's pretty compelling to get to shape this part of your admissions packet in its full entirety."

—Sarah Langberg, Princeton University

Connect to the Rest of Your Application

"Take stock of what you've done in high school, and try to find something that you have spent significant time on that has captured or transformed you, and write about that. It is also important that this activity or event resonates in the rest of your application. For example, my application essay on the emotional paradigm shift I experienced resonated in the fact that I was a member of several different bands (local, regional, and all-state) and music clearly permeated my life."

—Devin Nambiar, Columbia University

Your Essay Topic Is Individual

"Don't try changing your skin. If you don't have an interest in something, don't write about it. If it's something you think about a lot, if it's in your blood, then that's probably a topic you should choose. I was surprised when I visited the MIT campus and asked the tour guide what she wrote about. Her essay was on a conversation between her fingers. I thought, this is not me. It says a lot about her, but it wasn't a topic that I was going to be able to do. Write about something that will allow your passion come out."

—Anonymous, MIT

Explain Your Goals

"For the personal statement I have to tell you what I was told, 'Write about what makes you different.' You have to do the best to describe who you are to the person who is reading your essay and make them feel like they know exactly what your goals and ambitions are and how you plan to reach them.

"Find examples of college essays and see what kind of details make a college essay memorable. I must also beg you to have your essays proofread by as many teachers who are willing to read them and go over them with you and make suggestions.

"If the application happens to be like the University of Chicago's Uncommon Application, pick the topic that you find most interesting. Chances are if the topic interests you, you will find that you have a lot to write about, and the essay will probably be interesting too."

—Angelica, University of Chicago

Have Editors for Different Purposes

"Allow plenty of time for editing and revision. Don't just sit down the night before the application is due and throw something together. Prepare a rough draft and then have numerous people read it over. I had my English teacher read mine for grammar and usage, my parents read it for relevance, and my guidance counselor read it for appropriateness all before I sent it in."

—Cameron McConkey, Cornell University

Don't Get Carried Away with the Topic

"Everyone always says that your college admissions essay should be about something you are passionate about. While I agree with this advice because it definitely comes easier if you love what you are writing about, it is just as important to remember not to get too carried away with the topic. Remember, that you have to find a way to relate the topic to you—your personality traits and your strengths. A lot of seniors choose great topics to write about but forget that the real purpose of this essay is to reflect who you are. You don't necessarily have to be direct in describing yourself ('I am a wonderful person'); you can imply things about the type of person ('I tried twenty different times and my perseverance paid off'), but make sure that you convey the important things about who you are and why you're a good match for the college."

—*Manika, University of Pennsylvania*

Give Yourself Enough Time

"Make sure you give yourself enough time to write a rough draft of your essay and time for someone to proofread it. Also, be sure that you feel confident and proud about the essay."

—*Ashley Mitchell, University of Chicago*

Don't Write for the Admissions Officers' Approval

"Don't write what you think the admissions committee wants to read. College admissions officers, I imagine, are tired of reading the same sorts of essays about how one fuddy-duddy person (used in many others' essays) is the applicant's hero or about how winning a school or academic competition was the greatest moment of an applicant's life. Write about what you know, and write something that includes of bit of your personality. If you want to write about how Mr. Fuddy-Duddy is your hero, that's perfectly fine, but just make sure you aren't writing about him because it seems like the proper thing to do."

—*Mariam Nassiri, Duke University*

Get Specific about the College

"Add a personal touch and emotions to your essay, regardless of what the topic is. Remember to give the reader an idea of you as a person, and replace ambiguity (such as "I work very hard", "I love subject X") with very specific examples or experiences.

"Also, if possible, relate your story to something unique to the school you are applying to. For example, I am passionate about environmental issues, and Duke University has one of the best environmental programs in the U.S."

—*Pen-Yuan Hsing, Duke University*

Don't Compromise Your Message

"This seems petty, but don't be afraid to swear or use verbally controversial words, as long as they serve a legit purpose. Many of my friends applying to college this year believe that an unnatural level of censorship is required for their essays. Never compromise your message to appear more clean-shaven."

—*Anthony Gouw, Duke University*

Tell a Story

"I know they always say not to write about tragic events or make 'sob stories' because everyone does it and the admissions readers won't pity you. However, I feel that you should write about an experience that is unique to you (for me, this was my first time ever performing on stage in a musical instead of playing in the pit orchestra or working as stage crew). Also, tell a story! If you enjoyed your experience and were inspired by it, chances are your writing will reflect that emotional aspect and reveal something new and intriguing to you. The admissions officer will learn a lot about you, too!"

—*Jean Gan, Duke University*

Write about What Drives You

"Definitely write about something you are passionate about. College recruiters want to know what drives and motivates you."

—*Jackie Liao, Stanford University*

Ask Others to Help You Find Something Differentiating

"Write about something that you are truly passionate about and care about because the enthusiasm and dedication you put into the essay comes across on paper. If you think there is absolutely nothing that distinguishes you from the rest of the bunch, nothing that makes you unique, ask your friends, your family members, and other people who know you well to describe one thing that they find interesting about you.

"Also, when you are writing your essay, don't focus too much on writing about what you think the admissions officers want to hear—everyone else is doing the same thing! Instead, focus on telling an engaging, well-written, and meaningful story that has true value to you. In your essay, show what that experience meant for you and how it has transformed you. How has it affected your present, and how will it affect your future?"

—*Oana Emilia Butnareanu, Stanford University*

Write Multiple Drafts

"Write as many drafts as necessary. I wrote draft upon draft in order to perfect my essay. Dedicate as much time to the essay as needed. This essay can determine whether you are admitted or not, take your time on it. There were countless weekends where I'd stay home just to work on my essay."

—*Enrique Vazquez, University of Chicago*

Don't Try to Follow a Formula

"Try not to follow any formula that you think admissions officers are looking for. You should write about something that is personal and paints a picture of who you are as a person. Provide an honest portrayal of yourself which outlines why you are going to be an asset to the university. Many of the people you are competing against to receive a spot at the school will have similar test scores, class rankings, and grades so the essay and interview is an opportunity for you to differentiate yourself."

—Anne McPherson, Yale University

Start Three Months Early

"First, start early. You want to spend at least three to four months editing and refining the essay to make it the best. Ask your English teacher, advisors, and parents to help you on it.

"Second, write the most interesting/creative introduction you can. Admissions officers read thousands upon thousands of essays, and if you don't captivate their attention with the first sentence, they may not be as inclined to read on.

"Third, remember, essays are the most important element to your application. Don't count on SAT scores to get you into Stanford, Yale, Harvard, etc. They do not matter anymore, especially when you need to stand out. Make a good impression on the essay, and spend most of your time on that! Remember, this is the only way for admissions to get to know you, so give them the chance to get to know you!

"Lastly, your essay should NOT be something you write a week before the deadline. College admissions officers are trained to spot out essays that were rushed and not well thought out. Don't rush this part of your application!"

—Brian Aguado, Stanford University

Don't Pass Judgment on Others

"Pick an aspect or event of your life that boldly shows an important part of your personality. If someone is very interested in human rights, I think they should write about that part of their personality and how they plan on fostering it with an education.

"Another overlooked but very important piece of advice that I really would like to share is: don't ever pass any kind of judgment about others in essays. I've read applications where people would write (only for a sentence) about how someone else is dumb or awkward (basically 'I am better than all of the other applicants because...' or 'My awkward looking friend did this...') and it always ruins it and makes the individual come off as arrogant, which I don't think is good."

—Mathew Griffin, Brown University

Feel Confident about Your Topic

"Leave plenty of time to write your essays. It took me a good two months to finally come up with my final product. I tried to use the topics provided first because I thought if I came up with my own topic they would not like it. I tried using two of their topics before I finally decided to take a chance and make my own. It was the best decision I made. I just did not feel confident about the other topics. I guess that is my other advice. Feel confident about your essay and the topic you choose. Make sure it highlights what you want everyone to know about you. Also, I would not recommend making up a story."

—*Victoria Tomaka, University of Chicago*

Aim for Uniqueness

"Write about something unique. Essays need to be both memorable and interesting, especially if you plan to apply to a school where applicants are numbered in the thousands."

—*Lauren Sanders, Duke University*

Treat the Essay Like It Matters

"Write something you care about—something that comes naturally and flows. Don't write about what you think the college admissions officers want to hear, and make it unique. If you're going to write about an important teacher, a memorable activity, etc. make it different and nuanced. Give stark and vivid descriptions and examples, and they'll know what you're writing is yours. Also, treat this essay like it matters. I know of so many friends who wrote down the first thing that came to their minds and submitted it. I spent probably three weeks on my essay, looking over it every other day and getting teachers to edit it. Nothing comes out perfect on the first try, and even if it's good, it can always get better."

—*Lisa Kapp, University of Pennsylvania*

You Don't Have to Write about a Tragedy or Curing a Disease

"I have several pieces of advice, but I suppose they all relate to one idea: Be honest in your essay. There is a myth that in order to get into a top ranked school, you must have a)endured great tragedy in your life or b)have cured a disease, have a geometric theorem named after you, be a published author, etc. While all of these are excellent topics to write about, they don't apply to everyone, and you don't need to make up a story if they don't fit your life. I've had an amazing childhood, my family is fantastic, and like most teenagers, I'm still waiting to do my world-changing work (assuming I have any in my future). So, I wrote about what was important to me: the small things I am doing currently to better the world and the bigger things I hope to do. Essay readers know when they're being played, and they also realize that we're just kids—we have the rest of our lives to do great things."

—*Suzanne Arrington, Columbia University*

Be Unconventional

"Use plenty of anecdotes, and be sure to start 'in the moment' to keep readers engaged. Admissions officers are skimming hundreds of essays each day, so you shouldn't be afraid to be unconventional (within reason) to grab their attention."

—Steve Schwartz, Columbia University

Shamelessly Promote Yourself

"I would say that you really need the essay to be in your voice and have it reflect how you feel not how you think they want you to feel. Don't set out to sound really intelligent and scholarly, this is your only real chance to let them know the real you, not the you on paper. Also, this is one of the few chances where it is acceptable for you to shamelessly promote yourself so play up your good qualities. Think of something original to write on. You want to be different and stand out. So many people have written 'my Grandfather inspires me because' or 'I was standing on the field watching the seconds count down with a tied game.' You should write something that only you can write."

—Anastasia Fullerton, Stanford, Brown

Make Them Smile

"Try to make it original and funny. Since the admissions officers are reading thousands of essays, finding a way to make them smile is a good thing."

—Samuel Linden, Harvard University

Stay True to Yourself

"Be yourself. There is no better way to delight counselors than with personal touches. If a senior is funny, it will naturally come out in the words. If a senior is the 'political activist' it will also be perceived in the writing. Still check for grammar, spelling errors, and unclear language, but also remember to stay true to yourself."

—Michelle Kizer, Cornell University

Brag

"I would say not being concerned about bragging. You have done so much, and this is your time to shine! Also, start early on writing the essays! It takes a lot more time than you expect. I started my essays about two months in advance, and I didn't feel as it was enough time. As time goes on, you'll learn to re-use essays and tweak them to make them work for different colleges and questions.

"Another good idea is to create a list of accomplishments, starting from as early as second or third grade. This comes in handy when filling out the awards/honors sections on the applications, although things really start 'counting' from ninth grade on. In addition to accomplishments, I had every club I had ever joined, every award I had won in every competition, every leadership position I held in a club, etc. It might sound far-fetched, but it is easy to forget everything you have done in the hustle and bustle of application season. It is much easier to have the list handy and to work off that."

—Ariela Koehler, MIT

Reflect

"Reflect. Think about what events in your life have shaped the way you are today. Think about what is important to you, who you are, and how you arrived where you are. Be authentic and creative. Remember to not only tell a story, but reflect on its meaning. And convey your thoughts and feelings emotionally as well as intellectually."

—Timothy Nguyen Le, Yale University

Focus on One or Two Major Things

"My best piece of advice would have to be to be genuine, go into detail, and focus on one or two major things, not every little thing you're involved in. I remember going to a workshop where people read their essays for discussion and a lot of them were more like lists. The ones that stood out were the ones that had a single passion and really explained it and gave an in depth perspective. Don't highlight what you think they'll like, highlight what you like because that will sound the best to them, if you do it right."

—Anonymous, MIT

Read Other Essays

"Start early! How? Select around eight schools. Three of them being schools which you have higher GPA/SAT scores than their average, two or three schools that you are right on average and two or three schools that are a reach because you may be on their average or not and it's a gamble.

"Then review when applications come out, so you can take advantage of as much time to write the essay prompts. Think of it as an essay that will let the admissions officer get to know you and see a true reflection of you in your essays.

"I would also suggest to read essays and see typical essay questions so that you can begin outlines or construct ideas of how you would answer these questions. This will allow you to take advantage of the time and short amount of space allowed to write as much about you."

—Andres Cantero, Stanford University

Don't Try to Sound Impressive

"Be yourself. Don't write what you think might sound impressive (or what was already listed in other parts of the application), just think about what experiences matter to you the most and what stories highlight your unique traits. I think what worked for me was talking about my weaknesses and showing how they have made me stronger. What also helped a lot was reading sample admissions essays from books like this one to get a feel for the writing they expect."

—Anonymous, Yale University

Going Negative Is Okay If It Highlights Growth

"My advice is to say things about yourself in a way that shows off your best attributes. Also don't be afraid to write something that shows you in a negative light if you show growth. Instead of writing how you're perfect, write about something negative that happened to show personal growth."

—Aditya Kumar, Brown University

Evoke Feeling

"Write about what you care about and what you know well! Do not write about what you believe the admissions officers want to hear. Instead, focus on something that you feel strongly about and try to translate those feelings onto paper.

"The best pieces of writing are those that evoke a feeling; I focused specifically on description and detail. I wanted to bring the reader into my essay and let them live vicariously through me for five minutes. If you can take the reader somewhere by means of the story you tell it will undoubtedly be memorable.

"One thing that helped me to begin writing after I decided upon the gist of my essay was writing down verbs and adjectives that came to my mind when I thought of the subject I was writing about. In my case it was the woods—I imagined it beyond aesthetics; I thought of smells, textures, and feelings. I wanted to make my writing as specific as possible."

—Mollie Mattuchio, Brown University

WHAT I LEARNED FROM WRITING THE ESSAY

What Makes Me ME

"The way I brainstorm is to just start writing and throw a bunch of ideas onto a paper, then toss out what I don't like and start over until I am satisfied. Sitting down and thinking about 'what makes me ME' was a really rewarding experience and helped me gain a lot of confidence in knowing what made me exceptional."

—Robert Lee, Columbia University

Nostalgia for the Family Business

"I learned that I actually had some nostalgia for the family publishing business, whereas I would have told you before that I did not like it AT ALL."

—Zachary Richner, Harvard University

Reinforced What I Thought about Myself

"The essay certainly framed my experiences more formally and made my life seem like it made a little more sense, but there wasn't anything I didn't already know or think about myself."

—Jason Y. Shah, Harvard University

The Role of Friendships

"I learned a great deal from writing my college application essay, more than I would have expected at the outset. Like most experiences, though, it was neither fully appreciated nor understood until processed reflectively.

"Writing my essay, which was about a trip to a science fair competition, gave me the opportunity—maybe even forced me—to reflect on the events and activities swirling around me at the time. Not only did I recognize the role of this trip in the greater context of my junior year, but also I found certain gems in several, seemingly minor, events. Distancing myself from my experiences was impossible—I simply found myself retelling my story with a refined lens. This new perspective taught me a great deal about myself as well. I discovered how much friendships, despite their apparent brevity, affected me.

"Additionally, I recognized the role of these friendships in molding my experiences and perceptions. Fred, the main focus of my essay, showed me how the role of genuine passion could trump physical disabilities. I expect that this lesson would have never revealed itself had I not written my essay on Fred and taken the time to study the nature of his character."

—Jonathan Cross, Duke University

Discovered Passion

"After I wrote my essay I thought, wow, I'm definitely not that deep—I wrote in a far more passion-filled and emotional tone than I normally think, feel, and live my life, but in the end, as I re-read the essay four years later, I am confident that the strong and perhaps out of the ordinary tone left a lasting impression on those who read it. I learned that I do have the power to create strong words and paragraphs, but that I don't necessarily have to live my life in such a passion-filled way at all times."

—Sarah Langberg, Princeton University

The Role of Others

"The thing I learned about myself while writing that essay is the role that people play in giving me a positive impression about something I am doing. I think this is true in all facets of life; clearly for example, you will dislike your job if you dislike your co-workers. I was privileged to be surrounded by individuals authentically committed to what they were doing. One's activities are not necessarily ends in themselves but rather are viewed as good or bad depending on the personal dynamic that accompanies them."

—Devin Nambiar, Columbia University

The Process of Writing

"I learned I'm not really good at time management. It's a great process. I really recommend for people in Egypt to apply to colleges in the U.S. because of the process of writing your essays. There's a lot of self discovery. You want to tell people who you are, what you want, and what you like."

—*Anonymous, MIT*

Cherishing High School Experiences

"I learned a lot about myself after writing my personal statement. I had never really thought about the many diverse experiences I had participated in and at the moment did not realize how they affected my ways of thinking. I definitely cherish my high school experience a lot more after writing my essay."

—*Angelica, University of Chicago*

Tying Activities to the Future

"I learned a lot about myself from writing my admissions essay. I spent some time thinking about what experiences were important and relevant to what I want to pursue later in life. This made me realize how important my extracurricular involvement was when it came to writing an essay for admission."

—*Cameron McConkey, Cornell University*

Writing about an Uninteresting Food

"I did not discover anything particularly earth-shattering about myself while writing this essay, but I did learn that I can write passionately about a food in which I have no interest."

—*Mariam Nassiri, Duke University*

Connecting the Dots

"Thinking about what to write made me think through all that happened in my life, where I am now, and my future. Writing this essay let me put my life into perspective and weave it into a structured story. I learned that in life, following your passions might seem risky, and looking forward you can't see where you're headed. But looking back years later, all the things you did are like dots that connect and form a beautiful picture."

—*Pen-Yuan Hsing, Duke University*

Looking for Yourself

"Sometimes you need to be looking for something to find it, and a lot of times you won't be looking for yourself until you try to write about it."

—*Anthony Gouw, Duke University*

An Epiphany

"My essay did turn out to be largely a reflection about my experience in the ensemble and what I gained from it. The piece tells my story of how I changed from a timid novice on stage into an enthusiastic performer—readers want to see this 'Aha!' moment, this epiphany. This shows admissions people that you grew in some way and you got something out of your experience more than just spending a summer with 70 other cast members. Then, they will know that you can learn from life in college, which is what school is all about."

—*Jean Gan, Duke University*

Evaluating My Goals

"The admissions essay provided a great opportunity to evaluate my goals and to really understand my passions in life."

—*Jackie Liao, Stanford University*

Believing in Myself

"I think the most important thing I learned from writing this essay is to stop doubting, believe in myself, and trust that I am making the right decision. When some of my family members read my essay, they scoffed at it and told me that if I wanted to get into Stanford, this was far from being good enough. I remember them saying this was nothing to be proud of, because there are millions of people in the U.S. and around the globe who speak Spanish, and having this ability is nothing unique and out of the ordinary. Usually, I was very keen on listening to what others had to say, but this time, I was sure that they were mistaken and that my love for Spanish would get me far in life. So despite their objections, I sent in my essay and proved them wrong."

—*Oana Emilia Butnareanu, Stanford University*

Embracing the Past

"I did learn a lot about myself. When I was writing my essay for the Common Application, I wrote about many incidents that shaped who I was. I never really embraced those events until that moment. When I was writing, I had to sit there and really look within myself and see who I was. It was nice to know how my personality came about by past incidents."

—*Enrique Vazquez, University of Chicago*

Reflecting on My Family

"I never really wrote about my family and my upbringing in such detail. It allowed me to really reflect on the uniqueness of my family and appreciate the values that my parents instilled in us."

—*Anne McPherson, Yale University*

Being Thankful

"You know you have written a good essay if you go through a period of self-reflection. I learned about myself in the sense that I explored my individuality and what life meant to me at that moment. The essay forced me to count my blessings, which is something most people don't do on a regular basis. I have been blessed with multiple opportunities in my life (i.e. being admitted to Stanford), and the essay made me realize how important it is to be thankful for everything in life."

—*Brian Aguado, Stanford University*

A Positive Attitude

"I learned that even though I never participated much in extracurriculars or made many friends in high school, I still had grown a lot and (to my surprise) had a relatively positive attitude about life."

—*Mathew Griffin, Brown University*

A Numbers Person

"I learned that I do not like the stress of writing a perfect essay. I am more of a numbers person. I always think everything I write is not good enough or could be better. I stressed myself out. It turned out ok because I got accepted to college but I would much rather take a multiple choice test than write an essay."

—*Victoria Tomaka, University of Chicago*

How to Transfer My Personality to Paper

"I learned to transfer my personality to paper. An admissions essay is a glance into the mindset of a student. I don't think previously I had to do this before the college admissions process."

—*Lauren Sanders, Duke University*

Reflecting on Changes

"With the completion of any major task, there's always a sense of accomplishment. However, finishing my college essay was different because it just felt right. It really made me reflect on my life and how much it's changed and how grateful I am for everything that has happened to me."

—*Lisa Kapp, University of Pennsylvania*

Shaped My College Career

"Writing the essay required me to analyze why I had become involved in the UN in the first place. It helped me to place my UN experiences within the broader context of my pre-college extracurriculars. It also helped me to determine my college major (political science)."

—*Steve Schwartz, Columbia University*

Reflecting on the Past Five Years

"I realized how far I have come in the past five years, and it was nice to have that time to reflect while I was preparing for such a large change in my life."

—*Anastasia Fullerton, Stanford, Brown*

Come a Long Way

"If anything, I've learned that I do not credit myself as much as I should. While writing, I realized that I've come a far way from eighth grade, and that my experiences have made me a very strong person."

—*Michelle Kizer, Cornell University*

Trouble Writing about Myself

"I learned that I have a lot of trouble writing about myself. It's a completely different experience than writing an essay in class. In addition, I learned to be proud of myself! I have done a lot!"

—*Ariela Koehler, MIT*

Thinking about My Brother

"In the process of writing this, I literally spent hours every day for months reflecting on my brother's death. I have learned that reflection truly can be a very powerful thing. I do it every day—when I'm walking to school, washing the dishes, doing the laundry."

—*Timothy Nguyen Le, Yale University*

Considered How I Sounded

"I did have to think about a lot of stuff when writing my essays. I guess all throughout middle and high school you write essays about books or history, etc. It's very different to write about yourself. You have to think about how you sound. I tried not to overplay or underplay things, that was hard to do. It was a humbling and empowering thing at the same time. I had to put some accomplishments aside and figure out what I was really proud of. I think it helps you figure yourself out to write these essays. I took a class about writing autobiographies during my freshman year."

—*Anonymous, MIT*

Figured out My Academic Passions

"I learned that I had a lot more passion for certain academic fields than others and saw what I considered my strengths. This helped a lot my first year in college, because I went with these passions and took classes that would revolve around my passion, helping me enjoy my first year very much. It also taught me that with hard work and sufficient time, that I could do real well in a lot of things. The essays also reminded me a lot of my struggles and how even if college would be a struggle itself, that I had made it so far all right, and that I could definitely continue to do the same."

—*Andres Cantero, Stanford University*

Scrutinized Myself

"I definitely learned something about myself when writing the essays. These questions really made me scrutinize myself and my life in order to pick out the most important events that best shows the person I am."

—*Anonymous, Yale University*

I'm Not as Boring as I Thought

"I learned that I am not as boring as I thought through writing my essay. While I haven't experienced anything horrific or accomplished anything on a global scale, I've done a lot of small, cool things that have made differences in both my life and the lives of others. I am unique and interesting, and writing my essay helped me realize that. I haven't written an opera, but I've trained my legs to ride a bike 180 miles in two days. That's something to write about."

—*Suzanne Arrington, Columbia University*

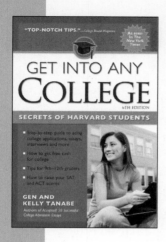

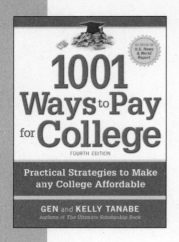

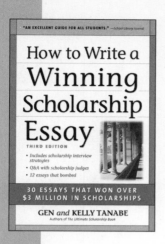

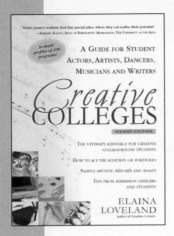

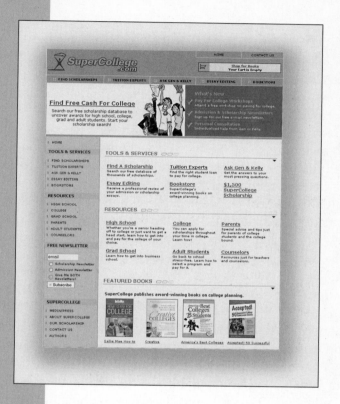

GET MORE TOOLS AND RESOURCES AT SUPERCOLLEGE.COM

Visit www.supercollege.com for more free resources on college admissions, scholarships, and financial aid. And, apply for the SuperCollege Scholarship.

ABOUT THE AUTHORS

HARVARD GRADUATES GEN AND KELLY TANABE are the founders of SuperCollege and the award-winning authors of eleven books including *The Ultimate Scholarship Book*, *Accepted! 50 Successful College Admission Essays*, *Get Into Any College*, *Get Free Cash for College,* and *1001 Ways to Pay for College*.

Together, Gen and Kelly were accepted to every school to which they applied, including all of the Ivy League colleges, and won more than $100,000 in merit-based scholarships. They were able to leave Harvard debt-free and their parents guilt-free.

Gen and Kelly give workshops at high schools across the country and write the nationally syndicated "Ask the SuperCollege.com Experts" column. They have made hundreds of appearances on television and radio and have served as expert sources for respected publications including *U.S. News & World Report*, *USA Today*, *The New York Times*, *Chicago Sun-Times*, *New York Daily News*, *Chronicle of Higher Education,* and *Seventeen*.

Gen grew up in Waialua, Hawaii. Between eating banana-flavored shave ice and basking in the sun, he was president of the Student Council, captain of the speech team, and a member of the tennis team. A graduate of Waialua High School, he was the first student from his school to be accepted at Harvard. In college, Gen was chair of the Eliot House Committee and graduated magna cum laude with a degree in both History and East Asian Studies.

Kelly attended Whitney High School, a nationally ranked public high school in her hometown of Cerritos, California. She was the editor of the school newspaper, assistant editor of the yearbook, and founder of a public service club to promote literacy. In college, she was the co-director of the HAND public service program and the brave co-leader of a Brownie Troop. She graduated magna cum laude with a degree in Sociology.

Gen, Kelly, their son Zane, and their dog Sushi live in Belmont, California.